the sound of utopia

the sound of utopia

MICHEL KRIELAARS

Translated from the Dutch
by Jonathan Reeder

PUSHKIN PRESS

Pushkin Press
Somerset House, Strand
London WC2R 1LA

Original text © 2021 Michel Krielaars and Uitgeverij Pluim
Published by arrangement with Cossee Publishers
English translation © 2024 Jonathan Reeder

The Sound of Utopia was first published as
De Klank Van De Heilstaat by Uitgeverij Pluim in Amsterdam, 2021

First published by Pushkin Press in 2025

**Nederlands
letterenfonds
dutch foundation
for literature**

The publisher gratefully acknowledges the support
of the Dutch Foundation for Literature.

1 3 5 7 9 8 6 4 2

ISBN 13: 978-1-80533-002-8

All rights reserved. No part of this publication may be reproduced,
stored in a retrieval system or transmitted in any form or by any
means, electronic, mechanical, photocopying, recording or otherwise,
without prior permission in writing from Pushkin Press

Designed and typeset by Tetragon, London
Printed and bound in the United Kingdom by Clays Ltd, Elcograf S.p.A.

www.pushkinpress.com

CONTENTS

Note on Transliteration   xi

Prologue   1

1. Richter's Secret   7
2. Yellow Shoes and Fancy Cars   46
3. The Lost Notes   101
4. The Russian Vera Lynn   125
5. Celebrated, Persecuted, Rehabilitated   147
6. The Vanished Singer   179
7. A Nun at the Keyboard   210
8. The Lost Legacy   230
9. Stalin's Last Lackey   249
10. Solidarity with Dissidents   279

Epilogue   307
Acknowledgements   311
Bibliography   313

for my muse Henriette

Work, play. You're living here, in this country, and you must see everything as it really is. Don't have any illusions. There's no other life. There can't be any. Just be thankful that you're still allowed to breathe!

—DMITRI SHOSTAKOVICH TO GALINA VISHNEVSKAYA

NOTE ON TRANSLITERATION

Music is a truly global language, and the artists and composers who devote their lives to it find themselves leading correspondingly international lives. In consequence, their names often go through a variety of permutations as they cross borders and into new languages.

There are many ways of transliterating Russian, but, because of the chequered histories of the persons the reader will encounter with in this book, many have become known to us in the Latin script under different systems, and so it would be a fool's errand to impose any single one on them. Preferences, where present, have therefore been respected, as have established conventions in the music world. Hence, for example, Tchaikovsky (rather than Chaykovsky) and Medtner (rather than Metner). Where no convention exists, this book employs a simplified version of British Standard, for the reader's convenience, except for bibliographic entries, which have been rendered using the more scholarly Library of Congress system.

PROLOGUE
MOSCOW, 2009

On a drizzly weekday evening in December, I walk past the Tchaikovsky Moscow State Conservatory on the Bolshaya ("Great") Nikitskaya Street. No snow has fallen yet this month, giving the low-rise eighteenth- and nineteenth-century houses a look of ennui, as though the usually bustling Russian capital has shut down. Even Coffeemania—the pricey coffee bar located in one wing of the conservatory, where the nouveaux riches treat their mistresses to Sachertorte and champagne, and the Bentleys queue up outside—is nearly empty.

Then a concert poster in one of the glass cases near the music academy's entrance catches my eye. That evening there will be a concert commemorating the seventy-fifth anniversary of the birth of the composer Alfred Schnittke (1934–98). I decide to buy a ticket, but at the box office I'm told the concert is sold out. Back outside, an elderly woman in a checked winter coat beckons me. Under the watchful gaze of the bronze statue of Tchaikovsky, she offers me a ticket for the equivalent of less than two euros—true, four times its face value, but still chickenfeed compared to a seat in the Amsterdam Concertgebouw.

I'm somewhat familiar with Schnittke's music. It's exciting, aloof and weird all at once. In 1992 I attended the premiere of his opera *Life with an Idiot* in the Amsterdam Muziektheater, conducted by his compatriot Mstislav Rostropovich, who for the occasion traded his cello for the baton. The composer was present as well. During the final applause, as Schnittke approached the stage to be embraced by an exuberant Rostropovich, Amsterdam was briefly transformed into Little Moscow, the auditorium roaring with Russian *bravos* and *hoorahs*.

For Schnittke, it must have felt like a victory over the totalitarian system that had frustrated his life as a musician in his homeland. Authorities in the recently collapsed Soviet Union had denounced his music as "avant-gardist" and banned its performance. So the aggrieved composer, who made his living mainly by writing music for films, had emigrated in 1990 to Germany, the country his Jewish father had left in 1927 for the Soviet Union. Alfred Schnittke died in Hamburg eight years after his Amsterdam triumph.

But in Moscow, on what would have been his seventy-fifth birthday, for nearly two hours he is very much alive. On the stage stands a large portrait, draped with flowers. Throughout the concert, someone will regularly walk up, their eyes solemnly teary, to place two red or white carnations before the late composer and stand for a moment's silence.

One of the soloists is Natalia Gutman, a world-class musician and a good friend of Schnittke's. Her playing fills the auditorium with the sombreness of his music. And yet, for her it is also a celebration, for her friend has been brought to life, the many listeners honouring him along with her.

From my perch up in the gods, I scan the vast, packed auditorium with its wood panelling and ceilings and its superb acoustics.

I am struck by the faces of the men and women listening intently to the music, as if they don't want to miss a single note. Many of them aren't even that old, but they're wearing those large plastic-rimmed glasses and the drab, ill-fitting suits you could get at the GUM department store on Red Square in the days of the Soviet Union. It makes these folks seem transplanted from another era, one that vanished when the Soviet Union was dissolved at the end of December 1991. They are the quintessence of the old Soviet intelligentsia, the teachers, the professors, the doctors and the physicists who did not benefit from the wild capitalism that spawned the New Russians, with their Coffeemania, their Bentleys and their insatiable hunger for luxury consumer products. It's as though I'm in some huge Noah's Ark, together with barely a couple of thousand survivors of a drowned civilization.

Next to me, a few earnest-looking conservatory students are feverishly taking notes. When, come intermission, they discover I'm a foreigner and hail from the Netherlands, they crowd around me for a chat. "Ah, Holland, land of tulips, Rembrandt and Diepenbrock," muses one of them, a beautiful, dark-eyed violin student. "I would so like to go there," she says. "And never leave."

Her fellow classmates also talk about emigrating to the West, because in Russia it's impossible to eke out a living as a composer. I tell them I'm not their man, that I always advise dreamers to stay put in their own country because that's where they're needed most—it's people like them who will help build a modern society. "And where else than in Russia," I add, "can you find such exquisite music and excellent musicians?"

After intermission I move up a few rows and find myself next to a father with his three young sons. He teaches organ at the conservatory; his boys study, respectively, violin, cello and piano. All four are enamoured of Schnittke, they say, just as they are of all great Russian composers. The father confesses to having idolized Schnittke even back in the Soviet days, and never passed up the chance to attend an illicit concert of his music.

I have always been fascinated by the admiration so many Russians harbour for classical music. In the Soviet Union, musicians and composers were revered as gods. They enjoyed a certain degree of immunity because they were unique in their creative urge. And yet, at the same time, dozens of them were persecuted, shipped off to labour camps or executed by the communist regime; their compositions and recordings were destroyed or banned; their performances cancelled.

Of course, this is nothing compared to the fifteen hundred writers executed under Stalin. But still, I'm intrigued by what was behind their persecution. Was it their music, or something else?

There were also composers and performers who acquiesced. And yet they, too, were often punished anyway. Because what was expected from them besides blind compliance, no one really could say.

The one thing they all shared during the first three decades of the Soviet Union was the misfortune that Joseph Stalin was a music-lover. He actively interfered in the nation's musical life and listened to every new release of a classical recording, noting his verdict on the record sleeve: "good", "average" or "rubbish". This last one could, in the worst-case scenario, earn you a bullet.

In 1932 Stalin decided to subject music, like the rest of the arts, to the artistic doctrine of socialist realism. Solace, beauty or amusement no longer mattered: art's sole purpose was to further the advancement of socialism. The regime's rationale (although many composers did their best to skirt around this edict) was that the positive energy radiated by this new Soviet music would lead to the betterment of the masses.

This book is about composers and musicians trapped in such an ideological system. What made them choose to make concessions—or not—in their work? Why did they risk their lives by being wilful or contrary? Were their actions purely the consequence of their creative urge, or did vanity play a role? And what about Tikhon Khrennikov, the powerful general secretary of the Union of Soviet Composers, who both aided fellow composers and made their lives miserable? Was he simply more power-hungry than talented, or was there more to it? Could his fickleness be understood only by someone who experienced the convoluted Soviet system at first hand? After all, musical life in the defunct USSR was of an unheard-of calibre: consider composers like Shostakovich and Prokofiev, and performers like Mstislav Rostropovich, Sviatoslav Richter, David Oistrakh, Leonid Kogan and Maria Yudina.

By the time I got to Moscow, many of these great musicians either were deceased or had emigrated to the West. On occasion I heard one of them—for instance, the cellist Mstislav Rostropovich—perform there. But for the most part it felt like all that was left were some faded memories of an exceptional bygone era.

At times I was lucky enough to be afforded a whiff of that glorious past, like in the small Moscow opera theatre built by the renowned soprano Galina Vishnevskaya, Rostropovich's widow, for her talented pupils. Vishnevskaya would sit enthroned in her own "royal box" and receive cheers from the singers and the audience after each performance out of gratitude for everything she "had done for Russia". Such moments not only validated my love of

Russian music, but also further piqued my curiosity. In the end, I decided to delve into a turbulent period in Soviet history, during which, to paraphrase the writer Konstantin Paustovsky, for every even slightly reasonable and not entirely insensitive person, life assumed the form of a daily ordeal. The fact that in this very country such marvellous music was composed and such outstanding performers graced the stage is nothing short of miraculous.

1

Richter's Secret

An attractive young man with the long, dirty-blond hair of a French singer approached me one summer morning in 2011 at the entrance to my Moscow flat. He was about thirty and had the kind of well-proportioned features you see in portraits of tsarist military officers in the Hermitage. A *papirosa*, a Russian filterless cigarette with a cardboard mouthpiece, dangled from the left corner of his mouth. It was a Belomorkanal, which always reminded me of Konstantin Paustovsky's books, in which everybody smokes them. The guy was drunk, but then, so were so many of the men in my neighbourhood.

The eleven-storey building on Goncharnaya Street, where I rented a spacious flat with huge rooms and glossy parquet floors while working as a correspondent for the morning daily *NRC Handelsblad*, had been built in 1948 by German prisoners of war. The façade resembled a neoclassical palace, with two imposing towers, one at either end, and a large archway leading to an interior courtyard. My neighbours were reverently impressed: German quality was a thing to be admired in Putin's Russia, be it cars, washing machines or houses. The building's first residents had been the high-ranking general staff of the Red Army whom Stalin had rewarded with a swanky apartment for their victory over Nazi Germany. After his death in 1953, the street became home to celebrity painters, entertainers, writers, musicians, dancers and scientists. They, too, had been rewarded for their services to the Soviet people. One category curiously high on the list was circus entertainers, like lion-tamers and wall-of-death daredevils. Once the red flag with the hammer and sickle came down for good, those original tenants vanished, as though they, along with communism, had been put out with the trash to make way for expats and the nouveau riche.

Some of the flats were still occupied by the now middle-aged children of those original tenants. Under communism they had lived like royalty, but after the collapse of the Soviet Union they suddenly had to survive in the new capitalist jungle. Those who failed often turned to the bottle, which could be had for a euro at the corner grocery. This young man must be one of these. He bowed deeply and addressed me in surprisingly impeccable Dutch with: "Good day, honourable sir! How do you do?"

He introduced himself as Andrei and told me he had spent his youth in The Hague and attended the Gymnasium Haganum high school. His mother had married a Dutch artist and wanted to make a go of it in the Netherlands. "Those were the best years of my life," Andrei said, his expression clouded over with wistful nostalgia for Holland. "I'd be happy to sing some Brel for you this afternoon! I invite you to my flat on the eleventh floor. Come whenever you like. I have all the time in the world."

He looked at me even more jovially than at first, as though we were old friends, so delighted was he to be able to speak Dutch again at last. But I suspected it was just as much an excuse to open a fresh bottle.

Andrei came from a family of artists. His mother, Natasha, was a watercolourist. His grandfather, Natasha's father, was Vladimir

Igoshev, quite a well-known Soviet painter. He died in 2007, and one can still admire much of his work in many Russian museums.

"Mama and I have lived in his apartment ever since," Andrei said. He adds, rolling his eyes: "We bought it in 1992 for a hundred and fifty dollars. Now it's worth a million, for sure. We're guarding grandpa's paintings, because, as you know, our country is run by desperados. They'll rob you blind. I don't want to come home one day and find out they've made off with everything."

Later that afternoon I rang Andrei's doorbell, more interested in his grandfather's paintings than in his drunken renditions of Jacques Brel. He opened the padded door to the flat and said, like a Dutch Pushkin: "Do come in, honourable citizen of the finest and most beautiful country in the world, where the democracy is as pure as her splendidly painted skies with their noble clouds."

I recognized the high ceiling and parquet floor of the entrance hall as identical to those in my flat. Only here, the space was filled with paintings, some of monumental proportions, stacked up against one another as though in a storeroom. I squeezed my way through into the living room and was transported to a Soviet residence from the 1950s. Antique sofas and armchairs jostled together. On a coffee table lay a few empty vodka bottles. The place smelt of a combination of dust, spoilt food, cigarette smoke and liquor.

On the walls were some excellent portraits of an older woman with a sun hat and a long white dress, drinking tea in a gazebo in a sumptuous garden. "My grandmother," Andrei said, pointing to the series. "Pretty, isn't she? And did you see this one?" He pointed to a portrait of an older, white-haired painter sitting in his studio. In his right hand he holds a paintbrush above a palette; a hunting dog rests its chin on his right knee. "Sierk Schröder, your fellow countryman. I knew him in The Hague. He posed there for my grandfather in 1991."

In a corner of the room, under a large portrait of an Asiatic hunter, was a light brown Grotrian-Steinweg concert grand piano. I had not even sunk into one of the armchairs before Andrei slid onto the stool and began playing the opening bars of Beethoven's *Moonlight Sonata*. Aside from the occasional wrong note, it wasn't half bad, for an amateur. But then he abruptly changed registers and hoarsely launched into Brel's "Le Plat Pays" and a soldier song by the Soviet singer-songwriter Vladimir Vysotsky. This genre was clearly his forte.

Just as abruptly, he stopped and plopped down next to me. After pouring himself a glass of Armenian cognac, he told me that, after he graduated high school, his mother (by then divorced from the Dutchman) took him to Milan, where she had started a gallery for Russian art. "I started driving a Porsche when I was twenty," he said. "When we got low on money, we'd sell one of my grandfather's paintings. But actually, life's best here in Moscow. Every night I'm in bed with a different pretty girl."

Andrei sat back down at the piano, this time taking a stab at a Chopin nocturne. After barely five measures he leapt up and hurried off to the toilet.

He returned five minutes later looking haggard. "Sorry, too much to drink." Now he went over to the vintage Rigonda stereo fixture and put on an LP. "Recognize this?" An impromptu by Schubert. "Sviatoslav Richter," I answered without hesitation.

He looked at me, surprised, and sank into the chair opposite me. "In the eighties I used to go to his house concerts and had to turn pages for him," he said. "And afterwards he would always caress my hair. He was in love with boys like me. You know he was..."—at which Andrei made the sound of a purring tomcat.

I've admired Richter ever since my student days. I played his CDs often but never heard him perform live, because he seldom did so. And if ever he did give a concert somewhere in Europe, it sold out in no time: Richter's international fans tipped one another off as soon as word got out. If the concert was cancelled at the last minute, then too bad for them. But their resolve to hear him play made it worth the risk.

He gave a concert in Musis Sacrum in the Dutch city of Arnhem on 17 March 1991. To this day I could kick myself for not standing in line at the box office to snag an unclaimed ticket. Judging by the reviews in the press the next day, I had missed something really special.

Just after eight p.m. Richter emerged from the wings, timid as always, as though unsure of what business he had there. He wore a grey suit and large glasses with clear plastic frames, emphasizing the angular look of his face. If you didn't recognize him from the robust head ringed with white hair and the long sideburns, you might mistake him for an usher who'd lost his way.

Once he sat down at the piano and the auditorium lights were dimmed, save a single reading lamp, all one could make out was his prominent jaw. After half a minute's silence, his huge hands abruptly struck the keyboard. The concert of Bach's English Suites Nos. 1, 3, 4 and 6 had begun.

Contrary to what one might expect from a pianist with such strong hands and an overwhelming physique, the sound was dry and measured. His control of the instrument and the notes commanded respect. The music sounded as if he put his unique and, most of all, vulnerable soul into it. And that was exactly what so appealed to me about Richter's playing.

The music critic Katja Reichenfeld was muted in her review in the next day's *NRC Handelsblad*, because in many ways the concert fell short of her expectations. She called the English Suites "less-than-accessible works that require a lucid and lively rendering", which she felt Richter did not deliver. She also wrote that his playing sounded like imaginary music locked mostly in the performer's own mind. The audience had to make do with monotonous playing, bereft of the many earthly joys that so typify Bach. This concert was a far cry from the lively, swinging interpretation of Glenn Gould. But then, in the Sarabande from the third suite, wrote Reichenfeld, something breathtaking occurred, as if "gifts suddenly fell from heaven": "A halting whisper rose out of a well-nigh tangible silence, and the listeners, caught completely unawares, witnessed a poignant intimacy between two great musicians: Bach and Richter." The "miracle" returned in the Sarabande of the sixth suite.

Richter's life, I later realized, coincided with an era in which a human life mattered little. Aside from being a giant on the concert stage, he was also an eyewitness to one of the grimmest episodes in Russian history: Stalin's reign of terror, which cost millions of innocent Soviet citizens their lives. His own father was one of them.

At the time of that concert in Arnhem, Richter was three days shy of his seventy-sixth birthday. Except that he had been the Soviet Union's greatest pianist for nearly half a century, I knew nothing about him. But I was fascinated by the combination of his ungainly posture and his delicate playing. As though his large body and pure passion—which caused him to hit plenty of wrong notes during live concerts—somehow melded with the subtle music he was performing.

My fascination intensified when I saw Bruno Monsaingeon's documentary *Richter: The Enigma*. The French filmmaker, who spoke decent Russian, had interviewed the pianist two years before his death in 1997. Richter was already a sick old man. He still spoke lovingly about his art but seemed otherwise entirely disillusioned with everyday life. He often expressed his cynicism about the Stalin era, although this was also when he enjoyed his first great triumphs on the concert stage. He recalled, with bashful nostalgia, his debut in 1941 in the Great Hall of the Moscow Conservatory with Tchaikovsky's Piano Concerto No. 1. It made him an instant star. The last notes had hardly died out when the audience broke into applause and hoorahs. He must have thought with pride on his parents, whom he had left behind in his birthplace, Odessa, in 1937. Little did he know that his father had been executed by Stalin's secret police, the NKVD, four months earlier.

Talking to Monsaingeon, he seems, all those years later, to have made peace with that traumatic event, almost brushing it off. And yet, from that moment on, it dominates the documentary. I figured it out soon enough: without his father, Teofil, he might never have become a world-class pianist.

Richter loved his father intensely. I gather as much from an audio recording a friend of Richter's made in 1988 at a New Year's party. Then seventy-three, Richter played a composition written by his father, "Alt Wien". It is a cheerful piece lasting about a minute. Richter gives it his all, as though it's a tender Mozart sonata that he doesn't want to end, and stretching it out allows him to hold on to the memory of his father. The little piece evokes images of an idyllic childhood, blocking out the reality of the violence of the revolution and civil war roiling the country.

It is exactly this incongruity of routine existence and occasional eruptions of violence in Russian history that has intrigued me for almost half a century. As though a storm obliterates your house, and you just keep on planting potatoes in your field.

Sviatoslav Richter's parents, Teofil Richter and the much younger Anna Richter (née Moskalyova), met in the Ukrainian city of Zhytomyr, where Teofil had spent the summer holidays. He gave Anna piano lessons, and they fell in love. For the previous twenty-two years, Teofil had been living in Vienna, the musical, libertine capital of Emperor Franz Joseph, where he had studied piano and composition at conservatory and never left.

They married in the summer of 1914, shortly before the outbreak of the First World War. A year later they moved with their newborn son Sviatoslav (nicknamed Svetik) to the more cosmopolitan Odessa. There, on the Black Sea, they were out of the war's reach. Teofil landed the position of vocal director at the opera house and was appointed to the conservatory's piano faculty. He also gave piano recitals and was organist and choir director at St Paul's Cathedral, the city's German Evangelical Lutheran church. His son thus had music etched into his DNA.

The Richters had just settled in to their new life when in February 1917 the revolution broke out and the tsar was deposed. Many people believed that with the rejection of autocracy, Russia would become a free, democratically governed, egalitarian society. That hope was soon dashed, however, when, just eight months later, Lenin's Bolsheviks staged a *coup d'état* and set up a brutal regime. Now a civil war broke out between the Bolsheviks and the tsarist loyalists, the White Guards; Ukrainian nationalists and anarchists also joined the fracas. The country was plunged into blood-drenched chaos that lasted for six years.

Young Svetik spent those turbulent years—during which looting, rape, harassment and dispossession of the owning class and the murder of Jews were rife—with his mother's landowning family in Zhytomyr, while his parents remained in Odessa. The violence passed him by, partly because Richter's maternal grandfather, Pavel Moskalyov, had always treated his farmers so well before the revolution that they continued to provide him and his family with food.

The family was reunited only in 1922. Russia was devastated, millions of citizens had perished or lost loved ones and possessions. And yet, life went on. This was clear right from when the seven-year-old Svetik started picking out tunes on the piano, and couldn't stop. In no time he had mastered a Chopin nocturne.

Cosmopolitan Odessa, with its hundreds of cafés, restaurants, music halls and theatres, flourished in the late 1920s as it had in the old days. Svetik was soon part of this bustling night life; at the age of fourteen he began accompanying amateur singers at the Palace of Seafarers. In this popular seaman's club (now home to a yachting academy and the haunt of well-heeled locals) things could get a little rough. Some time later, he started appearing for pay at various clubs around town, accompanying violinists, singers, a ballet company, even a circus. Sometimes he was paid in kind (it was shortly after the collectivization of the agricultural sector, and grain was scarce) with a sack of potatoes.

His father, who had stopped performing due to a neurological disorder, took him to the opera, where from the orchestra pit he watched Verdi's *Aida* and Puccini's *Turandot*. The stage, with its sumptuous decor, worked its magic on him, and soon enough Svetik was working as a répétiteur at the opera. His dream, especially after having worked with star singers like Sergei Lemeshev, was to become an opera conductor. But when he was passed over for a position, he changed course, although he would later tell the filmmaker Monsaingeon that his experience at the opera had been a formative one.

During the summer holidays of 1931 in Zhytomyr, Teofil introduced his son to the eight eccentric, elderly Semyonova sisters. They organized a concert in their white, columned house—it could have come straight from a Turgenev novel—for the young pianist. These sisters constituted the entire audience. They were thrilled by his performance of Schumann's Piano Concerto, and the next day they overwhelmed him with flowers from their own garden. Svetik himself was so excited by the concert's success that he began to consider becoming a professional pianist.

Two summers later, again in Zhytomyr, a concert given by David Oistrakh and Vsevolod Topilin heightened his resolve. In his memoirs he writes: "I went to their concert and became slightly bored by their purely musical performance—I had been bitten by the theatre bug and yearned to see a *scène* on stage, a plot… But I was bowled over when Topilin played Chopin's Ballade No. 4." The piece clearly struck a chord in the romantic seventeen-year-old.

His career gradually picked up steam. Svetik started going by his full name, Sviatoslav. On 19 March 1934 he gave his first real recital, in the Engineers' Club in Odessa, and the programme included Chopin's Ballade No. 4 and the Etude No. 4. No music critics attended, so there is no written account of the concert.

At the end of that same year, the popular party bigwig Sergei Kirov was assassinated in Leningrad, ostensibly by a disillusioned revolutionary. And the Kremlin faced the disappointing results of its first five-year plan, which had forced farmers into huge agricultural collectives and was meant to boost industrialization. Stalin, who had taken over after Lenin's death, needed scapegoats for both the assassination and the failure of the government's economic programme. He moved to eliminate his opponents and consolidate his power by means of a massive purge, initially aimed at those in the opposition but in subsequent years expanded to include the Communist elite, from local functionaries to party leaders. More than half a century later, Richter could vividly recall the nationwide, all-encompassing fear that suddenly burst forth like a storm in the desert, its ferocity even reaching as far as Odessa. "In 1935–36, people got a fright when the doorbell rang, especially at night," he told Bruno Monsaingeon.

The situation was no less grim at the opera in Odessa. Personnel could be fired on spurious claims of shirking responsibilities, corruption or licentious behaviour. Everyone was encouraged to unmask others publicly as "enemies of the people". In his memoirs, Richter describes the fate of the opera's music director: "A gathering was called in the main auditorium, and everyone had to contribute something against him. The prima ballerina, in fact a perfectly respectable person, was made to testify that the man was truly dissolute. One of the stage managers, also forced to denounce him, thought the idea so terrible that he passed out cold the minute he opened his mouth. This made it all the worse for the conductor, who was then only accused of more wrongdoing."

The upshot of this public trial was that photos of the conductor were placed throughout the theatre with the text: "Enemy of the People". Richter writes: "He was fired and replaced by an absolute son of a bitch."

For Sviatoslav and countless other Soviets, the purges were a perpetual nightmare. When he heard that the authorities in Odessa wanted to draft him into military service, he decided to leave his family, friends and the theatre behind and move to Moscow. By now it was 1937: the terror was about the enter its bloodiest year, in which more than 700,000 people were executed.

At twenty-two, Sviatoslav began to consider whether a career as a concert pianist was still viable. He was, after all, on the late side. So he paid a visit to Heinrich Neuhaus in Moscow, hoping to be admitted to his piano class at the Tchaikovsky Conservatory. Neuhaus (1888–1964) was one of Russia's foremost piano teachers. As for so many other artists, surviving Stalin's reign of terror meant proving his loyalty to the regime, so in a speech in 1936 he praised the *Pravda* articles denouncing Shostakovich's opera *Lady Macbeth of Mtsensk*. In his words, the greatness and splendour of the Soviet way of life must be expressed by music that was greater and nobler than everything that had preceded it in the arts. *Lady Macbeth*, with its "meaningless and petty sentiments" and "cynical, oafish music" was precisely an example of how not to do it. Even when you know Neuhaus didn't mean a word of it, his speech rings hollow. But it says everything about the climate of fear among the intelligentsia, which could drive even the most decent people to betray their friends to save their own skin.

Like Richter, Neuhaus was of German descent and was born in Ukraine, where he had spent the first forty years of his life. Both of his parents were piano teachers. He was, on his mother's side, a cousin of Karol Szymanowski.

And then there was that perilously German surname. Neuhaus, like Teofil Richter, would be arrested in 1941 on suspicion of spying for the enemy, although the official reason was that he refused to be evacuated. Thanks to an intervention by Shostakovich and his star pupil Emil Gilels (Stalin's favourite pianist), he was soon released, thus avoiding Teofil Richter's fate.

Having grown up in the privileged class of tsarist Russia, Neuhaus enjoyed a cosmopolitan education, which in turn would greatly influence his students. He had studied in Berlin, Vienna and Italy, in addition to Russia; he spoke fluent Russian, Polish, German, French and Italian, which was quite common among the pre-revolutionary Russian elite. He was also extremely well-versed in literature, philosophy and the visual arts. As a concert pianist, he was known for his poetic, refined playing, although he suffered from stage fright. His strength lay in teaching. He was the kind of teacher who, when his pupils were to play Debussy, told them to think of a blossoming flower.

Richter would become one of his top students and greatest admirers. In turn, Neuhaus recalled their first meeting: "My students asked me to come listen to a young man from Odessa who wanted to join my class. 'Has he completed music school?' I asked. 'No, he hasn't studied anywhere.' I have to admit this surprised me: someone with no formal training at all wanting to go to conservatory! I was curious to hear this plucky young man. An incredibly intense boy came in: tall, thin, blond hair, blue eyes, lively and extremely attractive. He sat down at the piano, placed his large, soft, and nervous hands on the keyboard and began to play. He played very modestly—I would even say he exuded simplicity and spareness. I was fascinated by the way he got right to the core of the music. I whispered to a girl in the class, 'I believe he is a musician of genius.' After Beethoven's Sonata No. 28 he played a few of his own compositions. Everyone wanted him to keep playing. That day Sviatoslav Richter became my pupil."

The two became good friends. Richter even lived for a while in his mentor's apartment, where he slept under one of the grand pianos in the living room. Via Neuhaus he met Boris Pasternak. The writer had left his wife Zhenya for Neuhaus's wife Zinaida in 1930, but that did not affect the two men's friendship: Neuhaus himself had fathered a child a year earlier with his former sweetheart Militsa Borodkina, whom he would eventually marry.

Neuhaus was a regular guest at Pasternak's dacha in Peredelkino. And in the 1950s, when Pasternak was working on *Doctor Zhivago*, Richter visited him often. They also lived more or less around the corner from one another in the centre of Moscow. It was a small world among the intelligentsia, and anybody who was anybody knew everyone else—something that hasn't changed much in Russia even today.

The amiable Neuhaus, with his white moustache and head of hair, was like a father to Richter, and as a teacher he inspired much in the younger man's piano playing. "He put great store in tone quality, and made my playing freer," Richter said a year before his death. "My tone had to be loosened up. In the Liszt sonata he taught me to bring out the pauses."

Neuhaus also taught him to take his time, especially at the outset of a performance. "Thanks to him I developed a little trick," Richter told Monsaingeon. "You come out on stage, sit down, don't move. You count silently to thirty. The audience is nervous, thinking, 'What is going on?' And then… bam! That first note, after a long silence. Of course it's theatrical, but music needs a certain element of surprise. So many pianists serve up the same old dishes. But the unexpected grabs the listener's attention."

Richter would later say that he had "three teachers: Neuhaus, my father, and Wagner. I loved the way Neuhaus played and behaved. He reminded me of my father, but then a light-hearted version."

No one was surprised that Neuhaus immediately took Richter on as a pupil. And Richter was a quick learner. In December 1941, four years after his audition, he made the debut at the Moscow Conservatory that catapulted him to stardom.

Six months earlier, on 22 June, Hitler had invaded the Soviet Union, his three million troops marching at a rate of 200 kilometres a day towards Moscow. They did not encounter significant resistance, because Stalin had ordered the execution of nearly all the Red Army brass in his large-scale purge of 1937–38, so there was practically no high command.

The German rout of the Soviet army only exacerbated Stalin's already extreme paranoia. At the outset of the war, he ordered the arrest of anyone on the front lines who could be accused of sympathizing with the enemy. And then when troops of Hitler's ally Romania headed towards Odessa in August 1941, it was the turn of Soviet citizens with German-sounding names. Richter's father Teofil was arrested, accused of espionage, and was shot two months later. Had Sviatoslav been in Odessa as well, and not in Moscow, he might have suffered the same fate. The NKVD had had their eye on Teofil since the early 1930s, because he had taught piano to the children of the German consul. This diplomat, having heard Sviatoslav perform the solo variations from Glazunov's ballet *Raymonda*, invited him to add some musical panache to the consulate soirees. The Richters became friendly with the consul and his family, and they celebrated New Year's Eve together several times. When the German president Paul von Hindenburg died in August 1934,

Svetik visited the consulate for the last time, to play Beethoven's *Marche Funèbre*.

Shortly thereafter, the NKVD summoned Teofil, wanting to know what he saw at these get-togethers. "You'll have had to shout 'Kheil Khitler' the whole time, surely," his interrogators taunted. Seven years later, his statements would be used against him and seal his death warrant.

Only after the liberation of Odessa by the Red Army in 1944 did Richter learn of his father's death. But the full story didn't come to light until 1961: on the night of 6 October 1941, ten days before the Germans entered Odessa, Teofil was taken to a rubbish tip seven kilometres outside of the city, where he and twenty-four others were shot in the neck. The false accusations of espionage were struck down by a Supreme Soviet military jury in 1962. Teofil, like millions of other Soviet citizens, had been wrongly executed and would now be "rehabilitated". Richter never set foot on an Odessan concert stage after that. "It is where my father died," he says in the documentary, "executed by the Communists." With these few words, he sums up all his loathing for Stalin and his henchmen. But something else had played a role as well.

The only person who could have told Sviatoslav in 1942 about his father's death was his mother, Anna. She had, after all, played a significant role in Teofil's death. This was the other secret Richter carried with him.

In the late 1930s, Anna Richter had started an affair with Sergei Kondratyev, a professor of composition at the conservatory. Richter had studied with him briefly but was so bored by his lessons that he for ever lost interest in composing. Kondratyev himself harboured a secret: he had been a high-level civil servant under Tsar Nicholas II, and his family had consorted with the nobility. After the revolution, he concealed his tsarist past from the Bolsheviks, continually changing his surname and feigning a disability so as not to have to appear at the conservatory.

Teofil Richter knew of Kondratyev's affair with his wife, as well as his aristocratic past. In 1941, with the region on the brink of war, Richter wanted to evacuate Odessa with his family, but his wife refused to leave her lover behind, because of his invented "handicap". So, they remained in the city until there was no escaping. Shortly after Teofil's murder, Anna married Kondratyev, who then took the surname "Richter" to further conceal his own identity. When the occupation ended in 1944, the couple fled to Germany, where they would remain the rest of their lives.

Richter never forgave his mother's betrayal and considered it the darkest chapter of his life. He refused to speak to her after she and Kondratyev fled the country. Although a sort of reconciliation took place during his American tour in 1960, where his mother came to meet him, things never really healed between them. Richter did, however, on occasion redirect his income from a foreign tour to his ailing mother, rather than, as was customary, to the State.

Meanwhile, musical life in Moscow went on, unhindered by the war raging in the west and the south of the country. Richter still slept "under pianos", his answer to anyone who asked his address. At first these were Neuhaus's, but later they were at regular people's homes, such as that of his childhood friend Vera Prokhorova. Some people ascribed his nomadic life to a sense of insecurity because of his German surname.

A month after Richter's debut at the Tchaikovsky Conservatory, Sergei Prokofiev heard him perform his Sonata No. 6, and immediately asked him to play his Concerto No. 5: the piece had had little success thus far, but perhaps Richter's virtuosity could change all that. Richter, thinking that Prokofiev was joking, agreed and performed the work in March 1943. It was the beginning of a long but uneasy friendship, for, despite his admiration for Prokofiev, Richter was always wary of him. In the Monsaingeon interviews, he calls Prokofiev a dangerous and cruel opportunist who was only concerned with his own political future. He points to the cantata *Zdravitsa*, which Prokofiev composed in 1939 on the occasion of Stalin's sixtieth birthday. With lines like "Hail Stalin, father of us all" it is now an absolute no-go. Nevertheless, he told Monsaingeon, "It is a brilliant work. A monument, but then to Prokofiev's own glory. He was a man without principles, whose motto was, 'You want it, I'll write it.'"

I suddenly wonder about Richter's own attitude to the regime. Did he, like so many others, denounce his colleagues, or was he too young to have been drawn into all that? And what did he witness of Stalin's Terror, which had undoubtedly claimed victims within his own circle? No amount of searching unearths any answers, so I'll just assume he focused entirely on his music. Perhaps his situation differed from Prokofiev's in that he was a performer rather than a creative musician, and as such had no reason to fear being coerced into accepting compromising commissions.

Richter's star rose during the war years, partly thanks to his performances of Prokofiev's piano music. He also owed his popularity to his concert tours along the front. These were far from comfortable, but he was no stranger to bare-bones living. Once back in Moscow, he returned to sleeping under one of Neuhaus's pianos.

In 1943 he performed in the remote northern harbour cities of Arkhangelsk and Murmansk, where the Western allies delivered war materials by ship. They were thus a target for German bombs and were largely devastated. One grey, depressing day, Richter heard the violinist David Oistrakh play Tchaikovsky's concerto on the radio. It was the kind of melancholy bliss one can only experience when, in times of despair, you sense unexpected beauty that momentarily transports you away from the misery.

On 5 January, Richter performed in besieged Leningrad. He travelled there by military aeroplane, which was highly risky. The German siege, which had already gone on for nearly nine hundred days and claimed a million lives, was in its final phase. The windows of the Philharmonic's main hall were shattered as a result of a bombardment of the nearby Russian Museum. The audience was dressed in fur coats, but Richter, never cold while he played, wore his customary tails. He played magnificently.

Near the end of the war, a woman entered Richter's life: Nina Dorliak, seven years his senior. They had already met at a memorial concert for a clarinettist in 1937, in his first days as a music student. The frail, dark-haired lyric soprano appeared last on the programme, singing "Solveig's Song" and "Solveig's Lullaby" from Edvard Grieg's *Peer Gynt*. Richter nearly fell off his chair with amazement, not only from what he heard but from what he saw. She "was extremely pretty, a genuine princess", he wrote in his memoirs. "I started asking everyone, 'Who is she? Who is she?' And they told me her name was Nina Dorliak."

They met again in 1943, this time at the funeral of the stage director Vladimir Nemirovich-Danchenko. Again, she sang. And again, he was taken with her voice, even more than the previous time. He approached her and said, "I would like to give a concert with you." Dorliak asked him if he meant to share a concert, but he answered, "No, I want to accompany you."

They gave their first joint recital in Moscow in 1945. It was an all-Prokofiev evening, including the *Five Poems of Anna Akhmatova*. They were entirely open about Prokofiev being one of their favourite composers, even later, when his work came under fire.

I have a double-CD set of Dorliak and Richter, where, alongside Glinka, Dargomyzhsky, Mussorgsky, Rachmaninov and Prokofiev, they perform Schumann, Bach, Mozart, Schubert and Debussy. She sings all of it in Russian, including the German and French composers. The recordings were made in 1943 in Moscow, probably in the Melodiya studio located in the Anglican church, with its fine acoustics, around the corner from the Moscow Conservatory.

Dorliak's voice on this CD is light, tender and crystal clear. She sings for us, says the booklet, as though we are alone in the world; her voice offers us pleasure and joy, but it also torments the soul. Words that could have come straight from the mouth of her accompanist.

Even before her successful musical partnership with Richter, Dorliak had concertized with other big-name pianists such as Maria Yudina, Alexander Goldenweiser and Maria Grinberg. Like Richter and Neuhaus, she came from a musical family and had studied with her mother, the renowned Russian opera singer Xenia Dorliak (1881–1945), who, before the revolution, had appeared at not only St Petersburg's Mariinsky Theatre but also in Paris, Berlin and Prague, and had taught at the Moscow Conservatory since 1929. Her aristocratic family lineage—she was descended from the wealthy von Fehleisen family of St Petersburg and had been a lady-in-waiting to the Empress Maria Feodorovna—meant that Xenia was labelled an "enemy of the people" in 1937. Her career thus came to an abrupt end, and she gave her last concert that year in the conservatory's recital hall.

This aristocratic background did not prevent her daughter Nina from giving legendary concerts of Schumann, Brahms and Wagner under the French conductor Georges Sébastian in the 1930s. He had heard her sing Susanna in Mozart's *Le nozze di Figaro* and was so impressed that he insisted on teaming up with her.

Less than a year after rekindling their acquaintance, Richter moved in with Nina Dorliak and never left. They had a small, two-room flat on the Arbat, a fashionable pedestrian street in the centre of Moscow. It was a *kommunalka*, a communal living space, shared with three other families. Richter didn't mind. He and Dorliak never shared a bed, never married.

They were, however, inseparable friends. Everywhere Richter performed, whether in the USSR or abroad, she went with him. She was, it seems, a counterweight to his impulsive character. "I was his wristwatch," she told Bruno Monsaingeon. "I kept track of his appointments and managed his professional obligations."

I was surprised to learn that their relationship was purely platonic. Moreover, because the many photos of the pair seem to indicate just the opposite. To get to the bottom of it, a few days after my booze-laced visit to my neighbour Andrei, I rang the bell at a yellow brick building at 2 Bolshaya Bronnaya Street, where Richter and Dorliak lived from the early 1970s until the end of their lives.

Since Richter's and Dorliak's deaths in 1997 and 1998, respectively, the flat has become a memorial museum and intimate concert venue. But this time it was unattended; at least, no one answered the door. A few months later, one rainy, bored Saturday, I gave it another try. Again, no answer. So I gave up.

Only in 2019, seven years after my stint as Moscow correspondent, did I try again. It was springtime, the trees were in bloom, and the city exuded its typical Mediterranean atmosphere. On Bolshaya Bronnaya Street, the terrace of the chic Aist Café was packed with the now-ageing nouveau riche. Porsches, BMWs and Ferraris circled the block jadedly in the hope of spotting acquaintances. Young women in miniskirts and stilettos vied for their attention.

And again, no answer. But this time, not about to be deterred yet again, I waited until a resident came home, and sneaked in behind him.

An elderly, moustachioed man in a baseball cap was sitting in the concierge booth watching a martial arts film. Without looking up, he asked what my business was. "Richter's flat," I said, as politely as possible. "Sixteenth floor," he grumbled.

I got out of the lift on the top floor. A white cast-iron grating led to the double entrance to the Richter–Dorliak flat. I rang the bell at the door on the right, and it was opened by Yevgenia Leonskaya, a musicologist who gives tours of the museum apartment. She welcomed me and apologized for the broken downstairs bell.

After telling her I had lived in Moscow for five years and planned to write about Richter, she led me straight to Nina Dorliak's office, a space no bigger than three by four metres, with a lowered, soundproofed ceiling. Against one wall stood a grand piano, on top of it a framed photo of Richter and a bronze hand cast of Stanislav Neuhaus (Heinrich's son, who had died at the age of fifty-three). On the wall above the piano hung an attractive portrait of Dorliak in her younger years, a photo of Richter performing and a portrait of him drawn by Robert Falk.

We walked through to Dorliak's bedroom. Here, too: a lowered ceiling and photos of Richter on the walls, including one from 1945. "He had just won first prize in the third All-Union Competition," Yevgenia said. "But Shostakovich, the jury foreman, got a phone call from the Party Committee to tell him that Richter's passport said he was German, which so soon after the war was a very sensitive issue. Shostakovich was terrified at what might happen if Richter was awarded first prize, so they made him share it with Victor Merzhanov."

After passing through the modest dining room, we entered the great room, in fact the two adjacent living rooms with the separating wall taken down. The expansive view of the city centre, with the most attractive of Stalin's seven skyscrapers in the distance, was magnificent.

Two Steinway grand pianos stood side by side. On the wall behind them is Pyotr Konchalovsky's famous portrait of the pianist Verigin and his wife (given by her to Richter). "Richter's Yamaha is in the Pushkin Museum," Yevgenia told me. "Those standing lamps were a gift from the mayor of Florence."

We passed into the second flat, a mirror image of the first, and into Richter's study. Against the wall is a table with a score on it and a secretaire with built-in book recesses. In another bookcase, the titles betray his literary taste: Thomas Mann, Zola, Dostoevsky, Balzac. "But he loved Proust most of all," Yevgenia said. Proust, the gay dandy who shut himself up in his cork-panelled room to devote himself to literature, and whose character Swann kept elitist company but, as a Jew, was the eternal outsider. In retrospect, this seems to explain a lot about Richter himself.

The last stop was Richter's small bedroom. A single bed tucked into a corner. A photo of his father, Teofil, a handsome, nattily dressed man. "It was always a party at his parents' home," Yevgenia says. "He got that from them. It was in his nature; he was a passionate man."

Alone on a wall is the splendid portrait of him by Anna Troyanovskaya: Richter, red-haired, in an open-collared dress shirt at the piano. His fingers seem to glide over the keyboard. Keeping in mind the reverence of Russian museum personnel to the heritage they are charged with protecting, I gingerly enquired about Richter and Dorliak's relationship. Was it love? And what about those rumours of Richter's homosexuality?

"After the war there were a lot of informal relationships between men and women," she replies. "He and Dorliak were best friends, and inseparable. But of course, Richter was homosexual."

Her frank and prompt answer told me that in the Russian museum world, too, things had changed. Despite Vladimir Putin's anti-gay legislation and Russia's prudish, LGBT-hostile society, one could talk openly and plainly about Richter's homosexuality, even in a state-run museum like this. I was impressed.

"And what about Richter's depressions?" I hazarded now, emboldened by Yevgenia's openness. "He had his dips," she said. "But they passed as soon as he was able to make music. Once, in his later years, when he was in a depression after undergoing an operation in France, Rostropovich, who lived in Paris, rang him up and said, 'I'll come around now, and we can play something together.' And they did, the whole afternoon."

Just as I was about to leave, the museum's director, Yelizaveta Miroshnikova, came in. She was about to fetch her child from school but could spare me a moment. When I asked about Richter's friendship with the cellist Rostropovich, she confirmed what I already knew: that Richter didn't like Rostropovich getting mixed up in politics.

This made her answer to my question about his friendship with the widow of the writer Mikhail Bulgakov even more interesting. "Yelena Bulgakova and Richter were great friends," she said. "Back in the 1960s, she asked him to smuggle the manuscript of *The Master and Margarita* to Germany, which he did, so the first full translation could be published."

What Richter did was most certainly illegal, because the German translation, published in 1968, contained politically sensitive passages excised from the first Soviet edition, released two years earlier.

Yelizaveta also told me that Richter was mad about Boris Pasternak, whom he had met at Peredelkino. "It's no coincidence that there's a portrait of Pasternak in his study. Richter's archive includes early musical works by the author, who had dabbled in composition in his youth. But most of his best friends were the actors from the Moscow Art Theatre and the Vakhtangov Theatre."

I also questioned her about Richter's homosexuality. And, like Yevgenia, her answer was yes. "He probably had lovers, too," she added.

Richter's homosexuality could have affected his life story, I realized. Perhaps the KGB blackmailed him. His closest friends, Yelizaveta said, were in the know, of course, but it was a very well-kept secret. Prudish audiences might be unforgiving of his "deviant" sexuality. Moreover, homosexuality was punishable by years in a labour camp—it happened to plenty of Soviet musicians. The gay pianist Youri Egorov was terrified, and rightly so, when the KGB tried to lure him back to the Soviet Union from the Netherlands, where he had taken asylum.

"Richter was a mix of extrovert and introvert," Yelizaveta said. "As open as he was with friends, he was very closed-off to journalists and the authorities. He never answered the phone. Any discussions with officials, whether Russian or foreign, were conducted by Dorliak."

Richter's need for solitude came through in another anecdote, this one from Galina Arbuzova, the stepdaughter of the writer Konstantin Paustovsky. I was visiting her at her dacha in the town of Tarusa, on the Oka River, some 140 kilometres south of Moscow. We sat in her large garden, dominated by red, pink, purple and white flowers, and talked about the many writers, musicians and artists who had lived in Tarusa. And we landed on Richter, who had a small dacha (more like a log cabin) down the way, on the riverbank. She had been friendly with him. Sometimes, when he wasn't on tour, he would spend weeks on end in his cabin. "He was so depressed that he refused to see anyone," she recalled. "Once, after a concert tour in Poland, he brought back a whole train compartment full of pillows, which, like everything else, were hard to get in the Soviet Union. During one of those depressions, he would lie on those pillows on the floor the whole day."

In the lift going back downstairs, I thought of my neighbour Andrei, whom I had not seen since the end of my time as a correspondent. I hoped he would somehow resurface so I could share my findings with him.

I settled into a spot among the parvenus at the Aist Café and treated myself to a glass of white wine. Soon enough, not Andrei but two dapper, well-coiffed men—they could have stepped out of a French fashion magazine—sat down at the table next to mine. They held hands and gazed lovingly at each other. Just for an instant, Russia felt like a fairy tale where everyone lived happily ever after.

Back in the Netherlands, I visited the Russian conductor Lev Markiz one Sunday afternoon in May 2021 at his charming courtyard home in the Archipelago district of The Hague. Markiz was born in Moscow in 1930. His father, an economist at the People's Commissariat of Agriculture, was arrested during the 1937 purge, falsely accused of sabotaging production plans. "He spent two years in the Lubyanka prison," Lev says now, eighty-four years later. "He refused to confess, so they transferred him to the camps in Kolyma, way in the east of the country. He only returned twenty-eight years later. I was thirty-three, but it felt like he had only left the day before."

Markiz's mother, a doctor, was thus a working single mum. She worked day and night to make ends meet and send her son to music lessons, because "otherwise I'd have played outside with criminals". During the Second World War, she was sent to a field hospital on the front to tend wounded soldiers. Lev joined her in 1942 and was given the job of carrying amputated limbs to the skip.

As we sit drinking black tea in his comfortable, sunny living room, Markiz recalls the Great Terror as though it were something quite mundane.

"Even in those years," he says, "I did not know fear. The average musician could lead a perfectly normal life. But if you were famous... Take Shostakovich, permanently in the limelight—he was always afraid, even though his life was ostensibly successful and privileged, and he was showered with prizes. He had to manoeuvre through the system, and was good at it. Of course I hate Stalin. But he wasn't the one who made life difficult for composers, it was Tikhon Khrennikov and the committee members of the composers' union, themselves often third-rate composers. It was entirely arbitrary. One day you could get lambasted, the next day you were rewarded. Like when Shostakovich was excoriated by the composers' union, and the following day was given a five-room flat in Leningrad."

Markiz was not well off in the Soviet Union, but so long as he could perform, he could make ends meet. No one had money in those days. But a musician could eke out a living from radio recording sessions. In his Moscow years, Markiz made about five hundred recordings.

Musicians were paid per recorded minute. A symphony, for instance, paid ninety kopeks per minute, so a 25-minute work would bring in 22.5 roubles. Members of a symphony orchestra could even earn up to four roubles per minute. A return ticket by metro to the radio station cost Markiz ten kopeks, and lunch at the Radio Committee studio's excellent buffet, another ten.

Markiz studied at the Moscow Conservatory—violin with Yuri Yankelevich, chamber music with the pianist Maria Yudina, and conducting with Kirill Kondrashin—and later worked as a conductor in the USSR with many top musicians. In 1981, when the authorities relaxed emigration rules for Jews, he moved to the Netherlands, where Kondrashin had been given political asylum years earlier. There, he founded the chamber orchestra New Sinfonietta Amsterdam and was its leader until 1997.

In Russia, he was a regular visitor chez Richter and Dorliak. Perhaps he could tell me: was Richter gay? "Of course he was," Markiz answers. "But then, so many of the great musicians were. Sometimes they'd get arrested for it and would disappear into prison for a year and a half."

He also underscores Richter's complicated, unpredictable nature. The pianist always decided himself what, when and where he would play. "For instance: if he was in a good mood, he might waltz into the Moscow Conservatory concert manager's office in the morning and say he wanted to play a concert that same evening. Everything had to be organized and rearranged on the spot. But come evening, the hall was packed. Richter the man was very modest, but Richter the pianist was God."

In Moscow I thought I'd stumbled upon a secret, because no one, not even Monsaingeon, either mentioned Richter being gay or had wondered how it affected his relationship with the regime. But for a Russian living in The Hague, it was the most normal thing in the world. Everyone in Richter's circle apparently knew, and even they adhered to a sort of "don't ask, don't tell" policy—not much different than in Dutch artistic circles in the 1950s.

Yet another cup of tea and *stroopwafel* later, Markiz pulls another rabbit out of his hat when he tells me that Dorliak was a lesbian. "She was a prudent woman, and steered clear of intrigues. She was Richter's 'fixer'. For instance, she very tactfully organized for him to play a concert every year on Police Day. Remember, he was surrounded by admirers. Natalia Gutman, the cellist, was one. When she wanted to get married to the painter Vladimir Moroz, who was bisexual and with whom Richter was in love, Richter and Dorliak cut her off. In the end, that marriage didn't go through and

Gutman married the violinist Oleg Kagan, who was friends with Richter, so everything was all right again."

Once Markiz and I have said our goodbyes and I cycle back to the train station, I'm reminded for the umpteenth time that, in Russia, there's more to everything than meets the eye. Talented musicians and composers like Richter and Shostakovich might have lived comfortable lives under Stalin, but at the same time their nerves were frayed by the constant fear of being arrested or denounced for some misstep or another. It was a hopeless situation, and the only way to suppress their anxiety was to pour all their energy into their work. They just wanted, after all, to live.

Between his concerts and social life, Richter led a busy life in Moscow. He was friends not only with Boris Pasternak, but in fact with the entire intellectual and musical elite. There's a home movie of Richter and Dorliak receiving guests for a Christmas get-together, where they listened to the *Christmas Oratorio* together. Richter hugs everyone, lifts a lady friend off the ground. What a difference from the shy, serious persona of his later years. There's always a bit of disconnect with images like these, because you know they were made in a time when the cultural and political elite always had to be looking over their shoulder. Merriment and mortal fear don't tally. And yet…

What also strikes me is that Richter's artistic life was hardly impacted by Stalin's decision to tighten his grip on the intelligentsia after the war. He had needed their support during the war, and accordingly eased off the repression. And in the immediate aftermath of the war, which had cost twenty-eight million Soviet lives, people yearned for better times. Stalin owed the victory to them, and in return they wanted an end to the gulag, the forced collectivization, the arrests. Pasternak talked of an atmosphere of freedom. But because freedom is the greatest threat to a tyrant's power, Stalin reversed course, tightening the reins again in 1946. Soviet citizens were led to believe that the outside world—this time, the United States—was a pool of depravity with no other goal than the downfall of the communist utopia. Party Secretary Andrei Zhdanov, after Stalin the most powerful man in the Soviet Union, decreed a new path for the nation's spiritual life. He started by unleashing an assault on the poet Anna Akhmatova and the writer Mikhail Zoshchenko for the supposed Western influences in their work.

In four separate resolutions, the Central Committee laid out a new set of guidelines for literature, cinema, music and the stage, adding the one for music in 1948. Composers like Dmitri Shostakovich, Nikolai Myaskovsky, Aram Khachaturian and Sergei Prokofiev were accused of writing "formalistic" music, meaning their music emphasized form over communist ideals. This was, said the edict, an expression of anti-democratic tendencies that were "alien to the Soviet people and its artistic tastes". Remarkably, though, their music was not banned. The authorities only needed to convey their displeasure to the extent that no one would dare play it. Authoritarianism at its finest.

The smear campaign forced some composers to express openly their guilt at a specially organized meeting of the Union of Soviet Composers. At the congress, the younger generation of Soviet composers claimed a privileged position, and the ambitious thirty-four-year-old Tikhon Khrennikov was named general secretary, a post he held until old age.

Prokofiev, convinced of his own brilliance, did not sit back and take it. When he was accused of formalism, he marched up to

Zhdanov and demanded, "What right do you have to talk to me like that!" Zhdanov's response is not known, but the fact that no further punishment befell Prokofiev says enough.

On 28 January 1948, a month before the resolution was announced, Richter and Dorliak gave a concert in Moscow with songs by Rimsky-Korsakov and Prokofiev. The concert was a stunning success for the composer and performers alike. When Prokofiev was cheered by the audience, he went onstage and said to Dorliak, smiling, "Thank you for resurrecting the dead."

He was referring to a long-unperformed work of his. If there were two musicians who understood Prokofiev's music, they were Richter and Dorliak. Richter is said to have had no sympathy whatever for Zhdanov's criticism of Prokofiev.

Zhdanov died the same year as his campaign against Western influences in music began. A power struggle ensued, in which Politburo members Malenkov and Beria set out to eradicate Zhdanov's influence in the Kremlin by initiating a purge of his supporters in Leningrad, where he had been party leader.

Richter again managed to take no notice of this new wave of repression. This probably did not take much effort, seeing as he didn't read the newspapers. And even if he did know, he would have kept it to himself, because, in those days, silence was the best guarantee of survival. You could be betrayed even by your family or closest friends. As before, and as with many of his fellow artists, his answer was to bury himself in his work.

The Union of Soviet Composers' official hostility to Prokofiev's music continued even after Zhdanov's death, although a concert was given in honour of the composer's sixtieth birthday. But Prokofiev's poor health—he had recently suffered a stroke—made it impossible for him to attend. He listened to the concert over the telephone. Richter performed his Sonata No. 9.

In his memoirs, Richter recalls a kerfuffle that arose in 1952 concerning Prokofiev's Cello Concerto No. 2, featuring Mstislav Rostropovich as soloist. The Ministry of Culture opposed the performance, so no one dared conduct it. Until Richter suddenly offered. He had broken a finger during a fistfight with a drunken sailor on a train platform and was therefore taking a break from performing. He had, on impulse, offered to conduct—after all, his aspirations to stand before an orchestra dated from his gig as a répétiteur at the Odessa opera. His official reason for offering was that his injury might mean the end of his piano career. The authorities relented: since winning the Stalin Prize in 1949, Richter was the regime's golden boy, and he was given uncommon latitude. After three rehearsals, the concerto was performed on 18 February 1952.

Richter, somewhat miraculously, managed to conduct the orchestra after just ten days of lessons from Kirill Kondrashin. And, thanks in large part to Rostropovich's passion for the work, the concert was a success. Prokofiev was delighted to have finally found a conductor for his work. But it was not to be: after this one concert, Richter never conducted again. He said he did not care for two crucial elements of being a conductor: analysis and power.

Everything changed after Stalin's sudden death on 5 March 1953. No one described the shift better than Vasily Grossman in his novel *Everything Flows*, whose words I quote here:

> And then, all of a sudden, on March 5, 1953, Stalin died. This death was like an invasion; it was a sudden irruption into this

vast system of mechanized enthusiasm, of carefully planned popular wrath, of popular love that had been organized in advance by district Party committees.

Stalin's death was not part of any plan; he died without instructions from any higher authority. Stalin died without receiving personal instructions from comrade Stalin himself. In the freedom and capriciousness of death lay something explosive, something hostile to the innermost essence of the Soviet State.

Stalin had died! Some were overcome by grief. There were schools where teachers made their pupils kneel down; kneeling down themselves, and weeping uncontrollably, they then read aloud the government bulletin on the death of the Leader. Many people taking part in the official mourning assemblies in institutions and factories were overcome by hysteria; women cried and sobbed as if out of their minds; some people fainted. A great god, the idol of the twentieth century, had died, and women were weeping.

Others were overcome by joy. Villages that had been groaning beneath the iron weight of Stalin's hand breathed a sigh of relief.

And the many millions confined in the camps rejoiced.

Four days later, millions of Muscovites travelled from the workers' districts, either of their own accord or on orders from their bosses, to the House of the Unions in the centre of town, where Stalin lay in state. They were there, tears in their eyes, to catch a glimpse of the man whom they regarded as their father. The heaving crowds led to thousands being trampled.

Half hidden behind the mass of flowers around Stalin's coffin, Sviatoslav Richter sat at an upright piano. The previous day, while in Tbilisi for a concert, he had received an urgent telegram from Moscow ordering him to take the first available flight home. Tbilisi had been hit by a storm, and all passenger flights were cancelled. So instead he had travelled by military air transport, alone, in a plane full of wreaths from Georgian party leaders.

He was brought directly to the House of the Unions and had to start playing at once, accompanied by a small orchestra. He began with a long Bach fugue.

On a raised platform behind him was the coffin with Stalin's embalmed body. When Richter discovered that the piano's pedals weren't working, he decided to stuff a score underneath them. This alarmed the mourners, who thought the man kneeling next to the piano was planting a bomb under Stalin. Some of them began hissing, causing the police to panic and yank Richter away from the piano.

Although his view was largely obstructed, he did catch a glimpse of party leader Georgy Malenkov, who had a terrified look in his eyes. The struggle for succession among the various Soviet bigwigs was clearly already underway, and all signs pointed to the bloodthirsty Lavrenty Beria as the probable victor. Richter was disgusted by the radio eulogies those leaders gave in the days that followed. "I was no fan of Stalin," he would tell Bruno Monsaingeon years later, "but this [the phony behaviour of Stalin's closest comrades] was repulsive."

He denied having played at the state funeral as a form of protest against Stalin, as so many people claimed. He simply did not care about politics and lived only for music.

Stalin's death also affected Richter's professional life for the better, for now he could, at last, give concerts abroad, although until 1960 this was restricted to Warsaw Pact nations. His growing popularity made the authorities ever more wary that Richter, like so many other prominent Russian musicians, would defect to the West. A secret Central Committee document from the time read:

> The Ministry of Culture has requested permission from the Central Committee to send pianist S.T. Richter on a concert tour in the West. Research has shown that Richter is not a member of the Party, he is unmarried, and he has no children or family in the Soviet Union. His father was sentenced to death in 1941 by the Odessa military tribunal, his mother fled to West Germany. Richter is clearly one of the world's great pianists. Invitations stream in from major venues abroad. His tours in the socialist bloc have not led to warnings from KGB agents who accompanied him. [However,] based on the above-mentioned remarks concerning his parents, his solitary lifestyle, his lack of immediate family, and despite the obvious benefit to the state, the Central Committee has, with the approval of the KGB, determined that sending Richter to any capitalist country be given a negative evaluation. The official reasons to be given to foreign concert organizations are ill health and an overfull concert schedule. Other pianists are to be given priority.
>
> [Signed (on behalf of the Central Committee): Suslav, Brezhnev and Furtseva.]

In the Soviet Union, too, the KGB was shadowing him. He first got wind of it in Baku, the capital of Soviet Azerbaijan, where he tried to give his pursuer the slip. This game went on for months. One day, on a Moscow bus, Richter asked the man facing him if he was going to get out at the next stop. When the man answered affirmatively, Richter responded, "But I'm not." The man went pale and had no other choice but to get off the bus.

Richter would later tell Bruno Monsaingeon that the authorities' fear he would defect was unfounded. He simply loved Russia too much to flee, even though most of his émigré friends urged him to do so. But nowhere in the world could vie with Russia's nature, its vastness, its culture, its writers and its melancholy.

You can well imagine his love for Russia, especially when you consider Richter's life on the days when he did not rehearse or perform. He would go to his dacha in Nikolina Gora, outside Moscow, or the one in Tarusa, play a house concert or meet up with friends, mostly fellow musicians with whom he discussed or listened to music. For someone of his stature, life wasn't half bad.

And yet, I can't help wondering if there wasn't a moment when Richter considered leaving his homeland—for instance, when he learnt what had happened to his father on the night of 6 October 1941. And surely, didn't he worry that his homosexuality would eventually get him into trouble?

I take these questions to the cellist Dmitri Ferschtman, the Russian cellist who, like Lev Markiz, had emigrated to the Netherlands. As a student of Natalia Gutman, he first went to Richter and Dorliak's flat in 1969 to hear them rehearse Shostakovich's *Seven Romances on Poems by Alexander Blok*. As I had heard in the museum, Dorliak was in charge. "I soon figured out what was what," says Ferschtman, now seventy-five, on a sun-drenched terrace near the Amsterdam Conservatory, where he has taught for forty years. "Dorliak had the KGB eating out of the palm of her hand. It was, for instance, her idea to have Richter perform on Police Day. She covered for him. Thanks to her, his being gay never got out."

Other prominent musicians weren't as lucky, Ferschtman tells me. "The brilliant pianist Naum Shtarkman spent eight years in a labour camp in the late 1950s for the same thing. After he got free, they would only let him perform in remote, provincial cities. Only during Gorbachev's perestroika in the late eighties—Shtarkman was then sixty—was he given a position as professor at the Moscow Conservatory. But by then there was nothing left of his career."

After the United States and the Soviet Union signed a cultural exchange pact in 1958, the authorities abandoned their distrust of Richter. The perseverance of Sol Hurok, an influential American impresario of Russian descent, did the rest, although the green light for Richter's American tour was only given in March 1960.

In the ensuing years he appeared regularly in the West, mostly in France, where he established the music festival La Grange de Meslay, near the city of Tours, in 1976. He never felt as at home as in the medieval barn near the village of Parçay-Meslay, with its ideal concert acoustics. In a 1979 German documentary about the festival, Richter—a glass of wine in hand—flirts with the interviewer Johannes Schaaf, as if he is freer to be himself in France than in Russia. At the end of the film, another lifelong sore spot comes to light. When Schaaf asks him where he feels the most comfortable, Richter first shrugs and then names Italy as his top choice. He then ticks off his other favourite countries, saying that Germany is at the bottom of the list. He stops short of saying he hates it. Germany is where his mother and her lover lived. He had clearly never shaken off the trauma of the circumstances around his father's death.

At the end of his life, Richter spent a year in Paris. He loved the city yet felt estranged from his fatherland. He suffered from depression.

On 6 July 1997 he returned to Russia, going to his dacha in Nikolina Gora. Six days before his death, his childhood friend Vera Prokhorova sat with him on the veranda. Richter talked about the future: in a year he would start playing again. He wanted to set up a music festival in Zvenigorod. He died of a heart attack on 1 August 1997 in a Moscow hospital. His last words, a few minutes before he died, were: "I am so tired."

2

Yellow Shoes and Fancy Cars

I was seven years old when I first heard *Peter and the Wolf*. Not only was I immediately enamoured with the sound of the oboe (the duck) and the bassoon (the grandfather), but also of the voice of the Dutch singer-actor Ramses Shaffy, who narrated the story of brave little Peter, his grumpy grandfather, the various animals and the hunters. An entire symphony orchestra, introduced instrument by instrument, passed by. I can't think of a better way to demonstrate to a child how wonderful classical music can sound and what a grand spectacle a symphony orchestra is.

The delight of that seven-year-old me was only heightened at the close of the musical fairy tale, when Peter rescues the wolf from the hunters and takes it to the zoo. There was, in the end, only one victim: the duck, whom the wolf had gobbled up. But even he was alive and well in the wolf's stomach. Prokofiev's music made me happy, mostly because the menacing measures of the wolf's entrance were followed by light, carefree music that put that danger into perspective. What a nice man the composer must have been, I thought to myself, when I saw his picture—thin, bald and with a duck's nose—on the record jacket.

Years later I learnt that *Peter and the Wolf* had been written at the outbreak of one of the most brutal periods in Russian history:

the Great Terror. There was no sign of it in the music, although sometimes a television commentator would suggest a parallel between Stalin and the wolf. Nonsense, I thought, if only because the duck kept on quacking in the wolf's belly, while Stalin's millions of victims were dead and voiceless.

Meanwhile, I've learnt more about Sergei Prokofiev's life and personality. There is not much left of my childhood image of that "nice man". He was instead a cold, ambitious egotist who did whatever was necessary to ingratiate himself with the communist authorities. In return, he was able to enjoy an extravagant lifestyle and was the darling of the regime—the same regime that had sent his first wife to a labour camp.

His distasteful personality aside, I was still captivated by his brilliant, exhilarating music, especially because it evoked the edginess of those tempestuous days. So, I delved deeper into Prokofiev's biography, and had to conclude that his life was far from carefree. Contrary to what I had thought, he was perpetually high-strung, if not from his boundless ambition then from his relentless work ethic. It would be his undoing. While at first his compositions were performed regularly, his later work met with increasing censure and disappeared into a black hole. You can hardly imagine a more tragic downside to a career marked by success and glory; a more complex life than Prokofiev's is inconceivable. But it wasn't only his life that was a hell—equally tragic was his death and what followed it.

On Thursday, 5 March 1953, just before ten o'clock in the evening, Josef Stalin took his last breath in his dacha on the outskirts of Moscow. Just three months earlier he had celebrated his seventy-third birthday (not that old age prevented him from instigating a full-blown campaign of terror against the Jewish intelligentsia). On the Sunday prior to his death, the dictator suffered a stroke after a late-night dinner party with several Politburo comrades. When he did not appear the following afternoon, his bodyguards became uneasy. But fear of their volatile boss prevented them from entering his room unannounced—Stalin could just as well be fine, and their brazenness would not go unpunished. Only late that evening did they dare to go in, finding Stalin semiconscious, lying on the floor in his pyjama bottoms and undershirt. In a panic, they informed the previous night's dinner guests. They too wavered, terrified. What if Stalin recovered? So they did not appear at the dacha until three o'clock in the morning, knees trembling—twenty-three hours after their dinner party ended. And they waited until morning to summon a doctor. But it was too late. The dictator died three days later.

News of Stalin's death plunged the country into collective grief. Stalin had ruled the Soviet Union with an iron fist for almost three decades. Millions of his countrymen had been imprisoned or killed during his reign. And still, many could not hold back their tears—a not uncommon reaction in a dictatorship in which peer pressure and blind allegiance quash even the slightest measure of individuality.

Less than fifty minutes before Stalin's death and just a stone's throw from the Kremlin, Sergei Prokofiev passed away at the age of sixty-one. He, too, chronically ill for the past eight years, succumbed to a brain haemorrhage. But, unlike the dictator, whose death notice was read out loud to tearful listeners at schools, offices and factories, the death of the once-famous composer went more or less unnoticed.

Prokofiev's posthumous fame has reached an all-time high. I noticed it at once when I visited his former flat on Kamergersky

Lane, a museum since 2008. Nowadays the street, with its elegant nineteenth-century architecture, is pedestrian-only and one of the most pleasant promenades in Moscow's city centre. In the summer it's got the atmosphere of a Spanish "ramblas", full of fashionable young people promenading.

In 2016, the 125th anniversary of Prokofiev's birth, a bronze statue of him "walking" down the street, fedora on his head and attaché case tucked under his arm, was erected on Kamergersky Lane. This is a man in a hurry. The bronze Prokofiev seems to be leading us to a building entrance tucked among the cafés and restaurants. Behind the door, in a corner by the staircase, a policeman keeps guard. When I enquire about the museum, he gestures upstairs and answers with a sleepy "Third floor."

Once there, I pass through the two open white doors leading to a vestibule with a life-size front-on photo of a stylish yellow Opel Kadett sedan driving somewhere on Moscow's Garden Ring. It is the fireball in which the composer, always in a hurry, raced through the city. Nothing about the museum's interior betrays that at the time of his death it was a *kommunalka*, where he and his wife shared a kitchen, toilet and bath with other families. The atmosphere has been sacrificed to accommodate the demands of a modern museum. Walls have been knocked out to create one large room; in one corner, a nook of about two by five metres recreates Prokofiev's study: a sturdy wooden writing desk, his Bechstein upright piano and his bookcase with French and English novels are lined up against the wall. An open score rests on the piano's music desk. A grey vest is draped invitingly (it's chilly in the museum) over the back of a nearby chair. A huge Victrola gramophone demands the visitor's attention, and a leather suitcase sporting stickers like *Hotel Grande Bretagne – Le Petit Palais – Athènes* remind us of the composer's wanderlust. Is this, I wonder, the actual sofa on which Prokofiev expired?

No one in the museum can tell me, because the elderly guard is asleep and the woman at the ticket booth at the front says she doesn't know anything about Prokofiev. I'd have to ask the director, who won't be back until the following week, and I'll be gone by then. "You can always send her an email," she says.

In the main room is a poster for a concert on Saturday, 23 January 1943, the first in the series "Exhibition of Soviet Music" with works by Prokofiev and Shostakovich.

A flask of Kadine by Guerlain, Prokofiev's favourite cologne, catches my eye. The glass display case also holds one of the many brightly coloured scarves he wore with his green jacket, a plaid English cap, yellow gloves and boots, various types of hat, walking sticks and expensive wristwatches. He was a dandy in a country that no longer had any place for dandies.

Sergei Prokofiev and Mira Mendelson, his fiancée (later his second wife) occupied one of the two rooms in the *kommunalka* where Mira's parents lived. The space was big enough to serve as a living–dining–bedroom–study. During their first years there, Prokofiev was absent more often than not: he was sickly and spent much time in hospitals and sanatoriums. But the building, unlike many at the time, had the luxury of running water and central heating.

Only near the museum's exit does the visitor read anything of Prokofiev's Soviet-era vicissitudes. And even then, the information is sketchy at best. The biographical text makes no mention of Stalin's repression, although it does briefly refer to his first wife Lina's arrest and internment in a labour camp, as well as the banning of his compositions. These are more like casual asides, as if to suggest that arrests, incarceration and censorship were simply part and parcel of life in those days.

Prokofiev's last day started differently than usual. He decided to forego his customary morning walk. With an outside temperature of −12°C, it was obviously too cold for a man in his condition, so he rode instead to the Central State Archive of Literature and Art to pick up a manuscript of his. He also sent a copy of the revised version of the Piano Sonata No. 5 to the Union of Composers' music publisher with the request to assign it to the same copyist who had done the original version.

In the early evening, between six and eight o'clock, his wife Mira had read to him in her parents' room from *Gogol in the Memories of His Contemporaries*, one of his favourite books. Then he went to their room to rest. No sooner had he shut the door behind him than he came staggering back out.

Mira immediately called for his regular nurse and doctor. She also rang her father at his Economic Planning Bureau office, who hurried home and notified Sviatoslav and Oleg, Prokofiev's adult sons from his first marriage.

Prokofiev now lay on the sofa, complaining of a headache. He was feverish and asked for the doctor, as well as for water with lemon to combat the nausea. It all happened quickly: by the time his sons arrived, he was already dead.

That evening, friends and colleagues came by to pay their respects. The next day, his coffin was taken to the House of Composers on Bryusov Lane, a side street of Gorky Street (as it was called then). On 7 March, a memorial service was held there, in the recital hall. Only forty people attended: the House of Composers was more or less unreachable due to the crowds being channelled through the streets of Moscow to pay witness to Stalin's lying in state only a few hundred metres away.

Prokofiev's grieving friends were not deterred. Kabalevsky, Shostakovich, and Khachaturian read eulogies. Others performed music: the pianist Samuil Feinberg played Bach and David Oistrakh played the first and third movements from Prokofiev's Violin Sonata No. 1. The chairman of the Union of Composers, Tikhon Khrennikov—Prokofiev's longtime gadfly—saw to the logistics, out of posthumous respect and collegial admiration.

Prokofiev was buried on 9 March in the graveyard of the Novodevichy Convent, one of the most beautiful spots in Moscow and final resting place of the great writers Mikhail Bulgakov, Anton Chekhov and Nikolai Gogol. There were no flowers—these had been bought up entirely for Stalin, who was interred on the same day in the Lenin mausoleum on Red Square—so instead his coffin was surrounded by potted plants.

While a million Soviet citizens were drummed up to weep at Stalin's bier, Prokofiev's funeral cortège amounted to just fifteen mourners. And even that was something of a miracle, for *Pravda* had for three full days run non-stop news of the dictator's death and uttered not a word about the composer's. Ditto the leading music magazine of the day, *Sovetskaya muzyka* ("Soviet Music"), in which the first 115 pages were devoted to the great Kremlin music-lover. Only on page 116 did they mention Prokofiev.

So, on 9 March the Soviet music world mourned the loss of its colleague in silence. The tears of the string quartet at Stalin's catafalque were not for the despot, but for the composer. Colleagues of the violinist Veronika Rostropovich, the sister of the cellist Mstislav, tried to calm her after several hours, but she only wept even harder.

"Leave me in peace," she said to them. "I'm not crying for Stalin, but for Prokofiev."

No one knows how Sviatoslav Richter felt as he played before Stalin's coffin that same day at the House of the Unions. He never mentioned it. Richter may have regarded Prokofiev as a genius and championed his music even after it was banned in 1948, but at the same time he took a dim view of Prokofiev's compliance with the regime.

The truth of it all was more nuanced than Richter imagined. Like himself, Prokofiev was a wunderkind. Born in 1891, he learnt the piano from his mother and wrote his first composition, "Indian Gallop", at the age of five. When he was eleven, the head of the Moscow Conservatory recommended him for private lessons with the composer and pianist Reinhold Glière, who spent an entire summer tutoring the lad at the Prokofievs' home, the rural estate Sontsivka in western Ukraine. Prokofiev's father, an agronomist, managed the estate on behalf of an aristocratic friend. The family lived an idyllic life straight out of a Chekhov or Turgenev story, with dinners on the veranda and musical soirées lasting deep into the night. It is this agreeable world that I recognize in *Peter and the Wolf*.

In 1904, Sergei and his mother moved to St Petersburg so that he could continue his studies. In the stately imperial capital,* with its pastel-coloured Baroque palaces, he was introduced to the composer Alexander Glazunov, a professor at the conservatory. Glazunov was deeply impressed by the youngster and urged his mother to have him take the entrance exam. He did, and was accepted the following year.

* St Petersburg was the capital of the Russian Empire until 1917.

The ambitious upstart made himself unpopular at the conservatory. I picture him as a mama's boy, his hair neatly parted, well dressed, but as insufferable as a spoilt little prince. From day one, his professors and classmates alike (all much older than he) considered him an arrogant twit. But his fellow students really began to loathe him when he started keeping a tally of their errors. His bad reputation didn't seem to weigh upon him, because, despite his behaviour, they admired his compositions, which he performed for them with utter seriousness. I wonder if he ever smiled.

Nevertheless, he received only mediocre scores for his final examination in 1909. This too did not faze him, so sure was he of himself and his talent. He started dressing like a dandy, with plaid English suits, brightly coloured shirts and scarves and yellow shoes (the height of chic in those days), which only made him stand out and above his fellows even more.

By the time Prokofiev's father died of liver cancer in 1910, he was, at nineteen, already a musician of some renown. He performed his chromatic and dissonant piano pieces at the "Evenings of Contemporary Music" in St Petersburg, which so impressed the organizers that they invited him to perform the Russian premiere of Arnold Schoenberg's *Drei Klavierstücke*, Op. 11.

On 25 July of that year, he scored another triumph in the acoustically brilliant Great Hall of the Moscow Conservatory with his Piano Concerto No. 1. But although the audience was wildly enthusiastic, the reviews were disappointing. Prokofiev belonged "in a straitjacket", wrote the *Peterburgskaya gazeta* ("The Petersburg Gazette"), while *Golos Moskvy* ("The Voice of Moscow") said you could hardly even call it music. *Russkie vedomosti* ("Russian Reports") was slightly more nuanced, pointing to "the convincing freedom of his playing and the clear rhythms" to account for his success with the audience.

In the ensuing years, Prokofiev's compositions continued to make waves—and, not infrequently, to cause a furore. Consider the premiere of his Piano Concerto No. 2 on 23 August 1913. "To hell with this futuristic music! The cats on the roof make better music!" howled the conservatives. Opposite them were the modernists, who were taken with the piece. As usual, Prokofiev ignored his critics. Why shouldn't he? In 1911 the leading Russian music publisher Boris P. Jürgenson had offered him a lucrative contract. His music would be printed and sold at home as well as outside Russia's borders.

Two short years later, at the age of twenty-two, he took his first trip abroad to the bustling, theatre-rich cities of Paris and London. He saw Sergei Diaghilev's Ballets Russes and was so impressed that he decided to write ballet music himself.

His career was on the up and up. In 1914 he won the "battle of the pianos", a competition in which the five best piano students at the Moscow Conservatory vied for a Schroeder grand piano. Shortly thereafter, he returned to London, this time accompanied by his mother (with whom he had a close relationship); there he met Diaghilev, who extended him a ballet commission. But when he played excerpts from it for Diaghilev a year later in Italy, the impresario rejected it as too un-Russian. He did, however, give Prokofiev a second chance and offered him, on Stravinsky's recommendation, a ready-made subject: the ethnographer Alexander Afanasyev's folk tale "Chout". *The Tale of the Buffoon Who Outwits Seven Other Buffoons* (or, in short, *The Buffoon*) enjoyed a successful premiere in Paris in 1921.

By this time, the First World War had broken out, with Russia siding with England and France against Germany, Austria and the

Ottoman Empire. While the cannons roared and the Russian and Austrian hussars fought one another on the tsar's western border, Prokofiev performed wherever there were no hostilities, composed to his heart's content, went to the theatre and even travelled across the Balkans with some friends.

Thus, the war more or less passed him by. Even though he and his friends discussed the news from the front every day, he had no desire to enlist, nor did most of his privileged-class contemporaries. To secure an exemption from military conscription he re-enrolled at conservatory in 1915.

The war did considerably slow down Prokofiev's life. He spent the summer of 1916 on the Gulf of Finland, where the sea exerted a calming effect and inspired several new compositions. In July, as an intermezzo, he boarded a cruise ship for a trip down the Volga toward the Caucasus. For the first time he saw the Russia he only knew from the "mood landscapes" by the painter Isaac Levitan. He admired the picturesque towns along the river— Uglich, Yaroslavl, Kostroma and Plyos, with their wooden houses and small churches—but was undoubtedly also shocked by the poverty and drunkenness he witnessed among the farmers and peasants. This world was so completely different to the cosmopolitan St Petersburg to which he was so accustomed.

In February 1917, the Bolshevik revolution disrupted his comfortable, easy-going life. In Petrograd—St Petersburg had been renamed to rid itself of the German-sounding *-burg*—the tsar's reign came to an end. Drawn outside by the hubbub, he sauntered through town in his fur coat to take stock of the situation. In his autobiography, written during the Stalin days, he recalls the events as might be expected from one in his position under communism. His compositions of 1917, he writes, reflect more "the sentiment of the masses rather than the inner essence of the revolution". It sounds like an excuse to hide his lack of enthusiasm for the revolt. His later biographer Daniel Jaffé saw the irony in this: in those February days there was hardly any real "revolution" to speak of. Yes, a spontaneous countrywide uprising had broken out, but it had no leader and quickly disintegrated into anarchy.

The July rebellion against the Provisional Government made the unrest even more ominous. So Prokofiev and his mother traded their comfortable flat in Petrograd for the Grand Hotel in Kislovodsk, a fairy-tale spa city in the northern Caucasus. Aristocrats had been going there for decades under doctor's orders to immerse themselves in mud baths followed by a mineral-water cure (the name Kislovodsk translates to "sour water"), emerging as though reborn.

But the harmony of the perpetually sunny Caucasus was disrupted once again in October 1917 by the news that the Bolsheviks had staged a coup against the Provisional Government of Prime Minister Alexander Kerensky. For the first time in his life, Prokofiev felt real danger and realized his familiar world was about to crumble. In the weeks that followed, the revolution in all its violence rolled across the country. And it was clear that it had reached the Caucasus, too, when the Bolsheviks showed up at the Grand Hotel to cleanse it of loyalists to the tsar. They accosted Prokofiev, but let him go once they were convinced that he was not a White officer. Israel Nestyev, another later biographer (and a member of the Central Committee) wrote of the incident in 1957: "For the first time, the composer learnt that a Soviet man with a gun is merciless to his enemies but has the highest regard for the upholder of a truly great culture." As if to say: nowhere could an artist be better off than in the new Russia. It's no coincidence that for decades, so many progressive Westerners blindly trotted behind Stalin.

Prokofiev knew better. He left his mother safely behind in the Grand Hotel and went to Moscow to suss things out. He immediately looked up his old friend Vladimir Mayakovsky, the avant-garde poet who, full of hope, had embraced the new order. Prokofiev did not last long in this circle of artistic revolutionaries. In April 1918 he performed in Petrograd, but preferred to leave the country as soon as possible. Unfortunately, he did not have permission to do so.

At one of his concerts in the Winter Palace, the writer Maxim Gorky introduced him to the People's Commissar for Education, Anatoly Lunacharsky, who on behalf of the new regime was trying to win over the old intelligentsia. He got nowhere with Prokofiev. The composer in turn asked Lunacharsky for an exit visa. Now that the revolution had been followed by a bloody civil war, with the Reds and the Whites at each other's throats, he thought it best to try his luck in America. For the time being, he said, there was no place for music in today's turbulent Russia.

Lunacharsky was disappointed with the request. "You are a revolutionary in music," he said, "and we are revolutionaries in real life. We should therefore work together. But if you want to go to America, I won't hold you back."

Prokofiev's time abroad was, at first, no more than an extended foreign tour. His official reason for being there was to expand his cultural horizons. He probably intended to return home once the Bolsheviks had been defeated and the pre-revolutionary order more or less restored. But, so long as civil war raged, he might as well rack up some more musical triumphs abroad until the outcome of the war had been decided.

He spent the summers of 1920 and 1921 in London and Paris, both of which were teeming with Russian exiles. He was in his element among these old friends. And renewed contact with Diaghilev was the icing on the cake.

Back in America, however, Prokofiev had a hard time of it. His conceit and vanity were part of the problem. For one thing, he hated having to take a backseat to his compatriot Sergei Rachmaninov, who, while no more virtuosic a pianist than Prokofiev, played everything; in American concert venues Prokofiev only performed his own works, with an eye to making a name for himself as a composer. Moreover, he had to compete with the popular modernist Stravinsky, whose music the Americans had embraced. He was frustrated by not achieving the breakthrough to which he felt entitled.

Contrary to Rachmaninov, who had left Russia out of distaste for the revolution, Prokofiev told anyone who asked that his stay in America was only temporary. He even made a point of defending the new Russia in interviews with American journalists, as though to project his gratitude to Lunacharsky for granting him an exit visa. His stance earned him the nickname "the Bolshevik pianist". No one could have known then that this is exactly what he would later become.

Everything changed when Prokofiev gave his first solo recital in New York. With his name now cemented as an artist, the future suddenly looked bright. More performances followed, and soon enough his star power in the New World matched Rachmaninov's. His good fortune was augmented by a meeting with the twenty-six-year-old soprano Lina Codina, an attractive, dark-haired woman, the daughter a Spanish émigré tenor and a Polish-French soprano from Odessa. Her exotic beauty and adoration of Prokofiev certainly stroked his ego. They soon became romantically involved.

In 1920, after a period of financial hardship, Prokofiev returned to Europe, now with Lina at his side. Their first stop was Paris, where Prokofiev again looked up his old friends from St Petersburg. It was a bittersweet reunion, because, although the émigrés still held out hope for a return to Russia, it would be clear by the mid-twenties that the life they had left behind was gone for good. Their temporary exile had become permanent. Russian literature and music were their only hold on the past, so for some, Prokofiev must have had the allure of a prodigal son. His decadent swagger helped: you can just picture him swanning down the Champs-Élysées on a Sunday afternoon, glancing vainly over his shoulder to see if any of his old countrymen had spotted him.

To get a better idea of the atmosphere, I turn to the book *L'Émigration russe en photos: France, 1917–1947* and see the Russian émigrés in their new day-to-day lives. In the 1920s, 800,000 Russians fled to France, 45,000 of them to Paris. Only a handful had managed to get their fortunes out with them, so counts and countesses, princes and princesses had become regular citizens without their jewels, fur coats and top hats. For the first time in their lives, they had to earn a living as a taxi-driver, doorman, factory worker or seamstress. And at the same time, they retreated into their cliques, with Russian newspapers, publishers, orphanages and churches. Prokofiev felt right at home in this "Little Russia", if only because he was idolized as a priceless relic of a world now out of reach.

Still mindful to keep all commentary about the Bolshevik regime in check, he allowed friends of the new Soviet Russia to organize concerts for him in Paris. And, during a brief sojourn in America in 1921, when his comic opera *The Love for Three Oranges* was produced under his own direction, he even praised the musical situation in his homeland with the optimistic but hypocritical words: "The Bolsheviks have promoted the arts and are doing everything to allow them to flourish. [...] In my opinion, musical culture in Russia has a bright future." These were the words of an opportunist born of necessity.

I first saw *The Love for Three Oranges* in January 2010 in the auditorium of a shopping centre on the busy New Arbat Avenue in Moscow. The performers were the musicians of the Helikon Theatre, led by stage director and conductor Vladimir Ponkin. Their theatre had been under refurbishment since 2006, so the troupe performed wherever it could, even in a shopping mall.

The audience in the spacious auditorium, which has the feel of a cinema, was predominantly made up of older Russian women. When the orchestra launched into the rousing overture and the chorus entered in playing-card costumes—hearts, diamonds, clubs, spades—I immediately recognized what is so good about this music: it's an American musical with a dash of Russian drama.

The Love for Three Oranges, based on a 1761 stage play by Gozzi, is one of the jolliest operas I've ever seen and obeys Prokofiev's musical motto of "speed, energy and movement". It tells the story of a melancholy prince whose depression can only be cured by a fit of spontaneous laughter. His valet is assigned this task but fails. An evil witch sets the prince a challenge involving three oranges. Naturally it ends with a beautiful princess, "and they lived happily ever after".

I laughed all the way through the performance. I recognized some of the music, like the famous march, from the radio. The opera is humorous and tense at the same time, and could just as easily have been by a Western composer like Kurt Weill.

When the curtain fell, the old ladies clapped in unison as though they were at a Communist Party congress. Some shouted, "Hoorah!" Aside from *Peter and the Wolf*, I can't imagine a better introduction to Prokofiev's music.

Back in Europe, Lina, Sergei and his mother rented a house in Ettal, a small town in the Bavarian Alps. They were expecting their first child and were married that September. Shut off from the outside world in an environment that, in the winter at least, felt like Russia, Prokofiev spent the next year working on a new opera, *The Fiery Angel*, which would only be performed after his death.

Meanwhile, the Soviet authorities did everything they could to lure him back. They were keen to give him a starring role in their propaganda offensive touting the communist utopia as a paradise for innovative artists. But for now, Prokofiev declined: his future lay more in Europe than in Russia.

When their landlord sold the house in Ettal, the Prokofievs moved to Paris, where Lina gave birth to their son Sviatoslav on 27 February 1924. The death of Prokofiev's mother that December came as a blow to Sergei. They had a symbiotic relationship and he fell into a deep, lengthy period of mourning. As when his father died, he was unable to talk about it, even to his best friends.

He found solace in the Christian Science movement, a sect founded in America in 1879 and fashionable among the upper classes. They believed that prayer was superior to conventional medicine. This appealed to Prokofiev, whose hard-driving work ethic resulted in chronic health issues. Under the influence of Christian Science, he also abandoned his expressionist style in the late 1920s and nudged his music towards "new simplicity", a catchword for Soviet-era aesthetics. A diary entry from December 1925 indicates the level to which Christian Science's doctrine—real or not—had affected him. He had travelled to Amsterdam and The Hague for concerts with the Concertgebouw Orchestra and during the train journey he experienced heart troubles. "I tried to treat it via Christian Science," he wrote. "Noticed an improvement!"

While his music was a great success in stylish-but-stiff The Hague, Prokofiev preferred Amsterdam. He wrote in his diary about the Amsterdam reception to his Piano Concerto No. 3: "An uncommon success: the hall (three-quarters full) gave me a standing ovation; even some in the orchestra rose to their feet. That was a first in my life, and it excited me greatly."

Both cities—The Hague with its embassies and royalty, Amsterdam with its bustle and artistic progressivism—must have triggered some nostalgia for his former life in Russia. Perhaps this fed a longing to return, for he began to realize ever more strongly that his roots were in Russia and that he belonged there, among Russians. His music might, at times, sound wholly American or modernist German, but Russia was his inspiration. So, again, Lunacharsky did him a favour. With Stalin's blessing, the energetic people's commissar had embarked on a propaganda tour of Western Europe to forge cultural ties and promote the arts of the new Soviet Union. During his tour he stopped in Berlin and Paris to meet with already famous Russian émigré-artists like Stravinsky and Prokofiev. In his request for an exit visa, Lunacharsky stressed to Stalin that these emigrants were in no way anti-Soviet, and that some might be persuaded to return to Russia for good. It would be a good idea, he argued, for those who by now felt more German or French than Russian to return on occasion so they could share their work at home. Stalin went along with the idea, and, on 21 July 1925, Prokofiev, Stravinsky and the renowned concert pianist Alexander Borovsky were authorized to visit the USSR, albeit under strict conditions: "The government agrees to your return to Russia. It agrees to grant you full amnesty for all prior offences, if any such occurred. It stands to reason that the government cannot grant such amnesty for counter-revolutionary activities in the future. It likewise guarantees complete freedom to travel into and out of the Soviet Union as you desire."

Stravinsky and Borovsky, alarmed by the threatening undertones, chose not to accept. Prokofiev, on the other hand, was excited by the idea, all the more because, despite his successes in the Netherlands, he felt underappreciated in the West. Besides, he missed his former colleagues in Moscow and St Petersburg. The urge to return was strengthened when, in 1926, he met up with his old friend Vsevolod Meyerhold in Paris. Under the Bolsheviks, Meyerhold, an avant-garde director, had become a renowned theatre reformer. After Prokofiev took him to a rehearsal of the Ballets Russes, Meyerhold suggested staging *The Gambler* in the Soviet Union, inviting his friend to see what the Bolsheviks had accomplished there.

And so, on 19 January 1927, just a week after getting his driver's licence and after almost ten years' absence, Prokofiev and his family left by train for a tour of his fatherland that would last until 23 March.

Upon arriving at Belorussky railway station, Prokofiev was confronted with an impoverished Moscow. He noticed it at once when some friends came to welcome him in his carriage. In his diary he wrote of one of them, the musician Vladimir Derzhanovsky: "He's got felt boots on, and, by the way, all of them are wearing odd caps, sheepskin jackets, et cetera, in short, the kind of thing that puts off foreigners."

Meanwhile the authorities carried on with their charm offensive. Prokofiev was welcomed as a prodigal son and was showered with honours. After all, what more convincing affirmation of the socialist utopia could one ask for than the return of a star artist? Here Prokofiev got all at once what had only come his way in dribs and drabs in the West, and it was worth doing anything to keep it coming. This was perhaps the moment, now that he was considering a return to his mother country, that the vain, self-seeking Prokofiev was reborn and his ambition amplified many times over.

But his sober and unsentimental side also began to take notice of the socialist state's darker side. For instance, a high official from the Central Committee rang him at his Moscow hotel to ask if he would participate in a concert commemorating the Communist takeover of Shanghai. The call troubled him, because he knew that wiretapping was commonplace in the USSR and that people could be detained and interrogated over nothing. It had happened to his cousin Yekaterina Raevskaya, who was subsequently exiled to a city in northwest Russia. He had also heard tell of people being arrested at their place of work, committing suicide or simply disappearing. When he hung up, he experienced a fearful moment of it being his turn.

And yet, I wonder how afraid he really was. When another cousin, Shurik Raevsky, was arrested, his fear quickly turned into conceit and he intrepidly demanded his release. Perhaps Prokofiev thought he wasn't taking much of a risk, for the only reason the authorities detained Shurik was because he had studied at the Imperial Lyceum, a privileged breeding ground for the tsarist elite.

In any event, Prokofiev's intervention didn't help—Shurik spent years in prison.

After that, he started wholeheartedly playing the game. It was the price of fame. Just read his diary entry about an official reception during his tour: "It was one toast after the other, including one from a young Communist student. His speech was directed at me and enthusiastically declaimed. He included me among the young musical Communist vanguard. Well, all right then, come and conquer!"

For two months, Prokofiev performed in Moscow and Leningrad (as Petrograd had been renamed after Lenin's death in 1924). The highlight of his stay there was a performance of *Love for Three Oranges* at the Mariinsky Theatre. He was delighted with the playful, creative staging and eagerly anticipated a planned reprise in Moscow.

He recognized much of pre-revolutionary St Petersburg in Leningrad. During the opera's intervals he would hurry outside, happily ambling like a lovestruck youth through the streets and along the canals. Fits of nostalgia would take him back to the time when a revolution was no more than the dream of a small group of radicals. His journal entry on 9 February 1927 reads: "After years of gadding about abroad, I had lost touch with Petersburg and started to believe that patriotism had foisted [the notion of] her beauty on the Petersburgers, and that Moscow was truly the heart of Russia [...]. In this frame of mind, I was now bowled over by Petersburg's magnificence: so much more dignified and statelier than Moscow! The white snow and clear skies contributed to this image."

In Leningrad, Prokofiev met a number of younger composers, some of whom played their music for him at the piano. The one who made the greatest impression on him was a twenty-one-year-old with thick glasses. His name was Dmitri Shostakovich.

After his final concert in Moscow, he and Lina returned to Paris and a few days later continued on to Monte Carlo for the rehearsals of his new ballet *Le Pas d'acier* (known alternatively in English as *The Steel Step* or *The Age of Steel*). It was meant as an intermezzo for him to fulfil business agreements; during that time, his second son, Oleg, was born.

His fickleness was, however, starting to make the Soviet authorities nervous. So long as his return to Russia was uncertain, they gave him leeway in his movements. At the same time, the Russian émigrés in Paris regarded his trip to the USSR as a betrayal. They saw it as appeasing the Bolsheviks and furthering their propaganda. Perhaps this was Prokofiev's fundamental dilemma: on the one hand, he longed to return to Russia, but not to write music for the proletariat (even though it was still unclear what that was supposed to sound like). On the other hand, his true audience was the Russian aristocracy, but they had all left the country.

Prokofiev's ambitions outweighed his doubts. He brushed aside the criticism, although it's hard not to see the last segment of the ballet, in which the dancers become one great machine, as Soviet propaganda. Prokofiev somehow felt that he was on the right track as a composer and that he had found a happy medium between appeasing the authorities and realizing his own musical goals.

But with the tragic fate of his Raevsky cousins in mind, he put off a definitive return to Russia and extended (notwithstanding his Soviet citizenship) his French *carte d'identité* at the end of his Russian tour.

His time in America had made a keen businessman of Prokofiev. He now insisted on being paid as a foreign artist for performances in Moscow and Leningrad—that is, in dollars, not roubles. Moreover, he refused to let himself be a pawn of political Soviet music organizations, so concerts for labour organizations were for closed audiences only.

He returned to Moscow in October 1929, but, having injured his left hand in a car accident in France, he was unable to perform. A new wind was blowing through Russian musical life, which had gained momentum when the People's Commissariat for Enlightenment was disbanded and its head, Prokofiev's supporter Lunacharsky, was "promoted" to the post of envoy to the League of Nations in Geneva—in fact, a demotion. Prokofiev's brilliant future on the Soviet music scene was, it seemed, to be cut short. Soon after his arrival, he met with Meyerhold and Boris Asafyev, an expert in avant-garde music and a leading figure in the Association for Contemporary Music (ACM). They filled him in on the latest political developments and their consequences for musical life. Soon enough, he would find out first-hand what this entailed.

The ACM had been founded in 1923. Its directors included modernists like Nikolai Roslavets and Alexander Mosolov, who encouraged experimental music, but who also favoured giving their colleagues considerable artistic latitude. It was precisely this freedom against which proletariat groups protested. In that same year, these groups banded together to form the Russian Association of Proletarian Musicians (RAPM) and quickly moved to denounce the ACM's modernism and constructivism as products of the bourgeoisie and individualism. The ACM lost the struggle.

The RAPM's musical politics boiled down to promoting optimistic, bombastic and accessible "melodies for the masses" rather than experimental symphonies that employed things like turbines, sirens and factory whistles. Composers were squeezed into a petty, parochial mould where everything had to be hummable and, most of all, uniform. Everything else was banned. All that counted was that the masses be fed a diet of ironclad socialist repertoire. And it was the RAPM that started nipping at Prokofiev's heels.

On 14 November, while attending an orchestra rehearsal of *Le Pas d'acier* at the Bolshoi Theatre together with Meyerhold and members of the theatre's management, Prokofiev was accosted by musicians from the RAPM, who were by now holding the theatre's reins. They demanded an account of the ideology behind the ballet: did it depict a "slave factory" (i.e. a capitalist company) or a Soviet plant where the workers were in charge? And if it was indeed the latter, where and when had Prokofiev visited such a factory, seeing as he'd been abroad for the past nine years?

Prokofiev was furious at this impudent and aggressive interrogation. His reply was indicative of his artistic mindset: "That question concerns politics, not music, and therefore I refuse to answer it." The RAPM wasted no time in disparaging the ballet in its magazine *The Proletarian Musician* as "a crude and vulgar grotesquerie, a counter-revolutionary composition bordering on fascism". This left the Bolshoi no choice but to withdraw the ballet from its programming.

The RAPM's unjust criticism was no more than common bullying, and Prokofiev was crushed. He had to stay in Moscow to conduct a revised version of the Sinfonietta for a live radio broadcast, but afterwards he left at once, deeply disappointed, for Paris. He wrote to his friend Serge Koussevitzky in America that life in Russia had indeed become more difficult, but that there were still interesting things happening and that he was planning to return in the spring, this time with Lina. The restrained tone of the letter shows he anticipated a more welcoming attitude from the Soviet authorities. Only years later would he realize what an idle hope this was. One thing, though, was clear: the more he missed Russia, the more he hated its politics.

So long as his musical activities took place in the West, Prokofiev mostly managed to evade the wrath of the RAPM. But the Wall Street crash of 1929 put paid to that. The Great Depression took its toll on America and Europe alike. There was no money for expensive new opera and ballet productions. At first this was of no consequence, because Prokofiev's solo engagements showed no sign of letting up, especially in Europe. In a letter to Vladimir Derzhanovsky he wrote, "If it goes on like this, it's farewell to Moscow until the autumn." And, as a P.S.: "I am deeply distraught by the death of Mayakovsky."

In 1929 Vladimir Mayakovsky, the great poet of the Bolshevik Revolution, as one might call the tall Georgian, met more or less the same fate as Prokofiev. He, too, was being hounded by a Soviet artistic organization—in his case the Russian Association of Proletarian Writers (RAPP)—that branded him a "class enemy" whose work was unintelligible to the masses. The RAPP attacked his satirical play *The Bathhouse*, produced by Meyerhold, who himself was also increasingly coming under fire. Bitterly disillusioned with the new regime, Mayakovsky took his own life on 14 April 1930. His suicide only confirmed Prokofiev's doubts about Soviet Russia. Conveniently, his busy concert schedule in Europe meant that he could safely avoid returning to the USSR for the coming six months.

But when, on 23 April 1932, the Central Committee created the Union of Russian Composers and Stalin decreed "socialist realism" a general artistic policy, Prokofiev immediately adapted, even though he was living abroad. His music now exhibited the requisite "new simplicity". It all pointed to his desire to undertake a new tour of the USSR. But what he didn't realize was that Soviet musical life was to be entirely centralized. The new Union of Composers was to be patron, publisher and promoter, all in one; it also provided communal housing for its preferred members, these musicians being offered comfortable flats in the "House of Composers". The union's chairman had the power of a tsar. He was answerable only to the State Committee on the Arts, a department of the Council of People's Commissars. In exchange for "assistance" with their creative projects, the composers were expected to attend meetings where work by their colleagues was discussed and criticized—censored, if you will. Reports were published in the union journal, *Sovetskaya muzyka*.

In April 1933, Prokofiev again went to Moscow and Leningrad to perform, and now he gushed with exaggerated praise for the new Soviet Union. According to his friend Nicolas Nabokov, a Russian-American musicologist and a cousin of the writer Vladimir Nabokov, he even embraced the Central Committee's "socialist realism" ideology as his own. He claimed always to have striven to conceive "simple, singable melodies" easily grasped by the masses. This fawning immediately earned him a contract from the Lenfilm studio to compose the film music for a historical feature, *Lieutenant Kijé*.

His eagerness to court the authorities went even further. On 16 November 1934, he published in *Izvestia* ("The News") the article "The Direction of Soviet Music", in which he declared his readiness to adapt his own musical style to the dictates of socialist realism. "Most of all we need great music; that is, music that in conception as well as execution reflects the grandeur of our time. Such music could be stimulating for our own musical development and would reveal our true character to the outside world. [...] The composer must bear in mind that there are thousands of people in the Soviet Union who are discovering music, people who in the past were immune or indifferent to music. [...] Most of all, music must be melodious, but with melody which is simple and comprehensible, without becoming repetitive or trivial."

Despite his zeal to pander to the Soviet authorities, Prokofiev still did not realize that they were mainly using him as an ambassador for their new society. Regaling him with commissions and promising him the earth had but one goal: to gradually lure him into the socialist fold.

Nestyev's biography (itself a piece of Soviet propaganda) makes their intentions clear. Prokofiev was called "the bearer of the new Russian culture" and "the bearer of the people's song". In an attempt to do the truth at least some justice, Nestyev also cites a conversation between Prokofiev and the French music critic Serge Moreux. Here, there is no talk of political motives, only the classic yearning for Russian soil:

> Foreign air does not suit my inspiration, because I'm a Russian, that is to say the least suited of men to be an exile, to remain myself in a psychological climate that isn't of my race. [...] I've got to live myself back into the atmosphere of my native soil. I've got to see real winters again, and real spring. [...] I've got to hear the Russian language echoing in my ears, I've got to talk to

people who are of my own flesh and blood, so they can give me back something I lack here—their songs, my songs. Here I'm getting enervated. I risk dying of academism. Yes, my friend, I'm going back!

But there were also those opposed to his return, like the members of the Leningrad composers' union, who were dead set against his music being performed in Russia. Myaskovsky warned him that all his projects planned for the Mariinsky Theatre were now uncertain, and that he was better off settling in Moscow than in Leningrad.

Prokofiev's dilemma must have driven those close to him to distraction. His homesickness for Russia and his hard-as-nails ambition seemed to be in constant conflict with his fear of the authorities taking control of his art. In the end, his naïveté and inflated self-esteem won out. A period in the countryside, on the banks of the Oka about 140 kilometres south of Moscow, would nudge him toward a definitive decision.

I know that area well. It is the Russia of one's dreams, of the stories of Chekhov, Tolstoy and Turgenev, with green woodlands and a broad river flowing past high banks and the occasional cluster of wooden houses.

The town of Tarusa is my favourite. Years ago, I was visiting the stepdaughter of Konstantin Paustovsky there. The place was home to all manner of renowned artists, musicians, writers, and poets; you trod in the footsteps of Marina Tsvetaeva, Nadezhda Mandelstam, Joseph Brodsky, Sviatoslav Richter and Alexander Ginzburg. The artists and musicians came here of their own free will, but the writers had been banished to beyond a hundred-kilometre radius from Moscow.

Paustovsky's dacha is one of the most impressive I've ever seen. It's a blue-painted wooden house that perches on the edge of the picturesque town, high on the riverbank. Unlike in Paustovsky's day, trees now block the view of the river. Galina Arbuzova—Paustovsky's stepdaughter—had planted a sumptuous garden around the dacha, unlike any I had seen elsewhere in Russia. Rhododendrons and roses in abundance.

Prokofiev spent a similarly bucolic summer at Polenovo, an artists' retreat across the Oka and a kilometre or so upriver from Tarusa. He had brought his wife and young sons with him for the first time, probably to get them used to being in Russia. He had a small, private cabin in which to work, with nothing but a writing table and a balcony overlooking the river. After five hours' labour, he played chess or tennis, read, walked or went for a swim. It was almost like being back on his parents' estate in Ukraine, as if the revolution had never happened.

He would return to Russia for good in 1936, after another international concert tour. But during that tour, in late January, something happened that would seriously shake up Soviet musical life: Stalin's sudden antipathy for the young Shostakovich's *Lady Macbeth of Mtsensk*. At once, composers and musicians woke up to the fact that they were not immune to the repression that Soviet writers had faced for the past two years. Now, too, the authorities' only aim was to stifle the individual in favour of the interests of the state. Ever since its premiere in 1934, *Lady Macbeth* had enjoyed widespread praise, both in the USSR and abroad. Many regarded the opera as the apex of Shostakovich's output until then.

But when Stalin, Vyacheslav Molotov and Andrei Zhdanov hurriedly left their box during a performance on 26 January, the composer knew something was very much amiss. Indeed, two days later, the headline "Muddle Instead of Music" appeared in *Pravda*, a newspaper that normally never wrote about music. Its anonymous author decried *Lady Macbeth of Mtsensk* as "nervous, convulsive and spasmodic music borrowed from jazz". Its success with audiences abroad was dismissed as the desire to "tickle the perverted taste of the bourgeois". A week later, *Pravda* published a second attack on Shostakovich, now directing its fury at his ballet *The Limpid Stream*. Not only Shostakovich, but other "degenerate modernists" like Nikolai Myaskovsky and Aram Khachaturian came under fire. Shostakovich saw it as a sign of impending doom. There was no doubt that the articles had been written on Stalin's orders. And although the Great Terror would flare up only later that year with a large show trial of prominent Party members, the cogs of the repression machine were already spinning at full speed.

The music world shuddered. In early February, the two *Pravda* articles were the subject of debate within the official artists' organizations. In Leningrad, when the local composers' union brought it up, some composers at once showed their true opportunistic colours. Boris Asafyev, for one, withdrew his earlier praise of the opera, claiming a lapse of judgement. Worse yet, at a Moscow meeting in the House of Writers, the ambitious twenty-three-year-old Tikhon Khrennikov aimed his artillery not only at Shostakovich but at Prokofiev as well, accusing him of having called Soviet music "provincial".

On tour in Eastern Europe, Prokofiev read the disastrous news from articles Lina had sent him from Paris. He had earlier called *Lady Macbeth* "an example of first-class theatre" and was thus shocked at what he read. But Lina, convinced of the constructive role he would play in Soviet musical life, reassured him that the events posed him no threat. He hadn't, after all, been named in the *Pravda* articles. Prokofiev would undoubtedly have responded differently—and might even have decided to remain in the West—had he been in Moscow rather than Prague and witnessed at first hand Shostakovich being thrown to the wolves.

When Prokofiev moved back to Moscow for good, with high hopes, his colleagues welcomed him as the conquering hero fresh from battle. No one mentioned the *Lady Macbeth* affair, and he made light of politics. For instance, observing an election campaign poster of Stalin on the street—Moscow was hung full of Communist banners—he remarked to Lina, "Look, Birdie, they're all voting for the same fellow." Such a comment would have earned a regular Soviet citizen a bullet.

Until late June, the Prokofievs lived in the Hotel National, across from the Kremlin. Thereafter they moved into a luxurious four-room flat on the Garden Ring, made available to artists of repute by the State Committee on the Arts. Nearly all their neighbours—including the pianist Heinrich Neuhaus, the violinist David Oistrakh and the author of children's books Samuil Marshak—were cultural celebrities. Even today, next to the building's entrance, there are plaques with all their names.

For the first few years, at least, Prokofiev thoroughly enjoyed this new, very comfortable lifestyle. Acquaintances were being arrested left and right, but for now the Great Terror seemed to pass the Prokofievs by. At a certain point, however, they were forced to face facts: their safety was hardly guaranteed. Lina, as an American citizen, felt particularly threatened. Her singing career had stagnated, all her friends lived in the West, and she missed her mother. Their sons, Sviatoslav and Oleg, had a hard time of it as well; after changing schools several times, they were enrolled in an English school in Moscow, together with children of the Soviet elite. The school closed its doors in 1937—most of the students' parents had been arrested—and at their next school, with classmates of far more modest roots, the boys were bullied because of their privileged background.

The trial of high-ranking Red Army generals and marshals on 11 July 1937 for supposed collaboration with Germany was a wake-up call for Prokofiev. One of the defendants was Marshal Mikhail Tukhachevsky, a friend and protector of Shostakovich, meaning Prokofiev's fate was also uncertain. Tukhachevsky was executed the next day.

To ward off a potential threat from the authorities, Prokofiev contributed an article to *Pravda* at the end of that year, confirming that he had embraced socialist realism in his own music. He added, perhaps rashly, that a composer must never bend over backwards to please the listener: insincere music had no future.

At that time, he rented the top floor of a dacha in Nikolina Gora, a village some fifty kilometres west of Moscow, where the writers Chekhov and Gorky and the painter Levitan had once spent their summers. Again, the idyllic rural setting reminded him of the estate in western Ukraine where he had grown up. The Great Terror, which was now spreading mercilessly through Moscow, seemed so far away. There he spent two peaceful months working on the *Cantata for the 20th Anniversary of the October Revolution*, a huge work for orchestra, military band, accordion band, percussion ensemble, two mixed choirs and *musique concrète* (siren, alarm bell, a recorded speech and the sound of marching feet). It was the ideal opportunity to blare out his Soviet musical credentials.

He had already begun work on the cantata in 1932 in the south of France, where he had rented a villa from the French Communist and *Izvestia* correspondent Jacques Sadoul, one of the people who had convinced him to return to Russia. Originally conceived as an ode to Lenin, the work grew into a ten-movement story of the revolution, the civil war, Stalin's pledge to Lenin and the drafting of the Soviet constitution.

He had discussed plans for the cantata with Boris Gusman, director of the Soviet Radio Committee Arts Division, during brief visits to Moscow in 1933 and 1934. Gusman negotiated for Prokofiev the tremendous fee of 25,000 roubles in return for the promise that the cantata be suitable for radio broadcast. Additionally, the work had to be in line with Marxist-Leninist philosophy and follow the current artistic-political norms. The deadline: 15 October 1936.

It became a 200-page score for forces numbering some five hundred performers. But when Prokofiev played it at the piano for a group of non-musicians from the State Committee on the Arts, there was immediate resistance from its chairman, Platon Kerzhentsev, who accused Prokofiev of setting texts belonging to the people to "unintelligible music". And the music wasn't heroic enough. Kerzhentsev insisted that Prokofiev revise the libretto, which began with the opening line from Marx and Engels's *Communist Manifesto*: "A spectre is haunting Europe—the spectre of communism." Prokofiev had also mixed in with the music speeches from October 1917 and statements from Lenin's essay *What Is to Be Done?* The texts (according to the complainant) had been given musical, not political, significance, because their words were subordinate to the notes, and the composer had therefore wronged both the revolution and Lenin. Prokofiev, the censor continued, had portrayed the Bolshevik leader as mistrustful of the people and the revolution as a period of cold, hunger, disease and ruin rather than a heroic event. And the finale, in which the new Soviet constitution is presented, even felt like the prelude to a catastrophe.

Coincidentally, Kerzhentsev at that time was working on a monograph about Lenin, in which he mixed biographical details with out-of-context quotes from the father of the revolution. Prokofiev stubbornly refused to scrap Lenin's words from the libretto and submitted a complaint to Tukhachevsky, who still sat on the Central Committee. But Tukhachevsky was already fighting for his life, and passed Prokofiev's complaint on to Molotov, who ordered Kerzhentsev to stop criticizing the cantata—only then to start meddling with it himself. Kerzhentsev relented, but a few months later would retaliate by yanking Prokofiev's ballet *Romeo and Juliet* from the Bolshoi's programme.

While Prokofiev was wily enough to look out for his position in society, he was blind to the savagery of the regime he was slavishly trying to please. Some colleagues, who by now had seen the cantata's score, intervened. They knew, even if he didn't, that if this work were performed it could cost him his head. His cantata was a Pandora's box that must not be opened. And indeed, it stayed shut until 5 April 1966, thirteen years after Stalin's death, and even then it was performed only in part.

The ban on his cantata dealt Prokofiev a demoralizing blow. Lina noticed that while he would usually get up early, take a morning stroll and work for three hours, he now padded around the house for hours in his bathrobe.

At the end of November 1937, he and Lina embarked on a tour of Europe and the USA. It would be the last time Prokofiev was allowed to leave the country.

Old friends living abroad noticed that Prokofiev's once lively nature had turned into "deep, terrible insecurity". He perked up only occasionally, as he reputedly did when he saw the Disney animated film *Snow White and the Seven Dwarfs* in America.

The pressure he was under on the home front became clear when the impresario Vernon Duke offered him a contract with a Hollywood film studio for the (astronomical) salary of $2,500 a week, and Prokofiev turned it down. His excuse was that, much as he was flattered by the offer and enjoyed meeting movie stars, he could not stay in Hollywood.

The one highlight of his American tour was the purchase of a sleek new Ford auto, which he had shipped to Moscow. Private cars were an unheard-of luxury in the Soviet Union in those days, and, upon his return, he had to justify its purchase to the Union of Composers. His primary argument was that while he might have spent much time in the West, he hadn't become a Westerner.

At press conferences in America, he was always positive about the Soviet Union. How hollow his words must have sounded in the ears of his émigré friends, when he never once brought up the repression and the purges, but boasted of his easy life thanks to royalties, fees, commissions from film studios and theatres, and stipends from the composers' union. The rebukes came from both sides: at home, Prokofiev's jealous colleagues branded him a "Western bourgeois". Even his dandyish style invited criticism, although his taste hadn't changed since his last year at conservatory.

In a way, all this criticism was liberating. He felt free to speak his mind, openly dismissing his colleagues' behaviour as "provincial" and, after returning from his tour, engaging in the *Lady Macbeth* debate at a meeting of the Union of Composers. He warned his colleagues that in the West, where there was a growing interest in

Soviet music, one might see the stylistic rules as a sign that Soviet composers were stuck in a rut. He also argued that it was nonsense to see formalism as a struggle against perfection and technical improvements, and that socialist realism must not lead to lazy, self-indulgent music with no intelligent basis.

Between 1936 and 1938, more than a million and a half Soviet citizens, many of them prominent cultural figures, were arrested. Most were shipped off to the gulag, but some 700,000 were executed. Some semblance of calm returned to the country only in 1939, because Stalin had to focus on the inevitable war with Germany, which his non-aggression pact with Hitler postponed only temporarily. This was Prokofiev's chance to write a patriotic opera: *Semyon Kotko*, based on the popular novella *I, Son of Working People* by Valentin Kataev. The opera was to be staged by Meyerhold at the Stanislavsky Theatre in Moscow.

But fate struck. Meyerhold was arrested on 20 June 1939 while working in Leningrad on the choreography for a gymnastics display featuring 30,000 athletes. Prokofiev was involved as well: in just a week he wrote the music, the *Six Gymnastic Exercises* (or *Music for Athletes*), and was paid handsomely for it, too, to the tune of 10,000 roubles. The Leningrad display was to be the dress rehearsal for an even grander spectacle in Moscow at the beginning of July, but after Meyerhold's arrest the whole thing was scrapped and the music shelved. It would be premiered only in 2009 at Princeton University.

At the end of June, Prokofiev left for the Stanislavsky Theatre's holiday retreat in Kislovodsk, the spa city in the Caucasus where he had been when the revolution broke out in 1917. There he bumped into Mira Mendelson, a literature student twenty-one years his junior, whom he had met there the previous year during a working holiday with Lina. Mira studied at the Gorky Institute and was a fanatical Party member. They took long walks, where he told her about his music and she read him her poetry. Confronted by Lina, he dismissed Mira as "just some girl who wants me to read her bad poetry". Shortly thereafter, he referred to her in a letter as "a Jewish girl who's after me".

Having grown up in the Soviet Union among the Communist elite, Mira had a better grip on the new political and cultural norms than he did. And although Prokofiev was flattered by the attentions of an attractive young woman, she was mainly useful at first in providing suitably censor-safe texts for his compositions. But a few months after his return from the Caucasus, he admitted to Lina that they were also having an affair. His feelings for his wife had cooled; the pressure he was under had created an imbalance in their relationship. Lina—who until her death in 1989 claimed to love her husband still—could not give him the moral support he felt he needed. Lina in turn reacted coolly to his confession, telling him that Mira was a calculating opportunist.

In the meantime, Prokofiev worked non-stop on his opera. His only distraction was the actress Serafima Birman, who visited him in Kislovodsk. Soon thereafter, Birman received a request—entirely staged, as it happens—to stand in for Meyerhold, who had been detained. Nearly everything pointed to Birman being linked to the secret police and having been sent to Kislovodsk to ingratiate herself with Prokofiev. The prospect of having to complete his opera under the watchful eye of the NKVD deeply vexed Prokofiev. It was as though he had only now caught on to their game. Mira's presence and support was therefore all the more vital to him.

By now Prokofiev feared the worst for Meyerhold. Every reminder of him had been erased: his photos were removed from the walls of the Stanislavsky Theatre, and his entry in the *Great Soviet Encyclopaedia* was erased. (This was standard practice when someone fell out of favour.) A month after his arrest, his flat was broken into, and his wife, the actress Zinaida Reich, was killed. She had been stabbed twelve times, including in her eyes—a signature of the underworld. In fact, the NKVD had staged the burglary-murder, because she had written letters to Stalin's political police and the chief prosecutor, Andrei Vyshinsky, protesting her husband's arrest.

Lina panicked at the news of her friend Zinaida's death and would have travelled directly to Kislovodsk to be with Prokofiev, but was denied permission, as the residency had been assigned to "one individual" and was designated a place for persons of status and achievement.

Meyerhold was tried in secret by a military tribunal, convicted of espionage and executed on 2 February 1940. The trumped-up charge was part of the latest wave of purges within the intelligentsia. The writer Isaac Babel would become another of its victims.

No one knows exactly how Prokofiev responded to his friend Meyerhold's death. In those days, the best thing was to keep one's grief to oneself. But make no mistake: Prokofiev and others must have been well and truly shocked. Meyerhold was a talented artist who'd had his share of run-ins with the regime, but he was no spy. If this could happen to him, it could happen to anyone.

The premiere of *Semyon Kotko* was postponed due to a politically sensitive element in the opera that clashed with the Molotov–Ribbentrop non-aggression pact signed in 1939. In Prokofiev's telling of the civil war, the counter-revolutionaries are supported by Germany, which, in the light of the recent pact, was hardly a convenient plot element. So as not to offend Hitler by portraying the Germans as enemies of the Bolsheviks, the handiest solution was to substitute Austrians for the Germans. But Vyshinsky, whom Molotov had assigned to keep an eye on the changes, insisted that the Austrians in turn be replaced by *haidamak*s (Ukrainian nationalists). Finally, then, *Semyon Kotko* could be performed.

Fifteen performances after its 23 June premiere, the opera was suddenly withdrawn, for the critics did not know what to make of it and were afraid to commit any risky indiscretions in their reviews. They preferred to write about a much simpler opera: *Into the Storm* by Tikhon Khrennikov, composed that same year for the Stanislavsky Theatre. Khrennikov's "simple music" about the struggle between revolutionaries and counter-revolutionaries even featured Lenin in a speaking role and was much more to everyone's liking than *Semyon Kotko*'s "difficult notes".

Prokofiev treated the rivalry with Khrennikov like a tennis match. When Mira brought to his attention an eighteenth-century libretto for the comic opera *The Duenna, or The Double Elopement* by the Irish satirist Richard Brinsley Sheridan, he knew at once that this could be his match point. *The Duenna* seemed to him a safely apolitical work full of romance, intrigues and imbroglios and was thus the ideal basis for his musical comedy *Betrothal in a Monastery*.

Prokofiev angled for approval from the authorities while at the same time fearing for his life. He felt more and more like a dissident, because, although he had nothing against "music for the masses", he also believed his music need not be accessible. But, like many other Soviet artists, he took the safe route of self-censorship and from then on wrote mostly ideologically acceptable music. The chance to prove himself arose a few months after

Meyerhold's arrest: the commission for a cantata in honour of Stalin's sixtieth birthday. He gladly accepted, as it would allow him to prove his loyalty to the regime with an optimistic panegyric and would guarantee him a place among the Soviet artistic elite. The result was the repulsive *Zdravitsa*—literally, *A Toast*, but also known in English as *Hail to Stalin*. The piece blared from loudspeakers in the streets of downtown Moscow.

Trying to picture how it must have sounded, I recall the 1 May celebration I witnessed in Moscow in 2010. A procession, several thousand strong, made up of Communists, National Bolsheviks, anarchists and anti-fascists marched through the city streets. Two demonstrators carried a banner with Stalin's likeness. The former leader had risen in the estimation of some Russians in recent years—no matter that during his reign he had murdered some fifteen million innocent countrymen. He was increasingly being embraced by young people: one need think only of the Stalin calendar that was very popular among them.

The 1 May protestors were expressing their anger over rising utility bills, taxes, government corruption, unfair economic policies and bourgeois capitalism, as well as NATO and the French and British participation in the upcoming Victory Day parade on 9 May. But as the march snaked through the city centre, their mood was softened by the melancholy war songs and "The Internationale" broadcast through the cable radio loudspeakers. The sound had the crackle of an LP record and the music itself sounded old, as though it had rusted over time.

The easing of the Stalin terror during the Second World War suddenly gave Prokofiev the freedom to compose what he pleased. By now, his relationship with Lina was definitively over. In March

1941, seeking solitude in order to work, he hid himself from Mira, who telephoned the house for ten days running, to no avail. At the same time, Lina tried to cheer him up by organizing parties and bringing out champagne, vodka and caviar. But this only irritated him. His last days with Lina were marked by arguments. At the end of March, he walked out on the family. When his son Sviatoslav saw his father in the hall with his suitcase and asked where he was going, Prokofiev answered, "To save a life." He was referring to Mira, who, desperate because he was not answering her calls, had attempted suicide.

The continual bombardment of Moscow was hardly the peace and quiet he sought. When it looked as though the city would soon fall to the Germans, the authorities decided to evacuate the leaders of the intelligentsia, including Prokofiev. Lina and their sons could have gone as well, but, once it became clear that Mira would accompany her husband, Lina resolutely refused to leave. Yet foreigners who stayed behind voluntarily fell under suspicion of being sympathetic to the imminent occupation.

Prokofiev and Mira, together with a group of professors from the Moscow Conservatory, actors from the Moscow Art Theatre and other "artistic workers", left in August 1941 by a special four-carriage train to Tbilisi, the cosmopolitan capital of the Georgian SSR; on the invitation of the cinematic director Sergei Eisenstein, they travelled onward the following May to Alma-Ata (modern-day Almaty), the capital of the Kazakh SSR, where the Soviet film industry had relocated. Here, in "the Hollywood on the Chinese border", Prokofiev and Eisenstein collaborated on the film *Ivan the Terrible*, on a pseudo-biography about the Romantic poet Mikhail Lermontov, based on a script by Konstantin Paustovsky, and on the music for the war film *Tonya*.

In October 1943, when the Red Army broke the siege of Stalingrad and the Germans retreated, Prokofiev and Mira returned to Moscow, where they took up residence in the Hotel National. In February of that year, Prokofiev had won the Stalin Prize for his Piano Sonata No. 7, which he had completed in Tbilisi. The prize money, 100,000 roubles, made him instantly wealthy. (The average monthly wage was 200 roubles.)

While it looked as though he was once again in the regime's good graces, there were two sides to this coin. Prokofiev and his friends had not returned from Alma-Ata of their own accord, but on orders from Vladimir Surin, the deputy chairman of the State Committee on the Arts. He had summoned them to take part in a competition for a new national anthem that was to replace "The Internationale". The authors of the new anthem's text, Sergei Mikhalkov and Gabriel Ureklyan (better known as El-Registan), wanted Shostakovich and Prokofiev to write the music. But Marshal Kliment Voroshilov, chair of the anthem committee, felt that the competition should be opened to all Soviet composers. In the end, Shostakovich and Prokofiev competed against two hundred others. Neither won. The choice fell upon Alexander Alexandrov, the founder and leader of the renowned military ensemble bearing his name.

Prokofiev had to be content with just being back in Moscow. On 13 January 1945, he conducted the premiere of his Symphony No. 5 with the USSR Symphony Orchestra in the Great Hall of the Moscow Conservatory. But before he could give the downbeat, there came the roar of artillery fire. The Red Army had crossed the Vistula and was marching towards Berlin. Richter wrote of the incident: "When Prokofiev took the stage it went quiet, and suddenly there was the sound of celebratory artillery fire. He had already raised his baton. He waited until the cannon fire had ceased. It had something significant, very symbolic. It was as though all of us—including Prokofiev—had reached a shared turning point."

The incident roused the audience all the more, and the symphony's success catapulted Prokofiev to the forefront of the USSR's rank of composers. Elated, he invited friends for a party in his new flat on the Mozhaysk Highway (now called Kutuzovsky Prospekt). A few days later, in a fit of dizziness, he had a nasty fall and was taken to hospital with a severe concussion.

With the money from a new Stalin Prize that he'd won in July for his ballet *Cinderella* and a loan from the composers' union, Prokofiev bought his own dacha in Nikolina Gora. The deciding argument in securing the loan was that his poor health required him to live outside the city. Doctors' orders. Prokofiev appeared to thrive in these idyllic surroundings, but this was false optimism, for he had begun to come to grips with his mortality. Prokofiev had always presumed himself immortal, so this must have come as quite a blow. His reaction was to start writing his autobiography and, mindful of his legacy, completing unfinished compositions.

A new wave of political oppression exacerbated his unrest. It was like a return to the purges of the 1930s. On 14 August 1946, the Central Committee issued a resolution banning two Leningrad-based literary journals, *Star* and *Leningrad*, for having committed an unpatriotic act by publishing works by the poet Anna Akhmatova and the satirist Mikhail Zoshchenko. Prokofiev, too, had reason to worry, having set poems by Akhmatova to music pre-1917, and even more so when the filmmaker Eisenstein found himself in Zhdanov's crosshairs. Stalin had seen Part 2 of *Ivan the Terrible* and called it a "nightmare". In particular, the scenes with the *oprichniki*, Tsar Ivan's bloodthirsty bodyguards, drew unmistakable parallels with the Soviet secret police and aroused the dictator's ire. These were exactly the scenes for which Prokofiev provided suitably wild music. The composer dodged that bullet, but soon enough, despite all the honours heaped upon him, he would once again fall out of favour. A month later, the Central Committee banned Part 2 of *Ivan* for allegedly being both anti-historical and anti-artistic. Eisenstein only managed to deflect the growing criticism by publicly expressing his remorse—a humiliating but common ritual in those days.

By now, Prokofiev's doctors forbade him from working more than one hour per day. He mainly followed their advice, so it is no small feat that he still managed to compose several brilliant works, including the Violin Sonata No. 1.

When the work was completed, he invited the violinist David Oistrakh and the pianist Lev Oborin to Nikolina Gora to play it through. The piece is perhaps his most sombre work. Prokofiev instructed Oistrakh that the first movement should sound like "the wind in a cemetery"—referring, according to Prokofiev's biographer Daniel Jaffé, to the millions of Russians who had been arrested during the 1930s and the hundreds of thousands who had been shot. Ironically enough, this piece would win the Stalin Prize.

Demoralized and physically weakened, Prokofiev started churning out works to please the authorities. Getting back on their good side, he must have thought, would increase the chances of a performance of *War and Peace*. One of the few highlights of his later years was the October 1947 premiere of his Symphony No. 6 in the Leningrad Philharmonic, conducted by Yevgeny Mravinsky. Galina Vishnevskaya was present, and in her memoir she wrote of

Prokofiev: "Leningrad audiences adored him. The symphony was a great success and he was repeatedly called for bows. He wore a grey suit, his own Stalin Prize medal and, for some reason, light-coloured, knee-high felt boots. I was sitting quite far back in the auditorium so I did not have a good view of his face. But I do recall the music: sharp and ringing, like the dripping of snow in spring." When the news of its success reached Moscow, tickets for a performance in the capital sold out within a day.

But this triumph, too, was short-lived. A week later, Stalin attended the premiere of the Bolshoi Theatre's staging of Vano Muradeli's opera *The Great Friendship*, an ode to Stalin's birthplace, Georgia, and exploded in anger because the opera apparently fell well short of the propaganda demands.

I listen to the work on YouTube. Its five scenes last about half an hour and tell of the spread of Soviet rule over the Caucasus in the 1920s. The melodies are classical; they sound lyrical and folksy. What's there to complain about? one might ask. Moreover, the libretto is bombastically patriotic and extols communism and the Soviet utopia. But if you take off your twenty-first century glasses and put on those of a Soviet censor in 1948, the answer is clear. Aside from ignoring the role of the Russian people in spreading communism throughout the Caucasus, there is a key role for the Georgian party leader Sergo Ordzhonikidze, one of Stalin's earliest vassals. Only, he fell from grace in the 1930s, and committed suicide in 1937—probably on Stalin's orders—and since then Ordzhonikidze had been off-limits. Stalin recognized him in the opera and flew into a rage; after the performance, both the composer and the Bolshoi's director, Leontyev, got an earful. No sooner had Stalin left the theatre than Leontyev had a heart attack.

His death was mentioned in passing in the Moscow press a few days later. Various musicians were arrested in the wake of this new dust-up; others had to amend their concert programmes.

At the end of January, Politburo member and chief ideologist Andrei Zhdanov assembled all the Soviet composers for an informal summit devoted to Muradeli's opera. Prokofiev sensed what was coming and called in sick. But on day two of the summit a government official showed up at his dacha and convinced him to attend after all.

Mstislav Rostropovich recalls:

> Prokofiev was in the auditorium when Zhdanov launched into his tirade. Everyone was dead quiet, except Prokofiev, who sat chatting with his neighbour, who was to conduct *War and Peace*. When a Politburo member in his row leaned over and said, "Say, this is about you," Prokofiev replied, "Who are you?" The man replied, "My name's not important. But just know that if I tell you something, you'd better listen." Prokofiev: "I never listen to anyone I haven't been introduced to." At which Prokofiev leaned back in his seat, unfazed.

Muradeli was accused of "formalism" in his opera. He confessed, and then pointed an accusatory finger at Prokofiev, Shostakovich, Khachaturian and Myaskovsky, whom he claimed had contaminated all the younger Soviet composers with their formalist doctrine.

Zhdanov also quoted at length the 1936 *Pravda* article "Muddle Instead of Music" that had excoriated Shostakovich's *Lady Macbeth of Mtsensk* and explained that Muradeli's opera had fallen under the spotlight because "not a single new Soviet opera has been produced in the past ten years". This infuriated Prokofiev, precisely because he had written three operas in that period, and all three had been banned. He indignantly turned his back on Zhdanov. According to one of those present, he wore, in protest, a medal from the Royal Philharmonic Society of London on his chest instead of one of his Stalin Prize medals.

The auditorium was stuffy, and Prokofiev eventually dozed off. One of the organizers said to him, "Comrade Prokofiev, you are disrupting the meeting. If Comrade Zhdanov's suggestions don't please you, no one is stopping you from leaving the hall." Which he did.

The authorities, embarrassed that such an influential figure would show such disdain for a public gathering by walking out, simply removed his name from the minutes. Officially, he hadn't even been there.

There were more repercussions to come. At the end of the month, the board of the composers' union, led by Khachaturian, was dismissed. They were replaced by a temporary leadership, with Boris Asafyev as director and the ambitious Tikhon Khrennikov as general secretary. In August, Shostakovich and several other conservatory teachers were fired. This purge let up only when Zhdanov unexpectedly died on the last day of August.

It is unclear whether there was a concerted political effort to make life difficult for Prokofiev and other members of the artistic elite. The policy was more likely haphazard, arbitrary and devoid of any rational basis. Simon Morrison, in his excellent Prokofiev biography, *The People's Artist*, writes that artistic careers were mostly determined by swings in cultural politics and infighting within cultural institutions, miscommunication between those institutions and the government, and interpersonal rivalries. Prokofiev's demotion in 1948 had less to do with ideological issues than with the fickleness of policymakers, factions within the bureaucracy and financial crises. And then, of course, there was the widespread and overriding fear of Stalin. The result was the canonization of the run-of-the-mill and vapid in Soviet music. So long as a piece was undemanding and hummable, it could be performed. It was a wet blanket for any musical growth.

This haphazard policy seems to be the only explanation for the fact that on 10 February the Kremlin hosted a ceremony honouring Prokofiev's promotion to People's Artist of the RSFSR and on the very same day the Central Committee issued a resolution paraphrasing Zhdanov's attack on the "formalistic distortions and anti-democratic trends" in Muradeli's *The Great Friendship*.

The empty champagne bottles from that ceremony at the Kremlin hadn't even been cleared away before Prokofiev, Shostakovich, Myaskovsky and Khachaturian were expelled from the board of the composers' union. They were accused of "renouncing the fundamental principles of classical music" in favour of "confused, neuropathological combinations that turn music into cacophony". Additionally, like their colleagues Vissarion Shebalin and Gavriil Popov, they were said to employ modernist, anti-democratic creative techniques and to have traded accessible Russian folk traditions for unfathomable abstractions. Their music embraced "the spirit of the contemporary modernist bourgeois music of Europe and America".

Zhdanov's aim was not to silence these well-loved composers, but to tug them into line. This goal was underscored by a week of meetings on the future of Soviet music, led by Tikhon Khrennikov, the new general secretary of the union and a favourite of Zhdanov's. He, too, did his best to sully the reputations of the four great composers and ignore their successes and contributions.

As a result of these meetings, a whole slew of Prokofiev's works were banned. These included the Symphony No. 6; *The Year 1941*; the Piano Sonatas No. 6, 7 and 8; the *Festive Poem*; the *Ode to the End of the War*; and the *Ballad of an Unknown Boy*. The ballets he had composed abroad were likewise banned as "products of bourgeois behaviour". The fourth and fifth symphonies, *The Fiery Angel* and the Piano Concerto No. 4 met the same fate. Richter had to replace Prokofiev's Piano Sonata No. 9 with a Schubert sonata at a concert in January 1948. The revered People's Artist of the RSFSR was suddenly the Pariah of the RSFSR.

After this latest humiliation, Prokofiev stopped attending meetings of the composers' union and sent a written apology to Khrennikov. He gave him permission to read it at the meeting, should the general secretary so desire. The Soviet authorities took advantage of this and published the letter as validation of Khrennikov's critique.

Western commentators saw the letter as a capitulation and refused to believe that Prokofiev had written it himself. They must have dictated it and made him sign it. But the tone of the letter was unmistakably his own. He admitted to having fallen into the trap of atonality. But he had "happily" found his way back out by returning to tonal music. The atonality in some of his works was only intended to underscore the contrast with the tonal sections.

One can also read the letter as a show of deference to the regime in the hope that future works would be performed. It was therefore mainly a proactive manoeuvre to ward off criticism of his new opera, *The Story of a Real Man*. But it was in vain. Chafing at Prokofiev's international reputation, the Kremlin was determined to force him to adhere to its own musical dogma.

At this stage of Stalin's campaign of terror, Prokofiev had more than enough reason to be afraid. Unlike his upbraided "formalistic" colleagues, he had left the country after the October Revolution to pursue a career in the West. His marriage to Lina, a foreigner, was another nail in his coffin. Fearful of being branded a Western spy, as so many others had been since the 1930s, he started clearing his dacha of foreign books and letters so that nothing "incriminating" might be found. To further put the screws on him, on 20 February 1948—ten days after the ceremony at the Kremlin and four days after his letter to the composers' union—the authorities arrested Lina on charges of espionage after she attempted to send money to her mother in Spain. This, and her frequent presence at receptions at foreign embassies and her request for an exit visa to return to France, would prove fatal.

Lina lay in bed that evening with a cold when she received a call from a friend asking her to accept a package outside. She got dressed and went downstairs. In front of her building, she was shoved into a waiting car and was taken to the Lubyanka, the headquarters of Stalin's secret police. That night, they combed her flat, confiscating Prokofiev's Förster piano, a portrait of Lina by Natalia Goncharova, LPs, jewellery, photos, documents and even her son Sviatoslav's collection of postcards depicting Soviet leaders.

Because of her contact with foreign diplomats, Lina was accused of espionage and treason. After six months of interrogation, a military tribunal sentenced her to twenty years in a Siberian labour camp. Her arrest was an indirect attack on her ex-husband, who for the rest of his life felt responsible for her imprisonment.

She was released in 1956—three years after the deaths of Prokofiev and Stalin, having served eight years in the gulag. In 1974 she emigrated to England, where she managed her ex-husband's legacy. Mira had died of a heart attack six years earlier.

The Prokofiev boys were home the night their mother was arrested. She wasn't allowed to telephone them, but it was clear that something was amiss when agents from the Ministry of Internal Affairs (the MVD) searched the house that night. Afterwards, they hurried to their father's dacha in Nikolina Gora, but, as there were no night buses, they walked the sixteen kilometres in the cold. When they told Prokofiev what had happened, he fell silent out of guilt, powerlessness and fear for his own fate. He himself was not arrested.

The simple fact that no one came to Lina's defence says enough about the widespread fear among Soviet artists. Sviatoslav and Oleg appealed to Shostakovich for help, but he balked (even though he was at the time a member of the Supreme Soviet in Leningrad, a function he never wanted but had foisted upon him).

Now fully realizing that he had been marked as an "enemy of the people", Prokofiev gave up on seeing *The Story of a Real Man* staged. He had in all sincerity stuck to the official doctrine and deluded himself into believing in a false reality in which his artistry was being manipulated from without. But what was the point of writing any more, if it was only going to be banned?

Exhausted and in ill health, Prokofiev spent most of the last three years of his life at his dacha in Nikolina Gora. Fearing that the least agitation could be fatal, Mira shielded him from visitors. She answered the phone and took care of his correspondence. Only his friendship with Mstislav Rostropovich seemed to buoy him. While by 1948 everyone seemed to give Prokofiev a wide berth, the young cellist visited him daily; they developed a firm friendship, and Prokofiev regarded Rostropovich as a son. In 1949, he wrote the Cello Sonata in C minor for him, and on 6 December Rostropovich performed it with Sviatoslav Richter at a closed meeting of the composers' union.

Although seriously ill, Prokofiev dragged himself to the performance. In July of that year, he had suffered a stroke, which only exacerbated the chronic headache, fever and nausea that had plagued him since 1945. Mira and his sons feared for his life after the stroke; high blood pressure had made his head go red, he spoke haltingly and had difficulty concentrating. Mira had wanted to take him to a clinic in Moscow, but he was too weak.

He is said to have remarked to his friend Myaskovsky (who would die of cancer in 1950): "Is it possible that everything we wrote is unwanted, that they'll throw it all into the bin?"

Despite those doubts, Prokofiev persevered. When he asked one of his doctors, Rosa Ginsberg, for permission to work, she said to his friends, "You can't stop an artist from creating. Music will always be in his soul, but being kept from writing it will wear him down, morally and psychologically. So let him live the way he wants to, even it means a shorter life."

His condition improved later that fall, but by winter it had worsened again. Shostakovich intervened with Molotov at Prokofiev's behest, and he was admitted to the Kremlin hospital, the best health facility in the USSR. There, the political elite was cared for by Jewish doctors who, only a few years later, would all be arrested during an antisemitic purge. In the past he would have been welcomed at the clinic, but since his fall from grace he no longer automatically received such privileges. Molotov arranged for him to follow a six-week therapy for hypertropia. His doctors forbade him to work, but he did so anyway and hid his sketches under the pillow whenever they came onto the ward.

Upon being discharged on 20 April, Prokofiev recuperated in the Podlipki sanatorium in Barvikha, a health resort outside Moscow where the political elite had their dachas; he remained there until the beginning of the summer.

The Central Committee's resolution of 1948 had marked Prokofiev as a traitor and a pariah, putting an end to the prestige that since 1939 he had enjoyed among his fellow composers. His bank accounts showed it, too, and his high-end lifestyle, with its expensive cars, fancy suits and yellow shoes, was a thing of the past. Soon he was heavily in debt, sinking into poverty in his last years. He "only just" managed to stave off hunger, according to Rostropovich. So, one day the fearless cellist stormed into the office of the composers' union and demanded that General Secretary Khrennikov give his friend a stipend of 5,000 roubles.

The sad state of Prokofiev's affairs is at odds with the exuberant celebration of his sixtieth birthday on 23 April 1951. Two days earlier there had been a festive evening at the House of the Composers, complete with messages of congratulations from the composers' union and the Bolshoi Theatre and a brief concert at which Sviatoslav Richter played the premiere of his Piano Sonata No. 9. The composer was too ill to attend in person, so the organizers arranged for a radio connection between the venue and Prokofiev's flat.

Prokofiev was last seen in public, visibly exhausted, on 11 October 1952 at the premiere of his Symphony No. 7, a far less inspiring work than his earlier symphonies. An early version ends serenely, but the conductor Samuil Samosud urged him to write a more upbeat ending in order to win a first- rather than a third-degree Stalin Prize. Prokofiev did so, because he could use the 100,000-rouble prize money. However, he made Rostropovich promise to destroy the new, lively coda after his death. (It still exists in both versions.)

A few years later, Samosud was proven right. The Soviet authorities sought precisely such works from its composers, and in 1957 Prokofiev was posthumously awarded the Lenin Prize (as it had been renamed after Stalin's death).

In his final days Prokofiev complained of pain in his soul. He had made a pact with the devil in return for a comfortable existence in which he could devote himself entirely to music. Politics need not play any role; all that mattered were the notes, and the rules of socialist realism were at most a necessary evil.

Yet at the end of the day, Prokofiev is probably the most brilliant and best loved of all the Soviet composers, admired by young and old. I realized this when I was invited to dinner in the summer of 2011 by my friends Yelena and Misha, successful thirty-somethings who earn their living as translators from Japanese. They had invited a pianist to play Bach, Mozart, Prokofiev, Debussy and Menotti for us.

Yelena and Misha live in a small flat on the twenty-first floor of a modern, forty-five-storey skyscraper. Their neighbours are members of the Duma (with bodyguards), ultra-wealthy Chechens (with bodyguards) and slightly less wealthy but corrupt high-ranking police department functionaries (with their own weapons).

The pianist, a twenty-three-year-old named Sergei, had come especially for this gig from Vladimir, one of the old cities on

Moscow's "Golden Ring". It's about a four-hour bus ride. At the outset of his house concert, he visibly enjoyed the transparency of Mozart and Bach. But his performance really took off when he began the Prokofiev sonatas. It sounded as though the music came completely naturally to him, no matter how difficult the notes must have been.

Outside, the setting sun bathed Moscow in a romantic glow. We surrendered ourselves to Sergei's playing and Prokofiev's musical world. Afterwards, we all agreed that not only in a concert hall, but also in a high-rise flat, music is the unifier of souls.

3

The Lost Notes

Barely a year after Sergei Prokofiev decided to return to his homeland for good, his fellow composer Vsevolod Zaderatsky was sentenced to six years in a labour camp in Kolyma, in the forbidding far east of the USSR. Like Prokofiev and Richter, Zaderatsky was born in Ukraine and had a bourgeois upbringing. He also studied at the Moscow Conservatory, but, unlike Prokofiev, he was no wunderkind. Although the Moscow music world was a small one, it is unclear whether they were acquainted.

As a concert pianist in the 1920s, Zaderatsky did perform works by Prokofiev. But there the trail dead-ends. As much as there is to discover about Prokofiev, so little there is about Zaderatsky. None of the Russian musicians I know have ever heard of him. It was only long after his death that he attained a modest following, for the simple reason that his oeuvre had been banned during his lifetime and was largely destroyed. Until a few years ago, Zaderatsky was a forgotten composer.

The fact that he was born and died in exactly the same year as Prokofiev only heightens my curiosity. For if Prokofiev didn't toe the ideological line, what indeed were Zaderatsky's "crimes"?

❖

In early February 2020, I travel to Moscow, where I am to meet the musicologist Marina Brokanova, Zaderatsky's granddaughter, at the music conservatory. It's vile weather outside, the wind cuts through my clothing, and the cold even manages to penetrate the thick soles of my boots. So, I'm relieved when I cross the Bolshaya Nikitskaya Street and recognize Marina's face from her Facebook page. On her arm is a very tall older gentleman.

Her brown eyes glisten behind her large glasses. She smiles, glad to meet me in person after our telephone introduction. The tall man, likewise visibly excited, is her father. He has the same first name as his father so, as is the custom in Russia, he goes by Vsevolod Vsevolodovich. "Never mind the patronymic," he laughs, "otherwise you'll have such a time pronouncing it all."

Marina points to Coffeemania, the chic café in a wing of the conservatory. The conservatory is on holiday, so it's nearly empty. Marina suggests we go in.

Vsevolod and Marina hang their heavy winter coats on the coatrack. When the fur hats come off, Marina's blonde locks cascade over her shoulders and Vsevolod, with his spiky white hair, at once exudes more vitality.

It's clear when they sit down on a banquette at a black Thonet coffee table that they're a tight father–daughter team. The genial Vsevolod tells me that, like his father, he plays the piano and composes. And that, at eighty-five, he still teaches music theory at the Moscow Conservatory and manages his father's musical legacy. In 2015 he published a biography entitled *Per aspera...* (citing a quote on Vsevolod senior's gravestone). He's barely got the title past his lips when he pulls a copy of the book from a plastic bag, plus a few photocopied articles and CDs of Zaderatsky senior's piano music. He's excited that someone from the West will write about his father; it's high time his work gets the recognition it deserves.

Grateful for the gifts, I thumb through the book and pause at the photos of his father later in life: a tall, thin man with a pronounced nose, piercing eyes and a bald head. He looks much older than he really was, but it's to be expected, considering his years in the gulag. I'm surprised that he could smile at all, after everything he had been through.

The belated revival of Zaderatsky's music is itself a minor miracle if you compare his fate with other big-name composers from Soviet musical history—Nikolai Roslavets, Alexander Mosolov and Arthur-Vincent Lourié—whom the socialists likewise relegated to the scrap heap, but whose music was at least performed before their fall from grace. Zaderatsky's work, on the other hand, was almost never played in public prior to his death, nor was a single note published. His name was nowhere to be found in reference books or the press. And not only was he more or less invisible among Soviet composers, but he was also treated as a pariah in his day-to-day life as well. "My father had no civil rights, like the right to vote," says Vsevolod junior, still indignant.

From the very inception of the new communist society in 1917, there was no place for someone like Zaderatsky. "Men of yesterday," as the Bolsheviks called those from the former elite, had to be erased without a trace.

Another hurdle to wider recognition was that from 1934 until his death in 1953, Zaderatsky was forbidden to live in the music centres of Moscow, Leningrad and Kyiv. An official reason was never given. According to Vsevolod junior, even the civil servants at the Ministry of Culture who had to enforce the ban probably had no idea why. While the others were mainly "eliminated" because of the nature of their music, how could this have been the case with Zaderatsky if his music was never performed?

Strangely enough, Zaderatsky was never expelled from the composers' union. His son thinks he knows why. "It could be that the union had to carry out the regime's instructions regarding Zaderatsky, and it was therefore just more practical to keep him within their organization."

What was it that had sealed his fate, I wonder. Why destroy him as a composer, and yet let him live?

Reading Zaderatsky's biography, I realize that the answer must lie in his tsarist past and the years directly thereafter. His father had, in the twilight of the *ancien régime*, worked himself up from a clerk at a telegraph office to director of the Southwest Imperial Railways in Kyiv. An expert in railway construction, he was a confidant of the imperial minister of communication. And his mother's family was of the once-wealthy Polish aristocracy, which probably did their reputation under the communists no good.

Zaderatsky's youth was spent mainly in the provincial city of Kursk, home to the railway directorate's main office. He received his first music lessons from his mother. After graduating from *gymnasium*, he went to Moscow to study law and piano, composition and orchestral conducting. Sergei Taneyev, one of his teachers at conservatory, immediately recognized his talent and admitted him to his composition class.

Zaderatsky should have had a bright future ahead of him. Not only as a musician, but as a socialite, too. As a student in Moscow, he lodged in the immense villa of the aristocratic family Platov.

The eldest son, Fyodor, was a talented painter and Zaderatsky's best friend, and the youngest son, Boris, was a classmate of his at conservatory.

When Zaderatsky married a fellow conservatory student, Natalia Pasechnik, in 1914, the future looked rosy indeed. Their son Rostislav was born a year later. But soon enough, dark clouds began to gather: that summer, war broke out with Germany, Austria-Hungary and Turkey. At first, the Zaderatskys carried on with their life, but, after graduating in 1916, Vsevolod was drafted into the army. He trained as a military engineer, and, in early 1917, having earned the stripes of a second lieutenant, he marched off to war, full of patriotic fervour but unaware of the grim realities of modern warfare.

Zaderatsky fought on both the western and the southern fronts. These were bloody confrontations, with many thousands of casualties on both sides. He was nearly one of them. One day he was sitting on a Black Sea beach, working on a composition, when a German cruiser slipped past the Russian blockades and fired a few fierce rounds at the coast. One mortar landed right next to Zaderatsky but did not explode, although the impact was strong enough to knock him out cold.

And then came the revolution that would plunge Russia into an abyss. A staunch monarchist, Zaderatsky would have nothing to do with the Bolsheviks, and, after their coup in October 1917, he joined the counter-revolutionary White Army led by general Anton Denikin. He had for the previous two years been Tsarevich Alexei's weekly music tutor, a position he owed to his uncle, Baron Karl von Stackelberg, director of the court orchestra and a favourite of the tsarina.

When the Red Army racked up military victories and things looked bleak for the White counter-revolutionaries, Zaderatsky decided that he, his wife and son should emigrate. He would send them to safer havens and join them later.

In 1918, his family left by ship from Novorossiysk for Yugoslavia, from where they travelled on to France. In the chaos of the civil war, Zaderatsky lost track of them, and only a year before his death in 1953 did he learn through the Swiss Red Cross that Natalia was living in France and had remarried. She presumably thought her husband, who never joined them in exile, had been killed amid the tumult in Russia. During the Second World War their son Rostislav was in the French resistance, and after the war he trained as an engineer. Zaderatsky didn't re-establish contact with his wife and son.

Zaderatsky never talked about his life during the revolution or the civil war. Even his second wife, Valentina Perlova, had no idea. It wasn't until 1997 that the mist cleared, when Vsevolod junior received a telephone call from his father's old friend Boris Platov. He told him that his father hadn't been persecuted because he fought in Denikin's army, but because he had been the tsarevich's music tutor. He probably realized himself that being associated with the Romanovs could be fatal and that it was better if no one knew about it. Being drafted into the army, says Vsevolod, turned out to be a blessing in disguise: "It saved my father's life, because, at a crucial moment in Russian history, he wasn't anywhere near the tsar or his family."

After a defeat of the White Army in 1920, Zaderatsky fell into the hands of the Bolsheviks. He and dozens of other captured White officers were confined to the salon of a large villa that served as the headquarters of the secret police. During the sleepless night that the prisoners spent awaiting their death sentence, Zaderatsky sat down at the piano and played what should have been his "final notes".

The commander of Lenin's secret police, Felix Dzerzhinsky, was also in the villa. As he signed one death warrant after another, he heard the piano from the adjacent room—far from a usual sound in his blood-drenched daily routine.

The next morning Dzerzhinsky asked who the pianist was. When he heard, he gave the order to set Zaderatsky free and issued him with safe-conduct papers. All the remaining prisoners were executed that same morning.

The aristocratic, cultured Dzerzhinsky—whose erudition normally did nothing to temper his wanton cruelty—apparently thought a White pianist would pose no threat to the new Soviet state. "Dzerzhinsky was so taken by my father's playing that he let him go," says Vsevolod, his eyes sparkling with excitement, as though it had happened yesterday. And, in a sense, that is so, since he heard about it so much later. His father never mentioned the incident, well aware that any mention of his past could cost him his head.

After Stalin's death, Zaderatsky would acknowledge that his experiences in the revolution and civil war were the inspiration for the character Vadim Roshchin in the writer Alexei Tolstoy's novel trilogy *The Road to Calvary*. The 2017 Russian mini-series based on the novels offers a dynamic and ultrarealistic portrayal of the incredible chaos and misery of those years. As I watched the series on Netflix, I became convinced that ending up a Bolshevik, Menshevik, Liberal or White Officer must have been more coincidence than ideology, a momentary twist of fate. I couldn't help wondering in which camp I myself would have ended up, given the circumstances—but one only really finds these things out when they actually happen.

One telling event that Zaderatsky did relate to his wife was that he shot dead a fellow White officer who had systematically murdered prisoners of war in the courtyard of the army's division headquarters. It is a scene that could have come straight out of Alexei Tolstoy's novel. What happened to him after that, one can only guess.

After his release, Zaderatsky's past as a White officer meant he was denied permission to reside in Moscow or Petrograd. He was exiled to Ryazan, where he had to report at regular intervals to the secret police. From 1920, he worked there as a senior piano teacher at the State Music School, then as a lecturer in music history at the Institute for General Education. His tarnished past did not, for now, seem to get in the way of his career as a musician. In 1922 and 1923 he conducted the local theatre's house symphony orchestra, and from 1925 he taught piano, music history and music theory at the Ryazan Music Academy. Among his well-known pupils was the choral conductor Klaudia Ptitsa.

But in March 1926 things took a turn for the worse. Entirely out of the blue, Zaderatsky was arrested and jailed as a counter-revolutionary. Upcoming concerts were cancelled, and all his manuscripts were destroyed. It explains why Zaderatsky's earliest surviving compositions date from 1928, after his release from prison, even though he had written music from his earliest youth.

The exact reasons behind Zaderatsky's arrest remain a mystery. The Soviet authorities had forgiven him his participation in Denikin's counter-revolution. Even after his release, however, he didn't wonder about it himself—what mattered was that he was once again free to work. One does not, after all, ask questions in a system where truth matters less than ideology.

Zaderatsky's son believes that the events of 1926 represent one of the greatest of his father's heartbreaks: it was the moment he realized that the Soviets were planning to erase him by destroying his work. He was, and would always be, a "man of yesterday".

Shortly before his death, Zaderatsky confessed to his wife that during his imprisonment he had attempted suicide with the sleeping pills he had procured from the camp pharmacy. He survived only because his fellow inmates alerted the wardens in time. After that, the camp's directors, loath to have to answer for a suicide on their watch, took better care of him.

This story reminds me of the many former prisoners I've spoken to in Russia. Their experiences, no matter how disparate, all boil down to the same thing: innocent citizens were arrested, sentenced and exposed to unthinkable hardship.

My clearest such memory is my meeting with the poet and author Yuri Fidelgoltz (1921–2015). In 1948 he was a student at the Moscow theatre academy, where a friend of his, a soldier, gave a reading of poems critical of the Soviet regime. His verses included things like "fuck the Soviet sheep". The friend was arrested and charged with anti-Soviet agitation. During his interrogation it came out that he was part of an organization whose ranks also included Fidelgoltz, who was subsequently arrested.

While searching Fidelgoltz's house, they found diaries containing poems critical of, for instance, the 1946 expulsion of Anna Akhmatova and Mikhail Zoshchenko from the Writers' Union. A military tribunal sentenced Fidelgoltz to ten years of hard labour and stripped him of his civil rights for another five. His soldier friend would spend thirty years in the camp.

Fidelgoltz was sent to the Kolyma labour camp, above the Arctic circle. He was put to work in the tungsten mines; on his back he wore his camp number: 396. He came down with tuberculosis and, by the time he was discharged in 1954, his health was ruined. For another two years, until the end of his official ban, he worked as an actor in provincial cities: he knew the entire social-realist repertoire by heart and could play the perfect party leader.

When I spoke to him in 2009, he related his story with a big smile, as though the labour camp was an absurdist, surreal play. I remember thinking that there's no better way to survive hell.

With Fidelgoltz in mind, I ask Vsevolod junior how his father survived his prison time. He smiles and says his father had an instinct for survival. "He knew exactly how to act with the wardens and the criminals he was locked up with."

In the same year as his initial imprisonment, a second conviction followed. Where and for how long he was locked up are unclear, but his first compositions after being released from prison date from 1928. They were written in pen on scrap paper at the port of Stary Karantin near the Crimean city of Kerch. Corrections made later show that he did not have a piano at his disposal—he had probably just been released from the camp.

After serving his second sentence, Zaderatsky was given permission to settle in Moscow, where he arrived at the end of 1929. He joined the Association for Contemporary Music (ASM) and in 1930 found work at the All-Union Radio as a staff composer. He wrote piano cycles, songs and two operas for radio broadcast. His son said the musicians there recognized his talent: "They were prepared to do whatever they could to have his music receive the recognition it deserved."

A friend of Zaderatsky, the pianist Lev Mironov, commissioned several compositions from him for his Stanislavsky Trio. But these works were never performed and disappeared entirely. The same went for his compositions for the radio and larger concert venues. His two operas (one of which, *Blood and Coal*, complied entirely with the artistic dogmas of socialist realism) were never even staged. At most, a few bits of incidental music for stage plays were performed. Vsevolod sees, after all those years, a concerted effort to ensure that his father did not exist.

In the five years that Zaderatsky lived in Moscow, it was mostly the RAPM, the Russian Association of Proletarian Musicians, that made life impossible for him. Vsevolod junior believes that RAPM members hated his father because he had called them "demagogues of music" and "musical charlatans" to their face. He called the organization itself a "joke of international proportions".

Declarations like these came at a price. Until being replaced in 1932 by the Union of Soviet Composers, the RAPM was the country's most influential music organization, with the power to destroy its opponents. And, seeing as Zaderatsky was one of these, the RAPM, egged on by the secret police, waged open warfare against him. But now, chastened by his previous run-ins with the authorities, Zaderatsky was on his guard. When the government's first five-year plan proved to be a disappointment, he sensed the threat of a new wave of repression and took measures to protect himself against both the RAPM and, after it was disbanded, the new composers' union, by asking three influential musicians to write testimonials for him.

One of these, the respected conductor and composer Nikolai Golovanov, attested in his letter of 22 October 1933 to the importance of Zaderatsky's opera *Blood and Coal* as well as his *Foundation* Symphony and the symphonic suite *Avtodor*, all of them based on Soviet themes and proof of "fine craftsmanship and excellent orchestration". More crucial yet was the sentence, "In my opinion, provided the circumstances of Comrade Zaderatsky's life allow him to live and work normally, he will rightfully occupy a distinguished place among young Soviet composers."

But even such a glowing testimonial couldn't protect him from the authorities' belligerence, which of course had nothing to do with his music, but rather with his past. In 1934 he was once again exiled, this time to Yaroslavl, a provincial city on the Volga, where he found lodging at the home of the former businessman Perlov. He fell in love with Perlov's daughter, Valentina, a child psychologist, and they married. In 1935 the couple had a son, the same Vsevolod whom I would meet eighty-five years later at Coffeemania in Moscow.

Before that second marriage (although the first was never officially annulled), Zaderatsky had found work at the Sobinov Music Academy in Yaroslavl. There, too, they immediately recognized his talent. He made a name for himself as a mentor and taught classes in orchestral conducting, opera, music history, harmony, form, orchestration and piano chamber music. Elsewhere in Yaroslavl he found work as a music educator, and he again devoted himself to composition. In 1934 he wrote the 24 Preludes for piano, five movements of the unfinished oratorio *October* and other works. In Yaroslavl he had a star pupil, Veniamin Basner, who, as a prominent member of the Leningrad-based group of composers, would orchestrate part of Zaderatsky's setting of poems by Alexander Tvardovsky.

His main contribution to Yaroslavl's musical life was the establishment of an opera class and a symphony orchestra at the academy, both of which he led himself. The orchestra would eventually become the Yaroslavl Symphony Orchestra, one of the USSR's better professional orchestras.

Zaderatsky continued to grow in spite of his banishment from Moscow, the epicentre of Soviet music. In 1935 he began a study of stage direction at the Institute of Theatrical Arts, graduating two years later. There he met the great Russian director Konstantin Stanislavsky, with whom he would stage several productions.

In Zhytomyr, Ukraine, he put his new craft into practice by producing two children's operas. His hope of being able to stage his own operas, however, was in vain. He was, as ever, a "composer *non grata*".

Zaderatsky's activities made him one of Yaroslavl's leading cultural figures. There was something surreal about it, as he was officially a second-class citizen without voting privileges or other normal civil rights. Nonetheless, in August 1936 he mustered up the courage to go to Moscow and petition for their restoration.

It was a reckless and dangerous move—the Great Terror, after all, was just picking up steam. But his boldness paid off. Just to be on the safe side, he had asked his wife to put his musical and literary manuscripts into safekeeping. A wise move, for not long thereafter, in March 1937, Zaderatsky was arrested yet again. Things looked bad for him this time, as the purges were now also aimed not only at writers, but other artists too. He was accused of having engaged in "propaganda for fascist music". The meagre evidence for this claim amounted to a few posters for concerts advertising music by the German composers Wagner and Strauss.

His wife, Valentina, would later be told that he was suspected of propagating German music in violation of Article 58, Paragraph 10 ("anti-Soviet and counter-revolutionary propaganda and agitation") and was sentenced to six years in a correctional labour camp in the gulag. Correspondence with him was forbidden.

Valentina knew that such a sentence would certainly be fatal and put all her energy into securing her husband's freedom. She went to Moscow to plead her case in person to President Mikhail Kalinin, the "Little Father of the Peasants".

After a two-month journey, Zaderatsky arrived at a labour camp in Kolyma, 300 kilometres from the port city of Magadan on the Sea of Okhotsk. It is the same camp where the poet Yuri Fidelgoltz had been sent. Prisoners were brought to this barren corner of northeast Siberia to work in the silver, tin and coal mines; countless died under the harsh regime and sub-zero temperatures. Zaderatsky managed to evade forced labour—in essence, the death penalty—and found himself in a timber works. "But even then," his son says proudly, "he couldn't keep from composing."

He kept his mind active in other ways, too. He told Valentina that at the end of a workday he and his fellow prisoner-labourers and their guards would gather around the fire, and he would tell them stories—mostly about ancient Rome, but also about Soviet legal issues. Apparently, he wanted to enlighten his fellow convicts as to the reason for their imprisonment. His "lectures" evoked sympathy and respect among the guards as well: at times they would exempt him from hard labour, especially if he was ill (or pretended to be). But most importantly, he managed to get his hands on paper and pencils, so that he could write. This paper consisted of a stack of blank telegram forms, a small notebook measuring less than 4 by 8 inches, and a few pages torn from an even smaller notebook. Without an eraser, the notated music had to be right the first time around. These would become the 24 Preludes and Fugues for piano, a cycle based on Johann Sebastian Bach's *Well-Tempered Clavier*. In doing so, he joined the compositional trend of harking back to eighteenth-century musical forms. No one would hear them until decades later, however, by which time other composers—Shostakovich and Hindemith, for instance—had already taken this route. After his release, Zaderatsky transcribed five of the preludes and fugues in ink: he copied two of them verbatim from his sketches; the others, he revised in the process. There are a few performances of them on YouTube: in them I hear the better kind of Russian Impressionism, with hints of Debussy and Scriabin.

Meanwhile, Valentina had spent eighteen months waiting in queues for hours at a time at an annex of the secret-police headquarters behind Lubyanka Square, hoping for word on her husband's welfare. (As it happened, she was not alone. Anna Akhmatova was doing the same for her son in Leningrad. From her lengthy poem *Requiem*, one gathers how awful the situation was.)

At first, Valentina's efforts appeared to be in vain, but in the autumn of 1938, when hundreds of thousands of prisoners had already been executed, she finally managed to submit her request. To this day no one knows what happened, or why, but in 1939 Zaderatsky was set free.

There are two possible explanations for his release. The first is that the executioners of the many thousands of Yaroslavl residents had themselves been arrested or killed. (This fits neatly alongside the unsubstantiated story about Shostakovich's having been instructed on a certain Friday to report to the Lubyanka the following Monday; upon arriving there, he was told that the officer who had summoned him had been executed the previous day, so he was free to go.)

The second possibility is that Zaderatsky was one of the fortunate 290,000 prisoners to whom Stalin had decided to grant amnesty. In his biography of Zaderatsky, Vsevolod junior mentions a certificate his father had received that read: "Issued to citizen Zaderatsky, Vsevolod Petrovich, confirming that he was remanded in a penal camp from 17 July 1937 to 21 July 1939 and was released from SEVVOSTLAG NKVD due to a settlement being reached in his case. Permission granted to return to Yaroslavl."

Zaderatsky was suddenly a free man, but this did not mean that the authorities helped him get home. First, he had to make his way to Magadan, the capital of Kolyma. Then he could travel by ship to Vladivostok and from there take the train across the country to Yaroslavl. A fellow convict, a hardened criminal, pulled out a gold ring he had concealed in his cheek and gave it to Zaderatsky to pay for the journey. I cannot think of a more moving show of respect and admiration.

Zaderatsky arrived at his family home only in early 1940, six months after his release from the Kolyma camp. And, as though nothing at all had happened, he went back to work the next day. I imagine him quietly telling his wife what he had endured—but only in a whisper, wary of government eavesdropping, hardly an uncommon thing in those days. But perhaps he kept it to himself, because, for someone who had never experienced those camps at first hand, the stories would be utterly unfathomable.

He soon completed the opera *The Widow of Valencia*, already nearly finished in 1934. He also wrote piano sonatas, songs and a chamber symphony for piano and strings, which he performed in December, acting as both conductor and piano soloist. "My father was cheerful by nature," says the son over a second cup of coffee, referring to those days. "Despite all the hardships he had endured he was obsessive about composing. Even in the camp, he couldn't stop himself."

Proof of Zaderatsky's position among the artistic elite was the family's evacuation after the German invasion of the USSR on 22 June 1941. They and other prominent local figures were sent to Kazakhstan, where they would remain until January 1944. Their next stop was the recently liberated Krasnodar, in the southern Russian agrarian region that is the Kuban. There, Zaderatsky taught at the local music academy and conducted the regional philharmonic, which gave concerts on the front that stretched all the way to the Black Sea. In this period, he composed the piano cycle *The Front* and the song cycle *The Breath of War*.

These songs were performed in Krasnodar, but nowhere else, because, as usual, the authorities would not allow the score to be published. The professional restrictions, Zaderatsky must have realized by now, were to be a lifelong millstone.

With Germany defeated, the family moved back north—to Ukraine, the place of the composer's roots—in the summer of 1945. He would have preferred to settle in lively Kyiv, home to great orchestras and theatres, but he was still forbidden from living there, so he returned to teaching at the music academy in the provincial city of Zhytomyr. The war had ravaged the city, and, as most of the dwellings had been destroyed, the Zaderatskys and other families found accommodation in the music academy's building itself. The noise, which went on till late at night, must have been maddening, but it did not prevent him from composing.

Zhytomyr's music life proved too limited, so a year later the family returned to Yaroslavl. For two years he taught at the music academy, and here he set poems by Alexander Tvardovsky to music.

All hopes of a normal artist's life were dashed when the authorities resumed their attack on "formalism" and banned all musical innovation. This was underscored when he went to Moscow in 1948 as a delegate (he was Yaroslavl's sole member of the composers' union) at the first Congress of Soviet Composers.

At the congress he witnessed the onset of party ideologist Andrei Zhdanov's witch hunt against several prominent Soviet composers. He himself was not among them. How could he be?—his music was never performed and the authorities still saw him as an obscure and inconsequential composer. But back in Yaroslavl, the local powers that be sank their teeth into him, and the music academy convened a special meeting to denounce—and ban—his latest compositions. So, when the director of the Zhytomyr academy invited him to return, he accepted without hesitation. Back to Ukraine the family went.

In Zhytomyr, too, Zaderatsky was the only member of the composers' union. He came into contact with fellow composers in Kyiv, such as Boris Lyatoshinsky, whom he held in high regard. When the Central Committee put Lyatoshinsky in their crosshairs, Zaderatsky stuck up for him, publicly decrying the vicious criticism of his esteemed colleague. Surprisingly, there were no reprisals this time, and Zaderatsky was even promoted to an appointment at the conservatory in Lviv, western Ukraine's main city, in the summer of 1949. In addition to piano, he taught chamber music and the history of piano repertoire.

At first, none of his colleagues were even aware of his extensive oeuvre. His work was unknown to his colleagues, perhaps, but not the KGB, which dropped by occasionally to remind him of the ban on performing his music. These were businesslike meetings meant to spell out the rules, and Zaderatsky probably just nodded along politely.

Despite his high standing at the conservatory, the family lived in constant anxiety, recalls Vsevolod junior. "When we walked down the street, my mother and I hardly dared speak to each other, we were so afraid of being spied on. For myself, I mainly tried not to stand out in any way. So, I pretended to have complete faith in Stalin." He looks at me intensely, his eyes wide open, and says, "All I wanted was to live!"

Despite the prying eye of the KGB, Zaderatsky felt at home in Lviv, which until 1918 had been Lemberg, Austria, and still exuded the atmosphere of a European city. His colleagues treated him as an equal and respected both him and his music, which some of them had only heard in private gatherings. The Lviv Conservatory was a melting pot of Polish, western Ukrainian and Russian cultural traditions, and Zaderatsky incorporated all these currents in his more recent compositions. He hoped to appease the authorities and meet the new musical demands of simplicity, accessibility, faithfulness to classical tradition and the integration of folk music. To this end he composed two piano concertos for children in 1948 and 1949; the second of these contained Ukrainian, Belarusian and Russian themes. He took the piece to the regional congress of the Ukrainian Union of Composers held in Lviv in 1950. It was a success and the Union decided that the work should be performed at its plenary meeting in Kyiv.

The official response to this plan came some two months later, when a delegation of Moscow musicologists showed up in Lviv to appear as guest conductors. In reality, they had been sent by the all-union composers' union to sniff out and eliminate "formalists" and other composers who did not toe the party line. Zaderatsky's concerto bore the full brunt of their mission, writes Vsevolod junior in his biography. Still, it is not clear whether the musicologists went there specially to harass Zaderatsky, or if they were just happy to have discovered an "enemy of the people" so as not to have to return to Moscow empty-handed.

For Zaderatsky, this new attack on his work was the last straw. Here, in the distant provinces, far from Moscow, he had always felt freer as a composer. He accepted his lack of recognition as part of the deal. But this public humiliation was too much for him. Aware of what was to come, he withdrew his concerto from the union's plenary congress programme. The opportunity to present, for the first time in his life, his music to his peers in an official setting had evaporated.

With nothing more to lose, he wrote an open letter to Tikhon Khrennikov. It read: "As a composer, I have been long dead—I am neither played nor published. To try to strangle a dead man is absurd."

His act of desperation changed nothing. His work was still banned, says his son. "And if it was played anywhere, his name was never mentioned." His 1946 setting of a text by Tvardovsky, "Poem of a Russian Soldier", was published in Moscow as "the work of a Ukrainian composer".

When I ask about Khrennikov's toxic role in post-war Soviet musical life, the younger Zaderatsky is surprisingly mild in his judgement of the tormentor of his father and so many other composers. "He had to manoeuvre between Scylla and Charybdis," he says. "And in the end, he did help get my father permission to perform his music in the cinema."

Zaderatsky himself pulled no punches in a letter to Marian Koval, the editor-in-chief of the magazine *Sovetskaya muzyka*, after one of Koval's staff editors had savaged his children's concerto in a review. Zaderatsky claimed that this critic did not understand an iota of his work and demanded a retraction.

The authorities in Moscow immediately launched a counter-offensive and ordered the composers' union in Lviv to discipline Zaderatsky. They were to threaten him with expulsion if he sent any more such missives.

Zaderatsky, by this point, couldn't care less. He had declared war on his persecutors and was prepared to accept the consequences. His wife was baffled by his sudden, self-destructive belligerence—all this uproar about a trivial work, not even representative of his oeuvre as a whole.

His son reckons that his father snapped because in Lviv, at the westernmost tip of the USSR, he finally felt at ease. His colleagues' respect had allowed him to forget Moscow's tentacles, and, when they did finally ensnare him, he cracked.

Yet again, surprisingly, Zaderatsky was not expelled from the composers' union. And again, the reason was probably because they reckoned they could better keep an eye on him from within. His colleagues, taken aback by Moscow's merciless censorship of his work, did their best to comfort him. They loaned him a good-quality grand piano, and the conservatory gave him two rooms in a *kommunalka*—a great luxury.

The Lviv Conservatory would be his haven for the remainder of his life. He worked feverishly on large-scale compositions, including a symphony (completed in 1952) and a violin concerto (unfinished at the time of his death). The pleasures of students who looked up to him and of life in a city with a real symphony orchestra softened the doctors' news that he had developed a heart ailment.

On the evening of 31 January 1953, he was working on his violin concerto. Earlier that day he and his wife had celebrated her birthday. No sooner was the tea and cake finished than he rushed back to his desk. It was, he knew, a race against time.

At 11:30 that night, he fell ill and lost consciousness. He died at one o'clock in the morning. Medical assistance came too late; all they could do was pronounce him dead—the cause, a severe heart attack.

Vsevolod Zaderatsky's funeral was held on 3 February. In the main auditorium of the Lviv Conservatory, the Philharmonic Symphony Orchestra played a public requiem mass. Then the cortège proceeded through the city to the Lychakiv Cemetery, where the mourners laid him to rest in the bitter cold. A month later Joseph Stalin, who had spread such unspeakable misery over his people and made life impossible for thousands of artists, followed him to the grave.

Young Vsevolod—barely recovered from the shock of his father's sudden passing—was unsure what to make of reports of Stalin's death. "At first, I didn't understand what was going on," he says, after yet another refill of coffee. "But when it was clear that Stalin really was dead, I was elated."

But neither the death of the tyrant nor the cultural thaw under Stalin's successor, Nikita Khrushchev, could change his father's fate. Zaderatsky's music, as good as that of Prokofiev or Shostakovich, was still banned, and appeared likely to remain so for ever. This did not prevent his son from performing it occasionally: "I played a prelude and fugue by my father at my final examination at the Lviv Conservatory in 1959. And what do you know: my professors loved it. Apparently, they were familiar with it, too. In the sixties I played some of his piano music in Novosibirsk. Since we have the same first name, they mistook me for my father, as though he were still alive."

Undeterred, Vsevolod continued to perform his father's music now and then. "In Kyiv, I recorded an LP with his romances for piano, written in the 1930s. When I went looking for the sheet music, I discovered that everything prior to his arrest in 1926 had been destroyed."

The search for his father's lost notes continued unabated. One of his compositions from the 1930s recently surfaced in an archive in Tyumen, Siberia. "It came from an archive that had been evacuated to western Siberia during the Second World War," Vsevolod says.

For twenty years he kept silent about his father, whose past was still so tainted. But one day he had had enough. "I was the associate director of the Kyiv Conservatory and wanted to write a biography of my father. When I made this known, the authorities told me that it really wasn't necessary. I started working on it anyway, even though I figured it would probably never be published."

Vsevolod Zaderatsky junior himself enjoyed a successful career in music. He made it as far as professor at the Moscow Conservatory. But in 1985 he resigned, frustrated at the growing influence of communist ideology in musical life. "A large part of the music history curriculum in those days was about propaganda songs. As a result, music education got watered down. Musicians and musicologists just toed the official line."

To round off our conversation, I ask him what exactly "formalism" is. His answer is as convincing as it is shocking. "Nobody knew.

When I wanted to perform Debussy in 1946, they didn't let me do that either. Suddenly even Debussy was a formalist. Apparently, an over-zealous civil servant thought he was pleasing the authorities by outlawing his music." We have a laugh about it and, for a brief moment, forget how terrible those days really were, and how the lives of so many talented people were destroyed.

When we say goodbye, Vsevolod junior, who at this writing is still very much alive, says to me, "Next time, you'll come to our place and we won't drink coffee, but something stronger."

AUTHOR'S AND TRANSLATOR'S NOTE: This chapter is based largely on Vsevolod Zaderatsky junior's personal recollections, as told to the author in person, as well as on his biography of his father, *Per Aspera…* (see bibliography). All quotations are given with permission of the Zaderatsky Estate. A partial English translation of *Per Aspera…*, prepared by Anthony Phillips, is available online at: https://anttialanenfilmdiary.blogspot.com/2015/12/tales-from-great-terror-story-of.html (accessed 20 July 2023).

4

The Russian Vera Lynn

Moscow's Museum of the Great Patriotic War (also known as the Victory Museum) is of megalomaniacal proportions; its two-hundred-metre-wide concrete exhibition hall depicts the war in remarkable detail, from battle to battle, from siege to siege, ending at the capture of Berlin and the victory parade on Red Square. The only thing is: in Russia, the Second World War starts two years late.

It is December 2008 and it's −15°C outside. Victory Park has turned into a vast ice-skating rink. Clutching the arm of my friend Yulia, I glide toward the pompous entrance, barely managing not to slip and fall. At first glance, the monumental tribute housed in this 14,000-square-metre exhibition space is impressive indeed—until you realize that this overblown celebration of triumph and heroism offers no mention whatever of the Molotov–Ribbentrop Pact of 1939. This non-aggression treaty between Nazi Germany and the Soviet Union made it possible for Hitler to invade Poland unhindered on 1 September, after which Stalin could annex the east of that country as well as the three independent Baltic states.

When I ask the attendant, a lady with a bouffant hairdo, about the absence of the infamous pact, her frosty reply is, "There is a video documentary about it on that monitor over there, in the corner, but it's temporarily out of order."

Judging from the videos on the other monitors, I can well imagine what I've missed on the "broken" one. They are simply slide shows of archival photographs, with no accompanying story. And yet the Molotov–Ribbentrop Pact, together with the Spanish Civil War, was one of the determining events leading up to the war. For, without that devil's pact, Hitler would probably not have dared to declare war on England and France in 1940.

The treaty meant that Stalin and Hitler could leave each other be for two years, all the while expanding their territory at the expense of Poland, Estonia, Latvia and Lithuania. Their temporary alliance did not fit in the official post-1945 narrative and was meticulously airbrushed out of the story. Until lately, mention of the pact was no longer a historiographic taboo in Russia, although recent legislation has once again prohibited any comparison between Nazi Germany and the Soviet Union.

The Hall of Remembrance and Sorrow, where you walk under a sky of tears (an installation of chains strung with glass beads), displays the archives containing the lists of the nation's military dead. The numbers alone speak volumes about the Soviet people's sacrifice during the war: 190,000 of the soldiers who perished came from the province of Tambov; 273,000 from Saratov; 262,698 from Rostov; 199,975 from Volgograd province. On and on it goes, until you've reached more than eight million.

And then there are the nineteen million civilian casualties. There's not much sign of them here, for the Museum of the Great Patriotic War is all about the heroes. They confront you head-on in the domed Hall of Glory, where you can read the names of 11,695 heroes of the Soviet Union etched in gold letters on seventy-two white marble panels.

Likewise absent is any reference to Stalin's Order No. 277,

which forbade soldiers to retreat. It was known as "Not a Step Back!" and anyone who defied it was summarily executed by the NKVD. During the Battle of Stalingrad (21 August 1942 – 2 February 1943) this fate befell 23,000 Soviet soldiers. In one of the other rooms, the Stalingrad drama is portrayed as a massive victory celebration. An immense painting by Marat Samsonov depicts the battle's final hours: two million soldiers in close combat. A German soldier gazes blankly ahead; a few metres further, the Russians cheer.

The battle was a turning point in the war, energizing the chaotically led Russian troops so they could march on to Berlin.

"I don't think I'll bring my daughter here, though," says a disappointed Yulia as we walk down the long corridors on our way to the exit. "War is mostly about the suffering of the common people. And this exhibition ignores that."

In one of the last rooms, I suddenly hear sultry dance music. A woman sings something about a soldier's longing and a sweetheart left behind.

"What a beautiful voice," I say. "Who is it?"

"Klavdiya Shulzhenko," she answers. "Her songs are the only good thing I can remember about the war."

The next day I go to Transylvania, my favourite CD shop tucked in a courtyard off of Tverskaya Street. You can get anything there, from the grungiest heavy metal to ABBA to Soviet rock. Usually, I go to the small classical nook at the back of the shop, but now I head for the huge Russian popular music section, which is dominated by CDs by the folk singer Lyudmila Zykina.

Sergei, my usual salesman who has an impressive knowledge of classical music, is not surprised when I ask for Shulzhenko. "She was my parents' idol," he says. "I remember that in the summer, when everyone in our building had their windows open, you could hear her voice coming out of several flats at once. Don't forget that in the Soviet Union we were inundated with the Second World War. Every day there was a film on television about the invincible Red Army and their victory over the fascists." He laughs at his own words, but he's serious, too. And, to be honest, Russian war films are often quite good. Shulzhenko and her male counterpart Mark Bernes, one of my favourite light-music crooners, often acted in them.

Sergei gives me a CD from the series "Russian Chansonniers". It's called *Klavdiya Shulzhenko: Forgotten Waltz* and contains twenty-six of her greatest hits. At home I play it for days on end and get swept up in a life story that ran parallel to one of the Soviet Union's darkest periods.

A few weeks later, sitting in Club Masterskaya, located on a side street across from the FSB (the modern-day incarnation of the KGB) headquarters on Lubyanka Square, I'm reminded how popular Shulzhenko is. At Masterskaya you can eat, drink, dance and watch live performances by a wide range of bands. Tonight's act is a klezmer band, some of whose members are friends of mine. They've just returned from America, where they performed for Russian Jews who had left the Soviet Union in the 1980s and struck it rich in the USA. "We earned enough in one month to live for half a year here," says pianist and singer Lev Sandyuk. They break into a few numbers by Shulzhenko, starting with "The Blue Scarf", which by now I'm familiar with from my CD. The 200-strong audience, varying in age from ten to eighty, sings along at full volume. They know the lyrics by heart.

I ask the lady next to me, a sturdy woman in her forties, how this can be. She says, "In Russia everyone knows Shulzhenko. Our grandparents won the war thanks to her, so she is our friend. Her songs are so beautiful that you can sing them any time, no matter what kind of mood you're in. We love Shulzhenko, as my children do and my grandchildren will. Wherever you go in Russia, you'll hear her."

In her day, Klavdiya Shulzhenko's fame in the Soviet Union was unparalleled. My thoughts turn to whether the maddening whimsy with which the regime tried to ruin Prokofiev and Zaderatsky also went for lighter music, or the *estrada*, as popular entertainment was known in Russia. Cabaret artists like Alexander Vertinsky and Pyotr Leshchenko had left the country in 1917, together with much of their audience, and simply resumed their careers among Russian circles in Paris, Berlin and Constantinople. They were heroes to the anti-Bolshevik émigrés, but their popularity with that group resulted in the foxtrot and tango being banned in the USSR in the 1930s. The instigator of all this was the writer Maxim Gorky, who called the music an "insane cacophony", produced by creatures who were half human, half savage and performed by a "Negro orchestra". "This is music for the fat men," he wrote in *Pravda* on 18 April 1928, referring to the pre-revolutionary elite.

Like Prokofiev, Shulzhenko would spend a great deal of her career carefully manoeuvring her repertoire through a minefield of regulations, determined to continue performing, whatever the cost. And while the Second World War had secured her fame, she, too, was subject to the whims of the Central Committee, and after 1945 large portions of her repertoire were banned.

Klavdiya Shulzhenko was born in 1906 in Kharkiv, in what is today northeastern Ukraine. Her father worked as an accountant for the tsarist railways; in his free time, he was an active and enthusiastic amateur musician. He taught his daughter Ukrainian folksongs. Klavdiya gave her first concert from the balcony of their home. In her memoirs she writes, "I turned on all the lights in the room, opened the windows and started singing. Suddenly I heard applause. 'Come on! Show yourself!' people shouted. Well, naturally I stuck my head out of the curtains. And they applauded even louder. That gave me some confidence, a bit of courage, so I dared to sing some more."

As a youngster she showed a gift for drama, and she enjoyed performing for her classmates. Her specialty was reciting poems by Pushkin and Lermontov. Her parents were quick to recognize her talent and took her to the local music conservatory, where she auditioned and was promptly admitted.

At first Shulzhenko did not aspire to become a singer, but rather a silent-film actress—the dream of so many girls in the early days of cinema. Little did she know that, with the invention of the talkies in the 1930s, the combination of singing and acting would be her greatest asset.

After graduation she tried her hand at vaudeville, where she could exploit her acting and singing talents in short musical sketches. But in 1919 Lenin had placed severe restrictions on music halls and the circus in order to purge them of "unhealthy elements". Both genres were subjected to the same ideological and administrative oversight. For up-and-coming singers like Shulzhenko, these obstacles made it well-nigh impossible to perform and robbed ordinary Russians of a pleasurable evening out. For instance, one could no longer sing in the café of vaudeville theatres, sauntering among the tables as patrons ate and drank, like Alexander Vertinsky did during the days of the tsar.

Light music is a much-loved genre in Russia, regardless of age or social status. I notice this when my wife—a mezzo-soprano who sings not only early music but also songs by Kurt Weill, Barbara, Vladimir Vysotsky and Alexander Vertinsky—performs in the Moscow club Bilingua. I sit proudly on the balcony among tattooed and muscle-bound labourers and off-duty policemen. Down in the stalls I spot a government minister and a famous author with their girlfriends amid stylish older ladies.

Even before she has sung the last notes of Vertinsky's song "Madam, the Leaves Are Falling", the men burst into cheers. They stand on their seats and clap until their biceps hurt. One of them growls in a smoke-roughened voice how fantastic it is to hear a foreigner sing in his own language: "a sign of respect". Dutch–Russian relations have never been this good.

As with Vertinsky, Shulzhenko's strength lay in the theatrical combination of singing and acting. Her songs became miniature staged dramas; she told a convincing story with all the requisite gestures. Naturally, these vignettes were mostly about love, yearning and jealousy.

In 1923 she was contracted by a Kharkov theatre to appear with the then little-known pianist Isaak Dunaevsky. She also landed roles in operettas and acted in a stage version of Dostoevsky's *The Idiot*. But vocal ballads were her forte.

Dunaevsky advised her to build up a repertoire of her own. He introduced her to Soviet songwriters, who provided her with a trove of sentimental numbers. She traded the gypsy ballads, foxtrots, and tangos—genres that had made Pyotr Leshchenko famous before the revolution—for socially engaged music from the new Soviet songbook.

One of these songwriters was the gifted Pavel German. His songs, with proletarian titles like "The Brick Factory Song" and "Mine Shaft No. 3", would make Shulzhenko famous.

But do not picture Soviet cabaret music as an austere musical evocation of the industrializing USSR. On the contrary: industry, with its pounding machines and steam-belching factory chimneys, was only a backdrop. The lyrics and melodies were sappy in the extreme and nearly always revolved around love, a consistent theme in Soviet film, plays and private lives.

Shulzhenko had 1920s working-class club audiences swooning. "The Little Bricks", as the song was also known, was so popular that after the show people would ask her to write out the lyrics for them.

Shulzhenko's breakthrough came in May 1928, when she was one of the featured singers in a concert at Leningrad's Mariinsky Theatre honouring the Soviet press. The audience went wild over her performance, repeatedly demanding encores of songs such as "Red Poppy", "Grenada", "George and Katya", "Never", "Cigarette Girl" and "Procession of the Octobrists". The success of this concert earned her a job at the Leningrad Music Hall, where her mentor Dunaevsky was now director.

In October 1931, Shulzhenko appeared in the revue *Uslovno ubityi* ("Conditionally Killed") with Leonid Utyosov. The composer: Dmitri Shostakovich. Like German and Dunaevsky, Utyosov—then the Soviet Union's most renowned *estrada* singer—immediately recognized her talent. He recommended that she put together a repertoire of lyric numbers; audiences had a hard time remembering the words to her revolutionary songs and, moreover, couldn't dance to them.

In her memoirs, she wrote that the secret of her songs lay in the combination of an elegant melody, rhythmic freedom, a heroic figure with straightforward traits and an unexpected, upbeat finish. The end of every song had to elicit a laugh, or at least a smile, from the audience.

But there has to be more to it than that. A song's success depends on its performer: see the countless YouTube clips of young Russian chanteuses ruining "The Blue Scarf" by camping it up. And think of how Frank Sinatra's sense of timing gave his "My Way" precisely that extra charm.

To learn more about Shulzhenko's secret, I visit Leonid Rusanovsky, a seventy-one-year-old Russian-Jewish viola player who emigrated to the Netherlands in 1979, escaping the rising antisemitism in the USSR. He settled in Amsterdam and enjoyed a long career in the Netherlands Chamber Orchestra. In his youth he often saw Shulzhenko perform.

I cycle to his house at the edge of the Amsterdamse Bos, a huge park on the outskirts of town. There's snow on the way. Sitting at the kitchen table while his wife Irina serves Kyiv cake and tea, we speak Russian and chat about the Soviet Union; it's just like being back in a Moscow kitchen, where I would sometimes stay up till all hours with Russian friends, kibbitzing about life, with a bottle of vodka, a sausage and a hunk of cheese within reach.

"The author Somerset Maugham," Rusanovsky tells me, "once wrote about being a stage actor: 'Never pause unless you have a reason for it, but when you pause, pause as long as you can.' That was Shulzhenko's strength. She was a great actress. She had the looks of a Russian peasant, but that was also an asset." To illustrate this, he takes out his iPad and pulls up a YouTube video in one of her post-war performances. "Look here, you see her sense of timing," he says. "The same as you hear in the music of

Myaskovsky, Khrennikov and Prokofiev—they all listened closely to her, and to Vadim Kozin."

In this black-and-white clip you see Shulzhenko, in a full-length glittery gown, gesturing gracefully like a Russian Mata Hari. A woman with a firm bosom and round face. "You got goosebumps the minute she came onstage," he says. "She has such a smooth manner, as if she were gliding on roller skates."

In the early 1930s, the RAPM decided it was time to target light music, including the tango and foxtrot. It was only thanks to Stalin's love of the genre that cabaret got off easier than classical music and literature. Besides, it hardly seemed prudent to attack relatively simple melodies and lyrics about love and young people when you need those same young people for the advancement of socialism. And yet, performers still had to be on their guard. They never knew what tomorrow might bring.

Shulzhenko wanted to continue performing, so she—like so many of her artistic compatriots—adapted her style, adding to her repertoire the kind of folk songs that could count on the RAPM's approval. This was no great hurdle, because by that time she had had her fill of the classic ballads about lovesick gypsies and aristocrats. Her new numbers, she wrote in her memoirs, expressed the "everyday emotions" of the kind of folk you saw on the street. They offered reassurance in a time when the RAPM seemed determined to quash any form of spontaneity. With the disbanding of the RAPM and its replacement by the composers' union in 1932, musical life once again had to ride the waves of shifting state propaganda. Now music was allowed to be jollier and more spontaneous, and classical musicians and revue artists alike heaved a sigh of relief. And Shulzhenko's career surged.

In the mid-1930s she fell for the young, talented Jewish musician Vladimir Koralli. They married and had a child. Their performances as a duo led to their first recording in 1935: "Tanya's Song" from the comic film *On Holiday*.

While Stalin's purges from 1936 to 1939 terrorized not only politicians but the intelligentsia as a whole, Shulzhenko toured the nation with her Skomorovsky Jazz Orchestra. After the tour, she cut a second record, this time with more songs including the jazz improvisations "The Note", "Andryusha" and "Rendez-vous". It was melancholy dance music for anyone yearning for a momentary break from the threat of war, state terror or the treadmill of the planned economy.

She went on tour to promote the new album. While in Yerevan, Armenia, she heard that the war with Germany had broken out on 22 June 1941. She took the first flight back to Leningrad, where the very next day she and 42,000 other artists were assigned to regiments to entertain the troops on the front. She would remain with them until the end of the war.

For many on the front lines and in Leningrad, besieged by the Germans, her music was balm for the soul. It was even said that her songs were just as important as the whole arsenal of Soviet bombs and grenades.

Online videos show how her mannerisms and affectations intensified in those days, but still, with her slightly sturdy build, her voluptuous hair, powdered cheeks, bright-red lipstick and plucked eyebrows, she was a quintessential "everywoman". Klavdiya Shulzhenko was Katya, Nadezhda, Vera, Irina, and so forth. She was their sister, mother and daughter all in one, just as she was the sweetheart of all their husbands.

In 1941 she joined one of the 3,800 revue, theatre and circus companies established to entertain the troops. The armed forces considered her so crucial for the morale of the soldiers that she and her ensemble were given their own rehearsal space in one of Leningrad's Red Cross posts. It was a privilege given no other artist.

Shulzhenko travelled along the front by bus or armoured train, giving short, half-hour concerts to avoid becoming a target for German fighter planes. She sang in −30°C on frozen Lake Ladoga, which, being the only air route to and from Leningrad, was under constant German fire. A typical "stage" was the beds of two lorries parked end-to-end. Shulzhenko and her audiences risked their lives at these appearances, but she didn't care. As she wrote in her memoirs, "Soldiers travelled along kilometres of ruined roads just to see me; they would endure bombardments and being shot at, they hardly slept or ate; they would even forget their dire situation, forget themselves. There on the front I experienced an artist's greatest honour: that smile, that love and recognition from soldiers for whom your art […] is absolutely essential."

Her empathy for the troops of the Red Army was such that when she once performed at a military hospital in a white gown, she noticed how much she resembled her wounded admirers in their white bandages. It nearly brought her to tears. She never again wore that white dress on the front.

It was the themes of these songs in particular that brought such comfort during the war years. Naturally they were mostly about fidelity and lovelornness, but they also oozed patriotism and comradeship. The world Shulzhenko portrayed in her music was a dreamland of purity, beauty and the absence of evil—just what her fans needed to forget the misery of real life. When, out of solidarity, she donned a military uniform for her performances for the troops, they were disappointed. They wanted to see her in gowns and pearls, as in the old days before the cannons started roaring. As far as inciting that yearning for glamour, her counterparts Marlene Dietrich and Vera Lynn couldn't hold a candle to Shulzhenko.

"The Blue Scarf" alone earned her the adoration of millions of soldiers. Everyone must have known it, hummed it, sung it. I understand completely: the tune is a melancholy waltz, the lyrics are about a woman whose blue scarf slips off her shoulders and is picked up by her beloved just before he is sent to the front. The woman promises to cherish it at the head of her bed until the fascists have been defeated and he has returned to her.

The song itself had its origins in the war. One day in the spring of 1942, a lieutenant on the Volga front, one Mikhail Maximov, approached Shulzhenko with a new text—the sentimental tale of the blue shawl—he had set to an existing melody. Aside from being a symbol of the love of a woman for her absent lover, "The Blue Scarf" now also expressed the conviction of victory over the Germans. And Shulzhenko conveyed that hope like no one else could.

"The Blue Scarf" became what Lale Andersen's "Lili Marleen" was for the Germans and Vera Lynn's "We'll Meet Again" was for the British. It boosted the soldiers' morale. There was even a twenty-year-old officer who sent his regiment into the field with the battle cry "For the blue scarf!" instead of the usual "For the Motherland! For Stalin!"

The documentary film *An Evening with Klavdiya Shulzhenko* (1983) includes a moment from the early 1970s with Shulzhenko sitting in a television studio among marine veterans on Victory

Day (9 May). The officers reminisce about a wartime performance she gave in a military hospital in Novorossiysk, on the Black Sea. They were wounded but eager to hear her sing. The song "The Hands" was a particular favourite: hands were essential for everything from writing and kneading dough to holding a weapon and caressing a lover. So they asked her to sing it for them again in the studio, which of course she did. And, again, you see her secret: not only are her voice, the melody and the lyrics enchanting, but her elegant gestures convince you she is reaching out in a warm embrace.

During the war Shulzhenko was decorated often, even being awarded the Order of the Red Star—usually reserved for high-ranking officers—for her appearances along the Western Front, the Caucasus and Central Asia. Recognition like this encouraged her to keep going, which she did until the war's end.

The euphoria of the triumph over Hitler was overwhelming, but equally immense was the devastation and suffering the Germans left behind. The entire European portion of the Soviet Union was in ruins; cities like Minsk had been completely levelled. Twenty-seven million Soviets died in the conflict, including eight million soldiers. Every one of my Russian acquaintances lost a family member between 1941 and 1945.

That history was tangible as I stood on Red Square on 9 May 2011 to watch the annual Victory Day Parade. I was one of the few Western journalists able to secure a standing spot in front of the stage where elderly veterans sat, laden with tin medals. The active soldiers—twenty thousand of them at attention; boys of seventeen in combat uniform, weapons chest-high—applauded as the veterans arrived on Red Square and made their way to their seats.

I had reported at seven o'clock that morning, together with some five hundred other, mostly Russian, journalists, at the presidential staff building (in socialist times the home of the Central Committee). Two hours after receiving clearance, we were taken by bus to Red Square. Security agents ushered us to the pavement in front of the stands. "Standing room for the press," barked one of them.

I suddenly spotted the former spy Anna Chapman, then twenty-nine and a veteran of a different war, in the stands. She and nine other Russians had been unmasked a year earlier in the United States as members of a "sleeper spy" network and had recently been repatriated as part of a prisoner exchange.

Yet more veterans were brought out in golf carts. Some had their grandchildren in tow, dressed for the occasion in military garb as well. The incredible array of uniforms, large and small, in green, white and blue, underscored that Russia was still very much a militaristic nation.

For the veterans, it was already an unforgettable day. It was like reliving the victory over Hitler one last time. I thought of my elderly friend Alexandra Ivanova Prolygina, who dug trenches near Moscow in 1941 and from there, rifle in hand, defended her city. I rang her up to wish her a happy Victory Day and to tell her that I was standing on Red Square. "I am proud of you, my boy," she said. "You are giving me great pleasure by being there."

The parade began at ten o'clock sharp. Eight guardsmen marched onto the square, bearing a Russian flag and the victory banner of the Soviet Union. The rousing march "The Sacred War" blared from a 1,500-strong brass band. This alone was already far more impressive than what I was used to seeing on TV.

The tense anticipation kept building, even among the generals who stood near me on the pavement, for, despite the meticulous planning, anything could go wrong. Then the Minister of Defence congratulated all the regiments on this sixty-sixth commemoration of the war victory. The soldiers' mass "hurrah" washed over the square. President Medvedev gave a speech. His face wore the melancholy expression of someone who knew this was his last parade as head of state. He spoke of freedom and global stability, and promised to beef up the defence budget. Contrary to the previous year, he had conciliatory words for the Allies. (But this was 2011: the annexation of Crimea in 2014 and the invasion of the eastern Ukrainian provinces Donetsk and Luhansk in 2022 would spark a new Cold War.)

The national anthem was played, and the marching could begin. The veterans stood up and waved to the troops as though they were back in charge. Tanks, armoured vehicles, mortar launchers and intercontinental Topol-M ballistic missiles rolled across the square. This was the first time I saw them up close, and it struck me how dilapidated they were, spruced up with no more than a slap of paint. After the parade, a female veteran complained to me that it was a scandal how poorly the army was looked after.

The parade ended at eleven. The veterans fanned out through the streets of central Moscow, overwhelmed with red carnations and kisses from young women. Sentimental war songs were piped into the metro stations' PA system. That evening Russian students and a Don Cossack sang more of the same in the home of a Dutch diplomat on the chic Patriarch's Ponds. Out on the street, the party was in full swing—synonymous with mass drunkenness. It was as though the victory over the fascists was just a few hours old. And everywhere you heard "The Blue Scarf". Not only from the hundreds of speakers hung from trees and streetlamps, but from countless voices, young and old.

The previous year I attended the awards ceremony for a high-school essay competition about that period. During the event, the human rights activist Lyudmila Alexeyeva, then eighty-three, related how she experienced the end of the war. Even then, she got choked up talking about it. "When I heard the war was over, I ran to Red Square," she says. "The streets were packed with people. Everyone was elated. Not so much because we had defeated the Germans, but because the war was over. We, the people, had won. That's why I'm so ashamed of all the Stalin posters I see hung up everywhere. Because ending the war was our heroism, not his."

Alexeyeva (she died in 2018) hit the nail on the head. Her sentiments must have also reverberated with Shulzhenko and all those millions of soldiers. They had delivered Stalin the victory and, in return, demanded greater civil freedoms and an end to the terror. The dictator, however, took this as an attack on his authority and only further tightened the screws, instigating a new purge to quash civil unrest before it was too late.

The Soviet press suddenly declared war on the tango, the foxtrot and the waltz: "decadent" genres that would corrupt the youth. Jazz elements, too, were taboo. In 1946, revues were stigmatized even further: "doctrineless" entertainment would henceforth come under the scrutiny of the Central Committee. The same held for ballads. The committee issued a blacklist of three hundred ideologically "undesirable" or "foolish" songs—including Shulzhenko's hits "The Note", "Hands", "The Clock", "Rendez-vous", "I Don't Regret" and, yes, "The Blue Scarf". Recordings of these songs became harder to get and discs were no longer pressed. It was as though the entire revue repertoire had been outlawed overnight, for the simple reason that it was too frivolous and sentimental and flouted communist ideology.

So, once again, Shulzhenko had to reinvent herself. It was more difficult this time, though, and she was not really inspired. It's hardly surprising: on the one hand, she was idolized as the best of what light music entertainment had produced; on the other, she was belittled by the authorities for her "banal" ditties.

Shulzhenko adapted not only her repertoire, but her whole performing style. One element of this was to sing with only piano accompaniment, no longer with her husband Koralli's jazz ensemble. Without the lively musical liberties that jazz offered, her old songs took on a far more earnest tone. She also set aside the love ballads in favour of songs about student life and the messy existence of young people facing a serious future. She guilefully manoeuvred her way through the remainder of the Stalin years, although it would take until the late fifties or early sixties for her to make a comeback with her old numbers and be herself onstage again. In 1956, she said that in future she would only perform songs that were dear to her, and that herein poetry played an important role. When romantic ballads came back into fashion in the 1960s, Shulzhenko once again triumphed on the concert stage with new versions of her early repertoire.

The local Leningrad television station broadcast one of her concerts. I watched it online. It's 1962, a time when the bushy-browed Leonid Brezhnev was in power, and, despite the high price of petrol, Russians seemed generally content.

The programme Shulzhenko sang that afternoon was called *Songs of Love*. The camera glides, documentary-style, through Peter the Great's summer garden with its splendid trees and statues, along the Neva River with its high bridges and stately former palaces, and zooms in to presenter Igor Gorbachev, who recites a love poem as he strolls. He stops in front of the concert hall, gazes at a poster bearing Shulzhenko's name. And then, his cap tilted nonchalantly, he says, "I don't know about you, but I love Shulzhenko." This is the Soviet Union at its most romantic.

Gorbachev, still gushing, introduces her to the audience. Shulzhenko herself, joined by a trio of piano, guitar and double bass, is in full glory, wearing her usual elegant gown with a silk stole draped over her shoulders, a pearl necklace and long earrings. Her hair—no longer blonde but dyed black—is put up. She is heavy-set for fifty-six, but it was a normal build for many Soviet women in those days. Shulzhenko exudes self-confidence; she has outdone herself after all these years.

It occurs to me how many women must have seen themselves in her. They probably dreamed of wearing such finery. The hall is packed with couples, young and old, and men in uniform, all glowing with admiration before Shulzhenko has sung a note. They've come for their idol and, of course, for the trip down memory lane. Nostalgia is typically Russian, regardless of the times in which you live.

In between numbers, Gorbachev reminisces about Shulzhenko's early years. There are film clips of famous wartime appearances, including a blonde Shulzhenko singing "The Blue Scarf". Then we return to the concert, where she sings "Let's Have a Smoke". And then you see once again how she captivated her audiences. It's not her eyes, squinting as if to avoid the smoke, but her hands as they roll an imaginary cigarette. She flirts with the camera and her audience. The same happens during her rendition of "The Note". While she sings, it's as though she's reciting the text in her mind. Her gestures are so convincing, you hardly even need the music.

At the time of the documentary, she and Koralli had been divorced for seven years. Neither was particularly distraught at the break-up; they had simply grown apart over the years. The only downside was that Shulzhenko, now registered as "single", was assigned to living in a *kommunalka*.

Two years later, in 1957, she remarried. The lucky fellow was a thirty-nine-year-old admirer, Georgy Yepifanov, with whom she had been corresponding for some years. That marriage, however, ended in enmity in 1964.

Shulzhenko, single again, was more vulnerable than ever. Her loneliness manifested itself in a combination of perfectionism and capriciousness befitting a prima donna. Her behaviour estranged her from friends, who were afraid of not being able to meet her exacting demands.

Her only solace came from the official recognition she would receive in 1971: she was named People's Artist of the USSR, the highest possible accolade for a singer.

Leonid Brezhnev, a veteran of the front in the Second World War, was a great fan of hers, with a particular fondness for the song "The Note". With this in mind, she summoned the courage to approach him after one of her concerts to complain about the difficulty in finding a place to live. The party leader promised to help her, and shortly thereafter she was given a comfortable new flat in a respectable neighbourhood. And in 1976, on her seventieth birthday, her powerful admirer awarded her the Golden Star.

The concert given in honour of that birthday put her back in the spotlight in the sold-out Grand Hall of the Leningrad Philharmonic. Shulzhenko continued to perform for another few years—her popularity, especially among older audiences, was undiminished—but struggled with mass media like radio and television, which by nature inhibited direct contact with the audience. In particular, she had trouble with television, because broadcasts were continually interrupted by ice hockey updates.

Her health (and memory) deteriorated in her final years. But you don't notice it in *An Evening with Klavdiya Shulzhenko*. Her voice might have sagged a bit, but she sings just as beautifully as ever. The documentary opens in her home, where an amiable man comes to fetch her for a recording at the Melodiya studios, a stone's throw from the Moscow Conservatory. She's still rehearsing, leaning over the piano, as the cameras enter. The decor is typical of the Soviet elite in those days: kitschy antique furniture and lamps, gold flock wallpaper with a floral motif, mirrors, grand piano. On the wall behind the piano hang portraits of her in her younger years.

She is driven to the studio in a Volga (which along with the Lada dominated Moscow's streets back then) to St Andrew's Anglican Church on Voznesensky (Ascension) Lane. The typically English red-brick building was built in 1883, lost its religious function after the 1917 revolutions and resumed its role as a working church only in 1994, after a state visit by Queen Elizabeth II.

For me it is a familiar spot, because aside from being a must-visit for Anglicans in Russia, it is also where the Moscow International Choir rehearses. My wife sang there for five years during our time in Moscow, as both choir member and soloist. Its acoustics are fabulous. The fact that so many renowned Soviet musicians made recordings there gives the church an almost magical aura.

In the documentary, Shulzhenko reminisces about her time in Leningrad during the war, but also about that birthday concert in 1976. She first performed in the columned Grand Hall back in 1939, she sighs, in a competition for revue artists. Then come countless archival film clips of her wartime appearances. The troops are at ease and beam with admiration from the open field, the concert hall, the hospital ward. The images confirm that in those years her songs made her everyone's sweetheart.

When Shulzhenko died on 17 June 1984, the entire Soviet Union, from Brest-Litovsk to Vladivostok, was in mourning. She was given a state funeral; thousands of admirers accompanied her coffin to her final resting place at the Novodevichy Cemetery. Flowers are still placed at her grave every year.

Young and old still sing Shulzhenko's songs today—see the YouTube videos by young women in army uniforms. As Shulzhenko herself said, "As long as people remember me, I'll stay alive." And it's true: just turn on the TV on 9 May, and you'll hear "The Blue Scarf".

I first became acquainted with Shulzhenko that December day in the Museum of the Great Patriotic War, and from the very first notes I was smitten. After leaving the museum, Yulia and I danced across the plaza towards the three houses of worship—a synagogue, a mosque and a Russian Orthodox church—and in the middle of the plaza, the enormous obelisk dedicated to St George, the army's patron saint, towered over us. We descended the Victory Park hill towards the metro station, singing all the way. In our thoughts, we're surrounded by the Germans, but we're safe—protected by the blue scarf.

5

Celebrated, Persecuted, Rehabilitated

I first heard the music of Moisei Weinberg (1919–96) in the 1957 Russian film *The Cranes Are Flying*. Accompanied by melodies that alternate between light, dramatic and romantic, it tells the heart-rending story of two young Muscovites in love, whose happiness is disrupted by the Second World War. I saw the film, directed by Mikhail Kalatozov, in the late 1980s at the Amsterdam art cinema Rialto when Mikhail Gorbachev's perestroika allowed Dutch audiences to enjoy a wide range of top-notch Soviet cinema. The opening scene, in which the lovers run down the quay of the Moskva River in the early morning after a night of revelry and suddenly spot a flock of cranes flying overhead, is etched in my memory. The film music always brings joy to my heart and makes me long for a Moscow morning in early summer.

I only became interested in Weinberg the man later on, when I read that Dmitri Shostakovich was a great admirer of his string quartets. I listened to the younger composer's music and was immediately struck by the similarities with Shostakovich.

My Weinberg knowledge deepened in the summer of 2019, when the Muziekgebouw aan 't IJ in Amsterdam devoted an entire programme to his music for the centenary of his birth. The Latvian violinist Gidon Kremer and his Kremerata Baltica chamber orchestra were inspired by Weinberg's powerful, emotive music to create a performance they called *Chronicle of Current Events*, a retrospective of Weinberg's life and fate, which evoked some harrowing parallels with modern-day Russia. The performance's effectiveness was thanks in large part to the director Kirill Serebrennikov, who had been under house arrest in Moscow since 2017 and never passed up a chance to criticize the Putin regime.

The performance at the Muziekgebouw was named after *The Chronicle of Current Events*, the hand-typed dissident magazine in the Soviet Union during the 1960s and '70s that reflected the reality of Soviet life. Music, performance and visuals comment on Weinberg's fate and emphasize the extent to which his life was impacted by communist ideology. And the melancholy string dialogue in Weinberg's Symphony No. 21 ("Kaddish") reflects the horrors of the Second World War.

I also saw Weinberg's face for the first time: vulnerable and inward-looking, with thin, arched eyebrows. Everything about his appearance radiated fear, which his music only seemed to confirm. It was a far cry from the optimism of Klavdiya Shulzhenko and her upbeat wartime romances.

Judging from his surname (spelt variously as Vaynberg, Wajnberg or Weinberg), I concluded that Weinberg must have had Jewish roots. The fact that his first name is sometimes given as "Mieczysław" betrays Polish heritage; in Poland, Jewish surnames often referred to German cities.

In search of Weinberg's Jewish ancestry, I consult my friend Mikhail Zemtsov, a Russian violist and conductor whose family emigrated to the West. He has been living in the Netherlands for more than twenty years, where he leads the viola section of the

Residentie Orchestra in The Hague and teaches at the conservatory there and in Utrecht. I catch him during a CD recording of a Brahms piano trio with pianist Hanna Shybayeva and cellist Timora Rosler, in a church-turned-studio in Amsterdam North.

Mikhail recalls Weinberg as a superb composer with a unique style. "Not all of his compositions may be on the same level, but that's true for nearly any composer," he says. "For me, his string trio and piano quintet are absolute masterpieces. And if they say he was influenced by Shostakovich, then the opposite is also true. Especially Shostakovich's use of Jewish folk melodies can be traced directly to Weinberg."

I ask Mikhail about the general state of antisemitism in the Soviet Union. Did he ever personally experience it? His answer is short and to the point: "Being Jewish in the Soviet Union was for the most part as it was under the tsars. For instance, universities and conservatories had a quota for Jewish students. When you applied for a job, there was the notorious 'Paragraph 5' in your passport, which stated your 'nationality' [i.e. in the case of Jews, their religion]. So a lot of Jews changed their surname to something Russian- or Ukrainian-sounding. That really did help. There's a well-known saying: 'They can hit you in your face, but not in your passport.'"

It gradually dawned on me how tragic Weinberg's life was. He escaped the Nazis in Poland by the skin of his teeth. Fleeing to the Soviet Union, he soon made a name for himself as a pianist and composer, partly thanks to Dmitri Shostakovich, who immediately recognized Weinberg's talent. But in 1948, Weinberg also fell prey to Stalin's anti-formalist and anti-cosmopolitan campaign, which was mainly directed at the Jewish intelligentsia. Until the dictator's death in 1953, the secret police kept a close eye on Weinberg and twice sent him to prison. Both times, it was his friend Shostakovich who came to his defence and secured his release.

Weinberg's rehabilitation in the 1960s meant that his music would be performed by big names in Soviet music like conductors Kirill Kondrashin, Kurt Sanderling and Rudolf Barshai; soloists like Emil Gilels and Leonid Kogan; and the Borodin Quartet—some of whom, like Weinberg, had Jewish roots. His piano quintet in particular was a favourite among musicians.

A gifted pianist himself, Weinberg often performed with other Soviet luminaries. In 1967 he teamed up with Galina Vishnevskaya, Mstislav Rostropovich and David Oistrakh for the premiere of Shostakovich's *Seven Romances on Poems by Alexander Blok*, and recorded the four-hand version of Shostakovich's Symphony No. 10 together with the composer. When the spinal tuberculosis he had picked up during the war years cut short his performing career, he focused entirely on composing.

Curiously, Weinberg never achieved the kind of fame in the West that Prokofiev and Shostakovich enjoyed during the Soviet years. This was partly due to his Polish heritage (meaning he didn't count as "Russian"), but also because of his refusal to teach at the conservatories in Moscow or Leningrad, where most other renowned musicians were based. He thus never really became a household name and ranked low in the hierarchy of cultural ambassadors who were sent abroad to promote the socialist utopia. While his Symphony No. 4 and the concertos for violin and trumpet were issued by the record label EMI in the 1970s under licence from the Russian state recording company Melodiya, he never performed in the West, so he remained more or less unknown there.

The turnaround took place only after his death. Suddenly he was seen as Shostakovich's equal. His centenary in 2019 was celebrated worldwide with symposia, concerts and new CD releases. What a contrast with 1994, when Weinberg, a little more than a year before his death, celebrated his seventy-fifth birthday. His music already felt dead and buried; with the exception of a few friends, he was forgotten. The downturn had started twenty years earlier. Soviet musical life was stagnating and concertgoers, eager for anything modern, turned their attention from old-timers like Shostakovich and Weinberg to the younger generation of underground composers like Alfred Schnittke and Sofia Gubaidulina.

Between 1994 and 2000, the Olympia label issued Weinberg's major works on CD, which in turn spurred a flurry of performances in concert halls outside Russia. From 2006 there were international conferences dedicated to him, and studies of his music were published in English, German, Polish and Russian. Weinberg's name, no matter how you spelt it, was now a fixture of classical music.

Weinberg's family, both on his mother's and his father's side, came from the Russian governorate of Bessarabia, in present-day Moldavia. The family name was spelt as it is today: Weinberg. During the bloody pogroms of 1903 in Kishinev (now Chișinău), not only were both his grandfathers murdered, but two of his great-grandfathers as well. His father, Samuil Weinberg, escaped the massacre on time. But in 1943, he, his wife Sonia (Sura) and their daughter Ester, two years older than Mieczysław, were murdered anyway, not by Russian Cossacks and local mobs but presumably by the Nazis in a concentration camp.

Mieczysław was able to flee to the Soviet Union. But, like so many other Jews who had survived the Nazi terror, he was tormented for the rest of his life by "survivor's guilt"; this, he wrote in his memoirs, would be his primary impetus to compose. That way, day in day out, he kept the memory of his family members alive.

Samuil Weinberg had earned his living at the beginning of the twentieth century as a composer, violinist and conductor of the small orchestra at Warsaw's Jewish theatre. When the Great War broke out in 1914, Warsaw had 800,000 inhabitants, 300,000 of them Jews. That considerable Jewish population—Poland's Jews numbered some three million in 1929, more than ten per cent of the total population—meant that Warsaw enjoyed a flourishing Jewish cultural life.

It was into this artistic environment that Mieczysław was born on 8 December 1919. In his memoirs, he recalls his father taking him as a small boy to the theatre to listen to his music. He was a self-taught pianist and remembers joining his father at the keyboard at age ten or eleven in the orchestra pit; he even regularly stood in for his father as conductor from that time. His theatre experience would later prove invaluable when he composed film scores.

At the age of twelve, Mieczysław was sent to study piano at the Warsaw Conservatory, where he had lessons from the renowned pedagogue and international performer Józef Turczyński. Young Weinberg was soon one of his star pupils. He also wrote his first compositions (including songs for the Jewish theatre) but would only turn seriously to composition after emigrating to the Soviet Union. Until then, his focus was entirely on playing the piano.

On the evening of 6 September 1939, five days after the Second World War broke out, Weinberg was playing in Café Adria, a popular Warsaw dance hall. Few Poles saw anything to worry about, trusting the government's reassurances that the Polish army had successfully held back the German troops. But when he returned home, Mieczysław heard on the radio that the enemy was approaching Warsaw and that all men were ordered to leave the city. Half a century later, he would write in his memoirs: "The next morning my sister and I left Warsaw, heading eastwards. But she tore open her foot and soon returned to Mother and Father. And I continued on my way."

He manoeuvred his way eastwards through the fighting; where his journey would end, he didn't know. He had barely anything to eat or drink and had a few narrow escapes: once he saw a German soldier stop to ask a few Jews for directions, and, as he drove off, he tossed a hand grenade at them, killing them all.

Poland capitulated on 27 September. By that time, Soviet troops had crossed into Poland from the east (under the terms of the Molotov–Ribbentrop pact) to seize Polish regions inside western Ukraine. Over the next few days, thousands of Polish and Jewish refugees assembled at the Polish–Soviet border near the city of Brest. With machine guns pointed at their backs, they begged to be admitted to the Soviet Union. They were lucky: out of the blue, permission was granted, and the borders opened.

But before they could enter the Soviet Union, the refugees had to register. And that was when Mieczysław Weinberg became Moisei Vaynberg. When the border guards determined he was a Jew, he was told that he would no longer be called Mieczysław but Moisei. His response was simple: "Moisei, Abram, whatever you say, as long as I can get onto Soviet territory." He did not realize at that point that he would never return to Poland again.

Weinberg, with his new name, went to Minsk, the capital of Soviet Belarus. There he could continue, at the state's expense, his conservatory training. He took composition lessons from the renowned and prolific Vasily Zolotarev, himself a student of Rimsky-Korsakov.

Little is known about his time in Minsk. He was poor but not starving, health issues kept him from being drafted, and music made him forget the world's misery.

Then he heard Shostakovich's music for the first time, and it changed his life—apparently, he recognized something of his own soul in that music. It happened when Shostakovich's Symphony No. 5 was being performed, and there was no one available to play the piano and celesta part. Weinberg offered to play it and was smitten at once.

From then, he made great progress as a composer and became one of Zolotarev's top students, which was likely the reason he was sent to Moscow in 1940 to represent Belarus at a congress on "The First Decade of Belarusian Literature and Art".

At this conference he met the composer Nikolai Myaskovsky, for whom he developed a great admiration. After he moved to Moscow for good, three years later, he would always send new scores to Myaskovsky for his evaluation. Until his death, he kept an autographed photo of Myaskovsky on his nightstand.

Weinberg received his conservatory diploma on 21 June 1941 during a concert which included his *Symphonische Dichtung*, played by the Minsk Philharmonic under conductor Ilya Musin. What better send-off could a young composer wish for? But the celebratory atmosphere was short-lived: that same night, Nazi Germany invaded the Soviet Union.

As in Warsaw less than two years earlier, the people of Minsk at first had no idea of the catastrophe that was in store for their country. For instance, the Gorky Moscow Art Theatre made a guest appearance at the House of the Red Army for a matinee performance of Richard Sheridan's comedy of manners *The School for Scandal*, and the Philharmonic played an open-air concert of Belarusian composers in the city park. The orchestra manager rushed onstage during the jolly programme with the news that Molotov, the People's Commissar for Foreign Affairs, was about to make a radio speech. Everyone hurried to gather around the loudspeakers of the wired broadcaster on the main streets. They knew that if someone as high up as Molotov spoke, bad news was on the way.

These developments were especially alarming for the many Jewish longtime residents of Belarus. Those living in Minsk fled for safer regions. Most of those who stayed behind would, in the coming years, be murdered.

Weinberg, too, wanted to flee. But for someone with Polish nationality this was easier said than done, because, as a foreign refugee, he was not given official permission to leave Minsk. Fortunately, a conservatory teacher managed to secure him a last-minute spot on a goods train heading east.

After a chaotic two-week journey, he arrived in Tashkent, the capital of Soviet Uzbekistan, where a slew of actors, musicians, writers, scientists and artists from Leningrad and Moscow had already been evacuated. In October, Moscow-based composers including Khachaturian, Khrennikov, Kabalevsky and Shebalin, as well as most members of the Bolshoi theatre, would also arrive by train. Shostakovich was originally among them, but he was in poor health and could not bear the overfull carriages; he disembarked earlier in the city of Kuybyshev (today's Samara) on the Volga, where he would remain until the end of the war.

※

Tashkent had been a flourishing cultural centre since the beginning of the century and had both an opera house and, since 1938, its own symphony orchestra. Opera companies and orchestras came from all over Europe to perform here. Weinberg soon found work as a répétiteur at the Uzbek State Opera, where he met many young composers, including the Soviet refugees Israel Finkelstein and Yuri Levitan. He also became friends with Uzbek musicians like Tokhtasyn Dzhalilov, who led the Tashkent Philharmonic Orchestra from 1937 to 1940. His work from that time betrays their musical influence.

The city owed its excellent orchestra to the fact that many musicians and students from the Leningrad Conservatory had moved to Tashkent. In June 1942, the orchestra performed Shostakovich's Leningrad Symphony; Isaak Glikman, a close friend of the composer, travelled specially from Tashkent to Kuybyshev to pick up the score from Shostakovich.

One day, in the cafeteria of a block of flats, Weinberg met a young woman, Natalia Vosvi-Mikhoels. She was the daughter of the famous Jewish actor Solomon Mikhoels (born Shloyme Vovsi), who had made a name for himself as director of the Yiddish Theatre in Moscow. They married a year later and moved into one of the two rooms allotted to the Mikhoels family. In the other room lived Mikhoels and his second wife (his first wife, Natalia's mother, had died in 1932) and their daughter.

The Molotov–Ribbentrop pact at first spurred a rise in official antisemitism in the Soviet Union, but this situation was abruptly reversed on 22 June 1941, because Stalin realized how badly he needed the help of the Jewish intelligentsia, who played an essential role in many sectors of society. In autumn 1942, the dictator even approved the establishment of a Jewish anti-Hitler committee, which the following April was renamed the Jewish Anti-Fascist Committee (JAC). Mikhoels was chosen as its chairman.

The JAC's primary goal was to spread anti-Nazi propaganda abroad and collect money for the Soviet war effort. To this end, Mikhoels and a few other JAC members travelled to the United States to raise funds from American Jews. Ironically, this trip would later prove fatal to him, because after 1945 the Americans were Stalin's new enemy.

Israel Finkelstein, who before the war was Shostakovich's assistant in his Leningrad composition class, was so impressed with Weinberg's music that he brought it to the elder composer's attention. He encouraged Weinberg to send Shostakovich the score to his First Symphony—Mikhoels acted as courier—and a month or so later Weinberg received an invitation from Shostakovich to visit him in Moscow.

In autumn 1943, Weinberg and Natalia went to the Russian capital and moved in with his in-laws, who by then had also returned to Moscow. Their flat happened to be practically around the corner from Shostakovich's. Weinberg played the piano score of his Symphony No. 1 to Shostakovich, who was so impressed that he arranged for him to be able to remain in Moscow.

That meeting was the beginning of a lifelong friendship. From then on, Weinberg would bring all his new compositions to the master. They would also regularly sit at the piano together to study music: Bach, Beethoven, Mussorgsky and Mahler were among Shostakovich's favourites.

Although Weinberg was never officially his pupil, Shostakovich spared no effort in pitching his friend's work to other established composers. It is no exaggeration to say that in this way he contributed considerably to Weinberg's later success.

In the following two years, Weinberg composed his Third and Fourth String Quartets, a piano trio, a piano quintet, three sets of piano pieces for children and two song cycles. One of these song cycles is the *Six Jewish Songs*, Op. 17, settings of poems by Shmuel Halkin about the fate of Jews during the war. In the fifth song he refers to the massacre of Jews in the Babyn Yar ravine in Kyiv. He later transcribed this song for orchestra as the fourth movement of his Symphony No. 6. He would likewise devote his Symphony No. 21 to the victims of the rebellion in the Warsaw ghetto. This included many friends and acquaintances, so its composition must have been emotionally taxing. But, he felt, it had to be written. And if anyone knew the atmosphere of the Polish capital, it was Weinberg.

After the war, Stalin was afraid of losing his grip on power: millions of Soviet soldiers stationed in central Europe had experienced the benefits of life without communism. So, the communist propaganda had to be ratcheted up. While in the past only Shostakovich, Prokofiev and Khachaturian were used as mouthpieces for foreign cultural propaganda, now other composers, including Weinberg, were set to the task.

His usefulness to the regime was short-lived, however, and the year 1946 marked the beginning of Weinberg's troubles. Jewish candidates for the Moscow Soviet were pressured to withdraw from the race. This antisemitic move was followed by Stalin's instructions to his ideological vassals Andrei Zhdanov and Konstantin Fadeyev to weed out cosmopolitanism and anti-patriotism in the arts. This had everything to do the Jewish Anti-Fascist Committee, which had served its purpose during the war (to garner support in America and Great Britain for the Soviet military cause) but was now *non grata* for having revived the proposal to turn Crimea into an autonomous Jewish republic. Stalin apparently saw this as an attempt to wrest the peninsula away from the Soviet Union. Under the guise of combating cosmopolitanism and Zionism, he launched a barely concealed antisemitic campaign, stoking age-old resentments against Jews. And seeing as a large percentage of the artistic intelligentsia was Jewish, that group became the target for widespread harassment.

In an attempt to spare the music world the worst of the kind of repression that had befallen Soviet authors, the composers' union held a plenary meeting in Moscow in early October to encourage its members to engage in self-criticism. Weinberg was one of the first candidates. His accuser was Lev Knipper, whose reputation was built on music he composed for the Red Army, but who was in fact a secret agent for the NKVD. The work of Weinberg and Jānis Ivanovs had, he conceded, touches of brilliance, but also suffered from a "wealth of ideas" that had nothing to do with music. This was, in his words, "a dangerous tendency". He also acknowledged Weinberg's talent and that, unlike many of his colleagues, he had grown up in extraordinary circumstances. Knipper was not worried about Weinberg's future, but felt he needed a nudge in the right direction.

Shostakovich came to Weinberg's defence, expressing his complete confidence in his younger colleague. Nevertheless, apparently afraid of the consequences of his own words, he proposed offering Weinberg "friendly criticism and comradely assistance" to ensure he stayed on the right path. (This fear was not entirely unfounded, because when the authorities opened their campaign against formalism two years later with an attack on Muradeli's opera *The Great Friendship*, Shostakovich himself became a target of the Kremlin. For him, 1948 would be an *annus horribilis*.)

By then Weinberg had other worries connected with the latest political developments. On 13 January, Solomon Mikhoels was murdered by the secret police during a business trip to Minsk. The exact details are still shrouded in mystery, but what likely happened is that after having dinner with actors in a play he was to evaluate for the Stalin Prize, he and Vladimir Golubov-Potapov, a theatre critic and informant for the secret police, were lured to a dacha. There Mikhoels was poisoned, beaten and shot dead. Golubov-Potapov was likewise executed, and both bodies were taken to the centre of town, where they were dumped, driven over by a truck in a staged "accident" and left behind in a snowbank.

That same day, Weinberg was participating in a meeting of composers and musicologists to discuss Zhdanov's warning after the attack on Muradeli's opera. He was therefore oblivious to the tumult at home. His wife took one urgent phone call after another beseeching her husband to come to the Jewish theatre at once. They had apparently received word that something had happened to their director in Minsk.

As soon as the news broke, Shostakovich hurried to Solomon Mikhoels's flat to support his friends. In a telling comment that reflected the mood of those days, he said he envied the dead man—at least now he had nothing more to fear from the regime. Everyone assumed that this would not be the end of it, and that things would only get worse.

After the funeral, the cousin of the Politburo member and Stalin associate Lazar Kaganovich took Natalia aside. They locked themselves in the bathroom, the only place in the house out of earshot of the secret police. Aside from passing on greetings from Kaganovich, the only Jewish Politburo member, her friend urged Natalia not to pursue any inquiry into her father's death, as it would only exacerbate things. It was a clear warning, Natalia would later write in her memoirs.

These were no idle threats. Shortly thereafter, Miron Vovsi (a doctor and cousin of Mikhoels), Benyamin Zuskin (a prominent member of the Moscow State Jewish Theatre) and Boris Zbarsky (the pathologist who had embalmed Lenin) were arrested. All three had seen Mikhoels's corpse at first hand, before Zbarsky had been made to conceal the bruises on Mikhoels's maimed face.

The assassination of the popular Jewish director, who was highly regarded in the Jewish community and who had known Isaac Babel and Osip Mandelstam personally, was the first public move in the persecution of the Jewish intelligentsia in the Soviet Union. Only years later would it be confirmed that Stalin himself had ordered Mikhoels's liquidation.

From that day on, Weinberg and his family were under constant surveillance. Weinberg himself had to report regularly to the secret police. This harassment came to an end only twelve days after Stalin's death in 1953.

Weinberg would later recall the nightmare of those five years: "I wasn't allowed to travel, I was constantly being watched and the secret police would just show up at my door or I was ordered to report to them. It was worse than prison. When they did finally lock me up, it came as a relief, because I always knew it would lead to that."

His father-in-law's death prevented him from attending the rest of the composers' conference. He therefore missed the speech by the general secretary, Tikhon Khrennikov, in which his colleagues were urged (or, better say forced) to echo his criticism of Prokofiev and Shostakovich. When later asked to do so, Weinberg refused.

No one knows how Weinberg actually felt in those days. Anything he said, even at home, could invite trouble. His music was his sole emotional outlet. In 1948 he wrote his Sinfonietta No. 1. He dedicated it to the "friendship of all peoples of the Soviet Union"—a safe topic. But at the top of the score was a quote from Mikhoels on the equality of the Jews: "On the fields of the *kolkhoz*, now too a Jewish song was heard; not a long-ago folk song full of sadness and misery, but a new, cheerful song of labour and industriousness."

Speculation abounded as to the composer's intentions. According to Natalia, the sinfonietta was her husband's protest against his father-in-law's murder: "Weinberg wanted to make it clear that a man mustn't be killed just because he was a Jew. But the quote by my father was scrapped in the printed edition of the score."

Who knows whether she's right. Weinberg's biographer David Fanning sees the quote as everyday Soviet propaganda, because many people could well remember the successful labours of the Jewish colonists in Crimea, where they had been sent to work in specially constructed agricultural settlements. On the other hand, it's just as possible that friends and allies of Mikhoels read it as an expression of solidarity.

In any case, the fact remains that Weinberg employed well-known folk tunes to get his sinfonietta approved, because he knew the authorities expected this of him. Add to it "the friendship of all peoples" and official consent was a sure bet. Especially because the quote was reminiscent of a passage from Shostakovich's popular song cycle *From Jewish Folk Poetry*: "In bygone years I never sang songs about the fields [...], a song of grief and suffering. [But] the *kolkhoz* is now my home [and] I am happy."

Weinberg's strategy worked. The sinfonietta was unanimously approved and cleared for performance by the composers' union. From its premiere onward, the work was a nationwide hit.

The success of the Sinfonietta did not, alas, render Weinberg immune to the consequences of the 1948 composers' conference. In the second issue of the music magazine *Sovetskaya muzyka*, six of his works were criticized; he was ridiculed as "a little Shostakovich", whose works contained all "the negative characteristics [...] typical of modern-day Soviet music". The criticism was aimed primarily at Weinberg's supposed pursuit of originality.

Interestingly, the very same reviewer wrote positively about Weinberg's *Children's Songs*, Op. 13, praising not only the melody but the thematic content, which was based on Jewish folk music. His piano works for children, on the other hand, were given a sound thrashing.

Fanning, Weinberg's biographer, sees the contradictory criticism as a secret deal between the reviewer and Khrennikov, although he can't put his finger on who might have persuaded whom. The fact that Khrennikov would also later praise *Children's Songs* seems to indicate that each had tailored his critique to fit the other's. By basing his compositions on Jewish folk music, Khrennikov wrote,

Weinberg produced a "brilliant work [...] full of *joie de vivre* and [exhibiting the] dedication of the Jewish people to the shining, free working life of the Jewish people in the land of Socialism".

Mostly, the wildly swerving judgments concerning Weinberg's work underscore the fickleness of the regime. Whether his being an ally of Shostakovich was the real reason he was condemned, no one knows. What does seem clear is that no one really knew what "formalistic" music was, or what one could and couldn't compose.

To confirm my suspicions about the capriciousness of the Soviet music authorities, I contact the Russian pianist, composer and musicologist Jascha Nemtsov in Berlin. A respected Weinberg scholar, Nemtsov was born in 1963 in Magadan, a harsh, forbidding region in the far east of Russia. In 1938, at the height of Stalin's Great Terror, his father had been imprisoned in a forced labour camp in the gulag. Like millions of other Soviet citizens, his life was upended by the sudden accusation of counter-revolutionary activities. When he was released and rehabilitated after Stalin's death in 1953, he remained in Magadan.

The family relocated to Leningrad when Jascha was two years old. He graduated with distinction from the conservatory there, and in 1992, after the dissolution of the Soviet Union, he emigrated to Germany. Currently, he is professor of the history of Jewish music at the Franz Liszt University of Music in Weimar, although since the Covid-19 pandemic he has been based mostly in Berlin. There, he and his wife Sarah give concerts of twentieth-century Soviet composers like Zaderatsky, Shostakovich and Weinberg.

Regarding the fear Weinberg must have felt under Stalin, he says that "everyone, famous or not, was afraid in the forties and fifties. It didn't matter whether you were a cobbler or a renowned violinist. Everyone was terrified. It's nonsense to say that musicians were less vulnerable than others. Enough of them landed in the gulag. At most, they were fortunate in that the composers' union did not carry out purges the way the writers' union did."

This last fact has, in my opinion, everything to do with Tikhon Khrennikov. He stuck up for his members as much as he could, even though he was forced to stab them in the back now and again to maintain credibility with his superiors at the Kremlin. Hadn't Vsevolod Zaderatsky junior said that Khrennikov protected his father, even though he had to constantly manoeuvre between Scylla and Charybdis?

Nemtsov also has strong feelings about so-called formalism. "In reality, it didn't make a bit of difference what kind of music you composed," he says. "If you see which compositions were approved and which were rejected, there's no connection to the music itself. Muradeli's opera might have been used to launch the campaign against formalism, but the music itself was really very traditional and folkloric. It's proof of how totally arbitrary things were in those days. If you're capable of labelling folkloric music as 'formalist', what's left? What kind of harmonies can a composer use? Stalin's terror had absolutely no logic to it, which only augmented the fear, because nobody knew if they would be next.

"Initially targeting elite composers in the anti-formalism campaign was Stalin's way of showing that no one should take their privilege for granted. The cafeteria of the composers' union was very hierarchical: in the first-class section they served good-quality food, and in the second-class section it was inedible. But the diners in first class were the ones who were criticized. It was only to show that the terror was clearly aimed at the elite."

✽

In May 1948, shortly after the hatchet-job composers' congress, *Sovetskaya muzyka* suddenly published articles praising the very composers they had blacklisted not even three months earlier. In December of that year, works by Shostakovich (who'd had more than his share of critique) were performed, and he was even honoured with the title Folk Artist of the Russian Socialist Federal Soviet Republic, the second-highest honour possible for a Soviet artist. Three Stalin Prizes for his film music would follow.

But in 1949 the tide would turn yet again, and just as suddenly, albeit with their ire turned towards a different group Stalin's anti-cosmopolitan campaign now set its sights on theatre critics (most of them with Jewish roots) and members of the Jewish Anti-Fascist Committee (founded by the unfortunate Mikhoels). In the summer of 1952, Stalin ratcheted the campaign up further by executing thirteen Jewish intellectuals, five of them writers, in the Lubyanka prison.

Shortly thereafter, the regime announced the "discovery" of a conspiracy of Jewish doctors. On the night of 10 November 1952, the fifteen most eminent doctors in the Soviet Union, all of them residents of a block of flats near the Arbat, were arrested and taken to the Lubyanka. They were accused of plotting the murder of leading figures in the government and armed forces by intentionally giving them incorrect medical treatment. It was the beginning of a nightmare that several of them would not survive.

On 13 January 1953 (five years to the day after Mikhoels's murder) the official news agency TASS reported on the plot by the "killer doctors". The alleged gang leader was Professor Miron Vovsi, head doctor of the Red Army and a cousin of Mikhoels. They labelled Mikhoels a "bourgeois nationalist" and an agent of the

American aid organization Jewish Joint Distribution Committee (known also as Joint or the JDC), through which, after the war, he had supposedly received instructions for his cousin Vovsi as to which Kremlin leaders were to be assassinated.

A fortnight later, the secret police spent an entire day searching the Weinbergs' home. Nothing was left intact. The agents, in their leather jackets and blue caps, ransacked the flat, emptying drawers, bookcases and wardrobes. When they finally left, the place looked like the scene of a pogrom.

The year 1953, which had begun so auspiciously for Weinberg with the premiere of his cantata *In My Fatherland* and the performance of his *Moldavian Rhapsody* by the violinist David Oistrakh, would soon take a catastrophic turn. One February evening, after a concert, the Weinbergs were in their flat, chatting with another couple about the music they had just heard, when they were interrupted by the insistent ringing of their doorbell. Natalia opened the door, and two men forced their way inside, waving an arrest warrant. Behind them stood a trembling young soldier and the concierge, who made sure no one left the flat.

Weinberg said, "My dear friends, I have done nothing illegal…" And then, almost with a shrug of his shoulders, he left with them.

After that, wrote his wife Natalia, "[a] few KGB agents remained behind and searched the flat until dawn. They sealed his study and assured me he would be freed within forty-eight hours if he was found innocent. When I went to the KGB information desk two days later, they told me to come back in two weeks because they hadn't discovered anything yet. They added that I should bring 100 roubles twice a month, and it would be passed on to my husband. The fact that none of that money was ever returned was for me the only proof that he was still alive."

Her hunch was right, because care packages and money were indeed delivered to prisoners while they were alive. This is the insanity of a perverse system convinced of its righteousness.

As optimistic as Weinberg was when they carted him off from his flat, he was terrified now that he found himself in Moscow's notorious Butyrka prison. He later told a friend he immediately confessed to the craziest accusations for fear of being tortured.

Weinberg was arrested because he was a Jew. His Sinfonietta No. 1 was supposedly an expression of Jewish bourgeois nationalism. Another accusation was that he had conspired to create a Jewish enclave in Crimea. All Weinberg did was to discuss cultural matters with representatives of the Jewish Anti-Fascist Committee.

But there were other issues that contributed to his arrest. Valentin Berlinsky, the cellist of the renowned Borodin Quartet and a friend of Weinberg's, claimed that, on top of being an antisemitic move, it was also the work of jealous fellow composers who were only too happy to thin out the competition. Not impossible, but even then, Weinberg's links to Mikhoels and the JAC cannot be ignored.

Weinberg himself, in a 1995 interview with the music magazine *Russkoe utro* ("Russian morning"), said that his connection to the "killer doctors" was the reason for his detention and the basis for the accusation of Jewish bourgeois nationalism. He claimed to have been quick-witted enough to say to the agents, "Since I can't read or write a single letter of Yiddish, but have some two thousand books in Polish in my study, wouldn't you rather accuse me of Polish bourgeois nationalism?" Their answer: "We know that better than you do."

※

Once again Shostakovich came to his aid. A week after Weinberg's arrest, he wrote to Lavrenty Beria, the feared head of the secret police. He described Weinberg as an extremely gifted and promising young composer whose focus was entirely on music and nothing else. He could guarantee Weinberg's good reputation. He also mentioned that Weinberg had back problems, which was true. Finally, he paid a visit to Kliment Voroshilov, the dreaded chairman of the Supreme Soviet, who would later sign Weinberg's release.

Weinberg was released on 25 April, a month and a half after Stalin's death. He had spent more than three months in prison. Natalia believes Shostakovich's letter to Beria hastened his release.

Referring to his time in prison, Weinberg told *Russkoe utro* ("Russian Morning"):

> I was put in solitary confinement, in a cell so small I could only sit, not lie down. At night they turned on a bright light, which made it impossible to sleep. It was hardly pleasant. Sometime around 19 February the interrogator suddenly said to me, rather enigmatically, "Your little friends are sticking up for you." All right, I thought, but I did not ask any questions, for of course it could have been a trap. If I mentioned a name, that person could end up behind bars! Afterwards, though, Natalia Solomonovna told me that she and Levon Tadevosovich Atovmyan [...] had personally delivered a letter to the prison from Shostakovich, who said something to the effect that he swore on his life or his name that I was an honest man and harboured no ill intentions.

It's anybody's guess what would have become of Weinberg if Stalin had not died. I'll bet that Shostakovich would have felt it was too risky to stick his neck out for him yet again.

Weinberg spent that day, 5 March 1953, in his cell without any idea that the dictator had died. Only a few weeks later did he notice that the guards were treating him more courteously. What he also did not know is that, starting on 4 April, the falsely accused Jewish doctors were being released one by one. The last, on 14 April, was Miron Vovsi. Eleven days later it was Weinberg's turn. He left the Butyrka prison with his head shaved, severely malnourished and with fear in his eyes. A friend came to visit him a few days later. Weinberg greeted him with, "So, how're things?"

Olga de Kort-Kulikova, a Russian musicologist who has lived in the Netherlands for more than twenty years and who writes for all manner of music magazines about Russian composers and musicians, tells me that Weinberg did not take his release as lightly as people thought. "At first he was so scared that he didn't even want to leave his cell," she says. "He said to the wardens, 'I am a Jewish nationalist and must stay here in prison.' It's said they had to fetch his wife to convince him to leave Butyrka."

With Stalin dead, hopes for a cultural thaw began to take shape. But Weinberg, still reeling from his imprisonment, felt it wiser to lie low. At most, he continued to take on commissions for propaganda music from the composers' union.

Shostakovich, on the other hand, set out to capture the post-Stalin intellectual shift in music. This resulted in his Symphony No. 10, written not on a commission but as a manifestation of artistic independence. He asked Weinberg to play the two-piano version with him, which he did, even if it was just as a favour. The freedom Shostakovich granted himself in the symphony came with a price: he was roundly criticized for disloyalty to the Party. Meetings at the House of the Composers in Moscow in March and April 1953 were the scene of fierce debates. Khrennikov in particular lambasted the work as contrary to the ideals of both Soviet music and Russian musical tradition.

This time it was the composers Weinberg, Georgy Sviridov, Dmitri Kabalevsky and Nikolai Peyko who stuck up for Shostakovich. Weinberg argued in his friend's defence that the symphony was one of music's core genres and had been more or less abandoned by the capitalist world. Moreover, he said, the symphony's critics did not judge it objectively and in their shallow criticism were merely venting their own frustrations. But he saved his harshest words for a speaker who remarked that concerts with music by Shostakovich were attended by "a certain audience". Weinberg took him to task for this comment, saying that if Shostakovich's music contained themes that were not to his critics' liking, this did not mean they could self-righteously write off his many thousands of followers as a bunch of snobs.

After this confrontation, Weinberg became even more of a recluse. Participation in official music life was kept to a minimum: he took no active role in the composers' union, seldom appeared as a soloist, and did not teach at the conservatory. "After his time in prison, all he wanted was to duck away from reality by shutting himself up in his study," says de Kort-Kulikova. "This also meant he was spared the intrigues within the composers' union. He was skittish and entirely out of touch, to put it mildly. For instance, if he sat outside, he had to ask his wife where there was shade, and she had to move his chair there. And if he had to share the lift with his neighbours, he would retreat into a corner and not say a word, so as not to have to make small talk."

But when the composers' union invited him in 1955 to join a committee to rejuvenate the "genres for the masses" section, he accepted. His being asked for this function acknowledged his earlier work for radio, film and the circus. He was apparently the authorities' ideal "composer for the masses". At the same time, the invitation was a sort of rehabilitation.

After that, Weinberg mostly composed for the cinema and the circus. In 1956–7, he wrote the film score for *The Cranes Are Flying*, which made him famous in the West. But Soviet audiences knew him mostly from the circus as well as immensely popular animated films such as *Boniface's Holiday* (1965) and *Winnie-the-Pooh* (1969), both directed by Fyodor Khitruk.

De Kort-Kulikova grew up with those animated films in her youth. "Like everyone [in the seventies and eighties], I knew Weinberg's music without ever having heard his name," she says. "I can still hum the music to *Winnie-the-Pooh*"—the same way children in any country have cartoon melodies embedded in their memory.

That film music, she says, was Weinberg's salvation. "Through a simple medium like animated film, he could expose audiences to his music and make people happy, while so much of his other work is sombre and heavy. You can't listen to his serious compositions without being reminded of the dark side of his personal history."

Weinberg's reclusiveness did not mean he was suddenly poor. "Don't forget that his music for animated films and the circus was well paid."

It's not so strange that de Kort-Kulikova only learnt of Weinberg's existence after moving to the Netherlands in the late

1990s. "During my musicology studies in the Soviet Union, I never once encountered his name. There's no mention of him in books on Russian music from the sixties, seventies, and eighties. Even the *History of Russian Music of the Second Half the 20th Century* [a reference book from 2005, co-authored by Tamara N. Levaya] affords Weinberg just one page. And even then, the article mainly emphasizes Shostakovich's influence on him."

The post-Stalin cultural thaw entered a second phase after party leader Khrushchev's "secret speech" at the 20th Party Congress of 25 February 1956, in which Stalin's crimes were first acknowledged. Suddenly, cultural contact with the West was allowed and musical influences like the twelve-tone system were available to Soviet musicians. This did not mean, however, that now everything was possible. Socialist realism remained the norm and composers were still warned against "formalism". Still, Muradeli's opera *The Great Friendship* and other works abruptly banned in 1948 could now be performed again.

Weinberg's already precarious health worsened in the late 1950s, and his output diminished accordingly. On 11 September 1957, Shostakovich wrote to his friend Isaak Glikman, "M.S. Weinberg is quite seriously ill. He suffers from a heart condition and is completely exhausted. Awful for him." But ill health did not entirely prevent him from composing. He wrote mainly string quartets, which would rank among his finest works and were first performed by the Borodin Quartet. Of his seventeen quartets, the one-movement No. 8 was long a standard repertoire piece for Western ensembles.

In the 1960s, Weinberg wrote several song cycles, two symphonies and a requiem. His Symphony No. 8 ("Polish Flowers", 1964), considered to be one of his best works, has as its theme the war in his homeland. Based on a poem by Julian Tuwim, it not only reflects on pre-war poverty and the Nazi horrors, but also hope for the triumph of freedom, justice and humanism. Weinberg also underscores the solidarity between Poland and the Soviet Union—which tells us he had no knowledge of the NKVD's massacre in Katyn of Polish officers, priests and intelligentsia in 1940 or of the Soviets' betrayal during the Warsaw uprising of 1944.

The bitter irony behind the work becomes even clearer to me when I pay another visit to the violist Leonid Rusanovsky in Amsterdam. He tells me that Weinberg's family was probably murdered not by the Nazis but by Catholic Poles. "Weinberg's father-in-law Mikhoels never found any evidence that the Nazis were responsible for the fate of Weinberg's family."

In addition to composing and despite his spinal tuberculosis, Weinberg appeared every so often as a concert pianist, particularly as a favour to Shostakovich. On 23 October 1967, he and Mstislav Rostropovich, Galina Vishnevskaya and David Oistrakh performed the premiere of Shostakovich's *Seven Romances on Poems by Alexander Blok* at the Moscow Conservatory in a rendition that aficionados say has never been equalled.

Despite such highlights as a musician, his private life was a bumpy one. He and Natalia divorced in 1968; five years later he married Olga Rakhalskaya, a fellow student of his daughter Viktoria. "Olga was a girl with simple roots who, through Weinberg, climbed the social ladder of the intelligentsia," says musicologist de Kort-Kulikova. "When he left Natalia, he was already suffering from Crohn's disease, a severe intestinal illness, and could hardly eat. Natalia had always fed him, but Olga did nothing. One rather cynical bit of trivia was that they moved to a new flat that looked out onto the Butyrka prison, where he had been incarcerated, and where Olga's mother worked as a prison psychiatrist—not exactly the ideal mother-in-law."

After Natalia and Viktoria emigrated to Israel in 1972, Weinberg's Moscow friends more or less cut him off. Not so much because he had left Natalia, but because, for the Soviet intelligentsia, her family was an important symbol of propriety and honour. One after the other, all his friends except Shostakovich broke with him.

Weinberg's Jewish roots continued to play a role in his work. The 1968 opera *The Passenger* was, he felt, his most important composition, even though its semi-staged premiere would have to wait until 2006, ten years after his death.

The opera was based on a radio play (later a novel) of the same name by the Polish writer and Holocaust survivor Zofia Posmysz. In it, a former Auschwitz guard is confronted with her past by a camp prisoner, Marta. The climax of the work is the chaconne from Bach's second partita, played by the violins (in Posmysz's story, Marta's fiancé plays it before he is sent to his death).

At first, Shostakovich wondered whether the piece would turn out as a symphony or an opera. After hearing the piano version for the third time, he said that it had "become a true opera, a success for which all of Weinberg's earlier works have paved the way. And aside from its musical qualities, this is an extraordinarily important work in our days."

Musicologists note that *The Passenger* has striking points in common with Shostakovich's *Lady Macbeth of Mtsensk*, as well as with the operas of Benjamin Britten and Alban Berg's *Wozzeck*.

These are qualities that could have brought Weinberg to the upper echelons of the music world, but this did not happen, because, with very few exceptions, his music was almost never performed in the Soviet Union. The reason is that the Soviet authorities were reluctant to bring too much attention to the Shoah, as it might detract from the suffering of non-Jewish Soviet citizens.

From the late 1960s onward, Weinberg's life was trouble-free. In 1980 he was granted the title People's Artist of the USSR, and in 1990 he received the USSR State Prize. He worked day and night until his death; his wife Olga said inactivity depressed him, and the thought of giving up composing frightened him. In this, he was not much different from Shostakovich, who was also known for his drive.

Weinberg would come to the aid of his friend Shostakovich one last time: posthumously, after his death from lung cancer in 1975. They had kept in contact until the very end; Shostakovich continued to show interest in Weinberg's newest compositions. In a tribute published the year after his mentor's death, Weinberg wrote that "the greatness of his music consists in the fact that it is inseparable from the most burning problems that stir the consciousness of his contemporaries".

When Solomon Volkov, Shostakovich's assistant, published the composer's so-called memoirs in 1979, Weinberg signed an open letter to the *Literaturnaya Gazeta* ("The Literary Gazette"), decrying the book as a deception. Although it is unclear whether Weinberg actually read the book, his condemnation carried considerable weight.

Like Weinberg, Shostakovich had to make artistic concessions and compromises in order to get his music performed. And, like Weinberg, Shostakovich cared nothing for politics. The only thing that counted was his music. The fact that they both managed to compose music they could stand by is, in light of the general artistic repression, quite exceptional.

Weinberg was sombre in his final years. The break-up of the Soviet Union in December 1991 also meant the disbanding of the composers' union and thus the end of the generous financial support for loyal members. For a composer like Weinberg, for whom commissions from the composers' union were the only source of income, this was disastrous. When work from the film studios also dried up because producers began turning to younger, more modern composers, the situation became even worse. Weinberg did not have contacts in the West or in government from which he might ask for financial assistance. Nor did he have paying students. His poor health prevented him from emigrating to the United States or Israel.

It is not surprising, then, that at a certain point very few people beyond a small circle of friends even remembered that he existed. That he was a relic of Soviet musical life was painfully obvious when, on 8 December 1994, his seventy-fifth birthday, no single musical organization marked the occasion. He was well and truly forgotten.

In the coming months, he became frailer by the day; his heart was weak, and his arteries clogged. From March 1995 onward, he spent most of his time in bed. A month and a half before his death on 26 February 1996, he had himself baptized in the Russian Orthodox faith. It was a gesture to his wife Olga, who like him had Jewish roots but had been educated at a Moscow religious school. My friend Leonid Rusanovsky reckons the baptism was mainly due to Olga's stinginess. "Only if he was Russian Orthodox could she bury him alongside her mother," he said. "That saved her money on a separate headstone."

When I wonder aloud whether Weinberg's conversion was a betrayal of his murdered family members, Leonid says reassuringly, "Of course not, Misha. Remember that all his compositions end in a major key. He was an optimist at heart."

6

The Vanished Singer

Whereas the Germans have gone some way in devising a Vergangenheitsbewältigung ("way of coping with the past"), Russians still struggle with their communist history. So many families in the former Soviet Union include both perpetrators and victims of Stalin's terror that it makes talking about those bloody years, which cost millions of innocent people their lives, something of a taboo.

Unlike the lives of Vsevolod Zaderatsky and Mieczysław Weinberg, that of the successful singer Vadim Kozin shows how blurred the line between casualty and collaborator can be. And there's something else that makes him stand out. After serving his sentence in the far eastern port city of Magadan (he, like so many fellow Soviets, was falsely accused of "counter-revolutionary activities"), he decided not to return. As far as he was concerned, his career was in ruins; he had no business in Moscow. But why Magadan, where the sun doesn't show itself for half the year and where the decrepit concrete blocks of flats, eaten away by the sea air, could plunge anyone into a hopeless depression?

I soon realize how difficult it is to sketch a clear portrait of him. The interviews he gave at the end of his life to the local media are unreliable. His archives—including his diaries, which could shed some light on the many riddles of his life or disprove the myths he himself propagated—are locked away in a tiny, cluttered flat in Magadan.

Vadim Kozin is a slippery character. I have a photo of him as a young man: his round face, with its long, sharp nose and slightly bulging eyes with their gentle, questioning look, reminds me of the poet Osip Mandelstam. He is vain: this much is clear. But then, so were most of the other Russian popular singers from the first half of the twentieth century, like Alexander Vertinsky and Pyotr Leshchenko. I know some of their songs by heart. Maybe that's why I'm determined to learn everything I can about Kozin.

Most of the essential information about his life can be found in the biography *Vadim Kozin*, published in 2001 by his friend Boris Savchenko. Savchenko spent years interviewing the singer and spoke to countless friends and acquaintances. In 1968, at the age of twenty-seven, he first heard Kozin perform live to a packed auditorium of Magadan's Gorky Theatre. Audiences were so keen to relive his songs from the twenties, thirties and forties that they had even sold tickets for seats in the orchestra pit.

Savchenko first met him shortly before that concert, in the Magadan public library, where he was doing research for an article about the painter Ilya Repin and Ivan the Terrible. Kozin, also waiting to check out books, noticed the young journalist's interests and invited him to his home to look at a few issues of the magazine *The Capital and the Estate*. Savchenko regarded the man as a living legend, but hesitated, recalling an incident in 1959 during a concert tour, when the KGB had caught the singer in a Khabarovsk hotel bed with a male student. It crossed his mind that there might be similar motives at play now, too, but he decided to risk it. One didn't often get invited to the home of a celebrity like Kozin.

Kozin's one-bedroom flat in the centre of town was chock-a-block with books, newspapers, magazines and a prominently placed chess board. Two cats also strolled about. This was the beginning of a long friendship that would last until Kozin's death. Savchenko interviewed Kozin twice a week for three-hour sessions. At first, the singer was reticent, but he gradually loosened up and spoke openly about his life.

Savchenko's editor encouraged him to write a biography of Kozin. Easier said than done: Kozin was on a list of persons, one drawn up by the authorities in Moscow, about whom it was forbidden to write. This was strange, considering he was allowed to perform occasionally in Magadan. Apparently, the local authorities were well disposed towards him: he had been given a flat and a small pension. But that did not mean the press could write about him or that his name or music could be broadcast on radio or television. A local hero, maybe—but, in Brezhnev's Soviet Union, he did not exist.

That changed in January 1982. Kozin's loyal fan Savchenko contributed an article about him to the magazine *Sovetskaya estrada i tsirk* ("The Soviet Theatre and Circus") entitled "Still So Many Songs to Sing". This brought an end to the taboo on writing about him, and Kozin was suddenly deluged with fan mail from all over the country. For the previous half-century, people had assumed Kozin had been pulverized by Stalin's terror.

Other newspapers and magazines followed suit, his music was suddenly back on the radio, and record stores restocked recordings that had been removed from the shelves decades earlier. On 17 December 1987, state television even broadcast a programme about two famous pre-war singers: Izabella Yurieva and Vadim

Kozin. The entire Soviet Union could thus witness Kozin's resurrection. The question arose as to why in heaven's name he would choose to live in faraway Magadan, while Moscow had been the epicentre of his successes—which only went to prove that nobody knew what Kozin had been through.

In 1991 Savchenko published a short monograph about Kozin titled *The Disgraced Orpheus*. He spoke with an ex-KGB general whose father had been involved in Kozin's conviction. The KGB man could not fathom why anyone would write about the singer. "He is a born homosexual!" he exclaimed, indignant. He did tell Savchenko that although Kozin had been charged under Article 58 of the Penal Code (which criminalized political missteps), the real reason was that the singer was homosexual.

One of Kozin's self-perpetuated mysteries is his year of birth. His passport said 1906, he claimed it was 1903, and the birth registry of St Matthew's Church in St Petersburg says 1905. According to one theory, Kozin presumed he would live to be 100 and wanted to be around for the centenary celebrations. The truth, however, is much more practical: in the days of scarcity following the revolution, his mother pushed his date of birth back by three years in order to increase the family's ration allowance.

Another murky detail of Kozin's life concerns visits to Stalin in the 1930s. The dictator had invited him to come and sing for him—Stalin was particularly fond of the song "The Suffering of Pskov". This was all that Savchenko could get out of him on this subject, although Kozin had performed regularly for the dictator in the Kremlin or at his dacha. Perhaps he was ashamed of this. But, well, Stalin was a big fan of his, and, in those days, to refuse to give a private concert could have had fatal consequences.

There was also the question of Kozin's parentage. During his detention prior to his second arrest in 1959, he claimed his father had been a merchant and his mother a woman of Romani origins who sang in a mixed Sinti-Roma choir. The renowned Romani singer Varya Panina was his grandfather's second cousin.

Here, too, the truth is less exotic, but interesting nonetheless. Vadim Kozin came from a well-to-do mercantile family from St Petersburg. His grandfather had been a successful wholesaler of haberdashery and before the war was one of the few owners of an automobile—a Benz—and a telephone. Vadim's father specialized in trinkets and jewellery in Paris and later in Russia.

Young Vadim was tutored at home by the children's author Klavdiya Lukashevich, who instilled in him a love of literature. Later, during Stalin's Great Terror, she disappeared without a trace. Her books were likewise purged from libraries, as if they had never been written.

Kozin's mother had indeed earlier sung in a gypsy choir. With the introduction of "light music" in theatres at the end of the nineteenth century, gypsy songs became immensely popular in Russia. Even Russian composers contributed sentimental ditties to the repertoire with titles like "In That Quiet Hour", "In That Long Night" and "In the Final Hour".

The passage of time plays a crucial role in these songs of love and yearning, which feature regularly in stories by Anton Chekhov, the master chronicler of the daily life of the common Russian.

Moscow theatres like the Yar, the Hermitage, the Slavianski Bazaar, and the Buff in St Petersburg were, together with hundreds of café-restaurants, the primary venues for the performance of gypsy romances. Artists such as Alexander Vertinsky, Pyotr Leshchenko, Yuri Morfessi, Varya Panina and Isa Kremer were much-loved national celebrities. Most of them were regular visitors at the Kozin household. The one time that the renowned Morfessi visited, little Vadim sat on his knee. Years later he would call him "the idol of my youth", and, as a singer, he could perfectly imitate Morfessi's mannerisms in his singing and gestures.

Young Vadim soon discovered that singing was his passion. His mother had taught him the Roma and Sinti songs and coached him in the proper onstage movements: refined, feminine gestures *à la* Morfessi. Visits with his father to the many *cafés chantants* and vaudeville theatres that had sprung up like mushrooms after 1917 only fed his interest.

But his father's death in 1922 changed all that. The Bolsheviks had seized the flourishing family business, and his father had found work as a bookkeeper at a state-run company, earning a steady but modest income. It now fell to the sixteen-year-old Vadim to step in and help provide for his mother and four sisters. The civil war was only recently over and there was no work for those with an education, so Vadim, having finished school, took a job as a dock worker. His evenings were devoted to realizing his ambitions: he sang in amateur clubs and accompanied silent films in the giant People's House cinema across from the Peter and Paul Fortress, wearing out his fingers with endless tangos and blues at the piano.

After the film there was live entertainment. Among the songs were those from the repertoire of Alexander Vertinsky, who was immensely popular under the last tsar and had emigrated in 1920. Kozin's lucky break came when he was called upon to fill in for the headline entertainer, who had taken ill. His performance was a success and launched his career as a singer of light music.

In 1924 he was accepted by an agency in Leningrad that helped freelance artists find work and was promptly signed on by three major local cinemas. He recalled how he and his mother plastered the city's main streets with posters for upcoming concerts. The fact that gypsy songs were in those days normally sung by women was a plus: a man who sang these numbers was unique and attracted whole new audiences.

In 1931 he was taken on by the concert bureau House of Political Enlightenment in Leningrad's central district, which secured him a job at the Leningrad State Vaudeville Theatre. Now he could call himself a professional singer. He told Savchenko how proud he was to see a poster at the front of the theatre announcing "THE FAMOUS PERFORMER OF GYPSY SONGS VADIM KOZIN".

In 1936, Kozin decided to try his luck in Moscow. Famine was still rampant in the countryside—a consequence of the forced collectivization of the agricultural sector that would eventually result in the deaths of some six million farmers. But in the cities, too, Stalin's terror was running at full steam. In the years that followed, untold numbers of artists would be arrested and banished to the gulag. At the same time, hungry farming families migrated to the cities to look for work in the new factories.

Moscow had been the capital of the Soviet Union since 1918, and in those eighteen years it appeared to have become the nation's cultural capital as well. Artists earned more there than in Leningrad; this was a draw for Kozin, who by now had become used to a life of luxury and immediately set up residence in the chic Hotel National across from the Kremlin.

His money soon ran out. But a performance in the Central Park of Culture and Leisure (renamed Gorky Park in 1936) opened doors for him. After the concert, the conductor of the vaudeville orchestra that had accompanied Kozin introduced him to the park's director, who offered him a fixed contract.

Soon Kozin was giving solo concerts that started at nine o'clock in the evening and could go on until midnight, depending on the audience's demand for encores. He sang without amplification, and his repertoire included popular numbers like "The Wicket", "My Fire" and "Zhiguli". He also performed privately for Stalin at vodka-soaked receptions. The dictator, who had a weakness for gypsy and folk songs, sang along. Kozin's stardom under Stalin was equivalent to that of the heavily made-up crooner Joseph Kobzon, the "Russian Sinatra", in Putin's modern-day Russia.

Kozin undertook successful national solo tours, accompanied by his regular pianist David Ashkenazy (the father of the concert pianist Vladimir Ashkenazy). People adored his voice, and he sold millions of records. Music shops even sold his portrait photo; many a "Red Corner" (the spot in communist households where photos of socialist heroes were displayed) included Kozin's portrait alongside those of Lenin, Stalin and Marx.

The party looked likely to be over when the authorities determined that non-political themes in the arts could demoralize the masses. Personal and intimate music was now forbidden; from then on, the arts had to focus on the collective optimism of the "shining future of socialism".

But Kozin slyly skirted the decree by imbuing his repertoire with ethnographic elements; by singing about typical Russian cities like Pskov and Arkhangelsk, he gave his numbers the feel of folk songs. His repertoire would eventually grow to some two thousand songs, most of them Russian, but with a smattering of Sinti and Roma numbers as well as songs by Russian or Soviet classical composers. And then there were two hundred of his own compositions.

One peculiarity of Kozin's concerts was that they were never broadcast live on the radio because he refused to sing amplified. So, just before his performances in Chelyabinsk and Kazan, the radio announcers informed their tens of thousands of listeners that the singer would not be broadcast, because he was too nervous to sing into a microphone. His fans' bitter disappointment didn't bother him in the least.

Kozin drove a hard bargain when it came to negotiating his fees. For instance, for a concert in the city of Molotovka he demanded 20,000 roubles, while the theatre director already considered 5,000 too much. It led to much haggling, with the theatre finally offering 10,000 roubles. But Kozin turned it down, and the performance was cancelled.

Eager to hear his voice, I put on the CD *Vadim Kozin: The Final Concert* and listen to the famous number "Autumn", about a man trying to convince his lover not to leave him. "Do not go, for I love you so." Two and a half minutes of melancholy in the tradition of the Sinti and Roma. I immediately realize how good he is—he's even better than my hero Pyotr Leshchenko at expressing joy, heartache, hope and suffering. You could say that he was the male counterpart to Klavdiya Shulzhenko (not coincidentally, she too performed with the pianist David Ashkenazy).

Without Kozin, gypsy music would never have survived the Soviet authorities' later ideological attacks. This was because Kozin, who couldn't read a note of music, had memorized every number—he was a walking music library. At the end of his life, every last song was recorded and transcribed for posterity.

❁

The German invasion of 22 June 1941 took Kozin as much by surprise as it did most other Soviets. Even Stalin had not expected Hitler to break the Molotov–Ribbentrop non-aggression pact they had signed two years earlier.

Kozin showed his most patriotic side, calling upon the state impresario Mosconcert to set up a mobile concert brigade. He was thus one of the first musicians to go to the front to play for the troops, providing a sentimental moment amid the fighting. Both "Autumn" and "Moscow" were specially composed for this tour; soldiers were especially fond of belting out "Autumn" on their way to the front.

Not a day went by without Kozin performing somewhere. In addition to the front in Crimea and in Kalinin (modern-day Tver), he sang in hospitals and armaments factories, on battleships and at supply depots. A special train took him from one venue to the next. He even cut a record with songs on the "front" theme, like "In the Forest Near the Frontline" and "My Leningrad". While records by other artists were being requisitioned (the vinyl supposedly necessary for the war industry), Kozin's were left untouched.

That Kozin's reputation travelled beyond the USSR's borders became evident at the Tehran Conference on 30 November 1943. The Soviet Union, Great Britain and the United States met that day at the Soviet embassy in the Persian capital to discuss the war's progress and to begin hashing out the post-war partition of Europe.

It was Winston Churchill's birthday, and a party had been organized. Marlene Dietrich, Maurice Chevalier and Isa Kremer (an internationally known singer of Yiddish songs who had emigrated to the West in the early days of the Russian Revolution) were to provide the entertainment. Churchill asked Stalin also to invite Kozin. Stalin was surprised, but, being in good spirits, he gave the order to fetch Kozin to Tehran. The singer arrived that very afternoon in a specially chartered plane, sang for the British prime minister that evening and returned to Moscow the next day. In return, Kozin is said to have asked Stalin to facilitate the evacuation of his mother and sister from Leningrad (alas, it was too late).

There is something fishy about this story. Did it actually happen? Kozin's accompanist David Ashkenazy says it did not; surely, if Kozin had performed, he would have accompanied him? On the other hand, Kozin himself was an accomplished pianist, so he could have accompanied himself. And although Kozin had been reticent about sharing details of the concert with his biographer Savchenko, as though wanting to keep the myth alive, Savchenko went along with it. The story is revealing about either Kozin's international standing, or his desire for it.

The war forced Kozin to make some concessions. In 1944, for instance, he allowed concert producers in Yaroslavl to turn on the radio microphone so that his performance could be broadcast live, and in Tashkent he agreed to a concert being recorded on film and then shown on the various fronts. Kozin was giving his all for the motherland's victory over her enemies, and it made him a hero of the Red Army. Sentimental Stalin, who had been an avid choral singer in his youth, awarded him the Order of the Red Star, the Soviet Union's highest distinction. I wouldn't be surprised if Kozin sang "Suliko"—the dictator's favourite Georgian number—at the ceremony. He also performed at a banquet for members of the NKVD. Ironically, the general who raised his glass to Kozin would, the very next day, sign his arrest warrant.

That arrest came on 16 May 1944, one day after having performed at the State Vaudeville Theatre. His name vanished from posters, his photos were removed from the glass cases at theatres and concert halls, and his voice no longer graced the airwaves. At the front, he was replaced by new talent, the best-known being Mark Bernes and Klavdiya Shulzhenko.

Kozin was arrested at the height of his fame. Since the beginning of 1944, he had lived in the Metropol Hotel, like that other revered singer of light music, Alexander Vertinsky, who in 1943 had returned from abroad to contribute to the war effort. It was in this fashionable Art Deco hotel (which after the Revolution had served as Lenin's headquarters but was now mainly the haunt of foreign guests) that Kozin received his liaisons. He was taking quite a risk, because he was being watched day and night by the secret police, and the streets surrounding the hotel were the scene of mass arrests and disappearances. In 2007, construction workers digging in the street behind the hotel discovered a pit containing the remains of several hundred executed persons.

Unlike in parochial Moscow, in Leningrad Kozin had been able to live openly as a homosexual. In a post-revolutionary society that frowned on traditional marriage (the People's Commissar for Social Welfare was the feminist Alexandra Kollontai, who advocated free love), homosexuality seemed almost to become a new accepted lifestyle. At first, communism had no laws forbidding it, but this changed overnight when in 1934 Stalin declared homosexuality a crime. After that, anyone hoping to lead a gay life with any semblance of normalcy had to have reliable contacts within the secret police. But then, as in modern-day Russia, the ban on homosexuality was rife with hypocrisy. Many high-ranking men in Stalin's apparatus, including the NKVD boss Nikolai Yezhov (who was executed in 1940), were gay. The park across from the Metropol, in front of the Bolshoi Theatre, had long been a favourite cruising spot.

The new law criminalizing homosexuality, which resulted in some 10,000 men being sent to the gulag, was mostly used as an instrument of vengeance by the elite. To this day, little is known about the fate of those men charged with homosexuality because the FSB archives on this subject are still sealed.

In 1959, while again in detention, Kozin would claim in a written statement that his 1944 arrest was the result of a conflict with Lavrenty Beria, the dreaded chief of the secret police. Kozin's mother and one of his sisters had been killed during the German siege of Leningrad, while Beria had promised Kozin they would be evacuated in time. But in 1959, too, Kozin threw up a smokescreen that his dispute with Beria concerned his trying to protect Marina Raskova, the pilot who had petitioned Stalin to set up a female-led air battalion, from his (Beria's) advances. Beria had a reputation as a literal lady-killer: he abducted young women, raped them and then made them disappear.

A year before his death, Kozin told the Dutch filmmaker Theo Uittenbogaard in the documentary *Gold: Forgotten in Siberia* that one day Beria summoned him and said, "You sing for Stalin. And that's not all. Stalin sings folksongs with you." Kozin confirmed this, to which Beria asked, "But why only Stalin? Why not sing about Lenin?" Kozin replied, "That's not true. I sing one about Lenin too. I sing it at all my concerts. I sing songs about Stalin and one about Lenin by [the poet] Demyan Bedny."

When Uittenbogaard asks Kozin why he was sent to Siberia, the singer becomes irritated. "Don't spring that kind of question on me," he says. "I'm over ninety." He continues: "So Beria asks, 'Why?' and I say, 'I sing one song about Lenin, set to a text by

Demyan Bedny. It starts: 'It was a day like any other, the same dull sky, the same drab street.' Beria asked again, 'Just one number?' And I replied, 'Yes.'"

Kozin flares up again when Uittenbogaard mentions that he was exiled. "I don't know why," he grumbles, "but I had to leave at once for the Magadan health spa. Full stop. So I went. Someone came to tell me I had to go to Magadan. I wouldn't be locked up. I could live there. So I went."

This is the first time I see Kozin on film. A vain, frustrated man who enjoys reminiscing about his past glory, but bristles as soon as an interviewer brings up the touchier episodes in his life. The interview is held in his one-room flat on the fourth floor of a dreary Soviet block on Magadan's Shkolnaya Street. There's a Krasny Oktyabr (Red October) piano he purchased in 1956, which was delivered by boat from the factory in Kamchatka.

What Kozin says in the documentary about his meetings with Stalin is also interesting. He performed regularly at the Kremlin; he was invited to stay after performances, and then out came Stalin to sing a folk song, accompanied by Kozin.

The interviewer asks whether he thought Stalin was pleasant. "As a person, he was good to me. I don't know what he was like around other people, but to me he was friendly. And tactful. He could be very tactful."

Kozin's irritability with some of the questions speaks volumes: with this interviewer, too, he does his best to keep up the myth that he was not homosexual, no matter how clear it is that this was the reason behind his imprisonment. Secret police archives, made available in part to Russian researchers in the 1990s, clearly state that on 10 February 1945 Kozin was sentenced by a special tribunal of the NKVD, a "troika", to eight years' imprisonment for anti-Soviet agitation and homosexuality. In November of that year, he was sent to the labour camps on the Kolyma River in the east of the Soviet Union.

In his travel diaries, published posthumously and edited by Boris Savchenko, Kozin recalls his jail stay in the city of Ufa, where he spent some time on the way to Magadan. He describes the dirt-floored cell and the smell of *makhorka* cigarettes. The place was full of bandits, murderers, thieves, political prisoners and falsely accused citizens. Some were wholly dejected, others acted as though it were all perfectly normal. One man prayed non-stop, another related Alexandre Dumas's *The Count of Monte Cristo* to his fellow inmates. Kozin had to be constantly on the alert so as not to be robbed while he slept. At night they were woken by wardens calling out the names of those who were up for the next transport, and the men whose turn it was noisily prepared to go.

In 1989 he admitted to the newspaper *Gudok* ("The Whistle") that he would never have survived the camp without the help of friends and acquaintances. He also claimed that his singing helped others to survive. Truth be told, Kozin had it easier in Kolyma than most. Two years after the article in *Gudok*, he said in a newspaper interview that he was free to move about Magadan as he pleased, provided he stayed within the camp zone, allowing him to travel about and give concerts in the region's gold mines.

Magadan, a cluster of wooden huts and blocks of flats alongside a craggy rockface, had been built fourteen years earlier by forced labourers and idealistic communist youth. The settlement served as the headquarters for the NKVD's new camps along the Kolyma. The area surrounding this enormous river was rich in minerals and contained the world's largest gold deposits. In addition to prisoners put to work digging in the mines, the project also needed specialists, engineers in particular, and, naturally, marriageable women for them. Prisoners first travelled by train the entire breadth of the USSR to Vladivostok, where they boarded a ship holding between three and five thousand passengers that took them northwards past Japan and through the Sea of Okhotsk. Once they arrived in Magadan, they were transported to the camps by lorry, sometimes over thousands of kilometres, along roads built by forced labourers. The harsh, barren landscape was unsuitable for a railway.

The entire journey could take up to six months. Of the 16,000 prisoners sent to the Kolyma camps in the first year, only 9,928 reached Magadan alive. One famous casualty of this journey was the poet Osip Mandelstam. In 1938 he was sentenced to five years' forced labour, but en route to the gulag, in a transit camp near Vladivostok, he died of a heart attack.

Soon there were 30,000 forced-labour prisoners in Kolyma, but, according to Savchenko, from 1938 onward their number rose by between 135,000 and 225,000 each year. Between 1937, the onset of the Great Terror, and 1945, a total of some two million prisoners were sent to Kolyma, spread among 160 camps, each with a maximum of 15,000 inmates. Tens of thousands were executed. According to official figures, approximately 130,000 prisoners died of hunger or disease.

Although the prisoners were well fed and warmly dressed, conditions were nevertheless harsh. Winters were long, and temperatures could drop to −60°C. Death, from one cause or another, was never far off. Sometimes an entire barracks, accused of being "enemies of the people" would be herded up and executed.

Kolyma became a symbol for the hardships of the gulag, in the same way that Auschwitz has become synonymous with the murder of the Jews by the Nazis. But, unlike Auschwitz, the Kolyma gulag also brought some civilization to the wilderness. The writer Yevgenia Ginsburg, who was imprisoned there from 1937 to 1949 and, after her release, had to remain in Magadan for another five years, wrote in her memoirs about forests being cleared and swamps dredged, and about the construction of roads, houses, cities, factories and railways.

As throughout the gulag, a cultural life emerged. Each camp had its own cultural brigade. Musicians, singers and actors were assembled into song-and-dance ensembles that performed for camp supervisors. They put on shows which included favourites like "The Ballad of Stalin" or "The Song of the NKVD". Commandants even vied for the best orchestra. The city theatre in Magadan had such fine acoustics that musicians were actually happy to perform there.

But the preferential treatment given to artist-prisoners was not enough to assuage their fears. Their fellow inmates included hardened criminals. For instance, the violinist Georgy Feldgun, who was accustomed to performing in the concert halls of Leningrad, once had to play Vivaldi for a group of fifty criminals in a transit camp. The socialist idea behind it was that music could help even the most die-hard criminal to mend his ways.

The camps in the far eastern gulag were run by one Ivan Fyodorovich Nikishov, the "tsar of Kolyma". He was a stereotypical merciless NKVD lieutenant. However, his mistress, the much younger Alexandra Gridasova, was more culturally inclined. The author Varlam Shalamov, one of Kozin's fellow inmates, would immortalize her as "Rydasova" in his story "Ivan Fyodorovich".

Gridasova, a member of the communist youth movement Komsomol, had come to Kolyma as a volunteer. She was tireless in promoting the cultural life of the camps, having musicians and other artists provide entertainment for the prisoners. It is thanks to her that the Gorky Theatre in Magadan became one of the finest in the USSR. Vadim Kozin was one of her pet artists.

From the outset, he enjoyed certain privileges. He had his own cabin on the MV *Soviet Latvia* and could bring all the luggage he wanted, as opposed to the rest of the prisoners who were stuffed into cramped, shared quarters and were only allowed a single duffel bag.

At Magadan, he was met on the quay by Gridasova herself, who drove him straight to the Gorky Theatre. She had organized a surprise welcome for him there. When he walked onto the stage, dressed as always in a trim black suit, patent-leather shoes and a starched white shirt and bow tie, the musicians were tuned and ready. He could finally sing for an audience again. And it was a rousing success.

The Gorky Theatre was a project of the NKVD's cultural club, which regularly put on plays. The group had no home base, so in 1938 they decided to build their own theatre and name it after the recently deceased writer Maxim Gorky. The theatre was officially opened on 5 October 1941. It had a proper stage and orchestra pit and could seat an audience of six hundred. There was also a restaurant. The building's façade sported carvings of soldiers, *kolkhoz* farmers, mine workers and labourers, all produced by the nation's finest sculptors—themselves prisoners.

Because the Gorky Theatre was not an in-camp theatre, audiences were made up of camp guards and members of the general public. They had no idea whether the entertainers—renowned musicians, actors, and directors—were prisoners, volunteers or paid artists. They just came for a play, a concert, an operetta, an opera or a ballet. And these were generally top-notch performances.

An evening at the Gorky Theatre followed a set programme: classical music (a piano concerto or arias from well-known operas) before the interval, followed by light music or a stand-up performer. A regular was trumpeter Eddie Rosner and his jazz orchestra. (Rosner landed in Magadan in 1952—as a prisoner, naturally.) Kozin would round off the concert's second half.

Once, the programming deviated from its usual format, with Kozin opening a concert for policemen. Commandant Nikishov was in attendance as well. When, after only a few numbers, the audience loudly cheered the singer, Nikishov leant out from his box seat and yelled into the auditorium, "Who are you shouting hurrah for? Bunch of faggots! You're only to shout hurrah for your leaders. Not for that idiot onstage." To Kozin he hollered, "And you—get the hell off the stage!"

At first, Kozin didn't understand and asked, "Who, me?" To which Nikishov replied, "Yes, you. Off the stage. And into the slammer with you!"

The director Leonid Varpakhovsky tried to smooth things over by having the orchestra strike up a jazz tune. But Kozin had got a fright all the same. He realized how fickle fate could be with a camp inmate. Gridasova rushed backstage. "Don't worry, Vadim Alexeyevich," she reassured him. "There's no way you'll be put in jail. I'll take care of everything."

And indeed, thanks to his patroness, Kozin kept out of jail. But Nikishov's outburst terrified him so much that he attempted suicide. In the second part of *The Gulag Archipelago*, Alexander Solzhenitsyn wrote that they undid Kozin from the noose in the nick of time. He spent the next month rehabilitating in a spa—hardly the place for a gulag inmate, but this was probably also thanks to Gridasova.

So, for all those years in prison, Kozin was more or less a free man. Not only could he wear his own clothes, but after a conflict with jealous colleagues led to fisticuffs he was given (again, thanks to Gridasova) his own studio with a piano, so that he could rehearse undisturbed. He performed, toured the region with musicians from the Magadan Theatre, visited with other artists and camp personnel. And, at the same time, he lived in fear, because Gridasova always made it clear that he could fall out of favour if he did not show enough gratitude.

Kozin rarely talked about his time in the camp or in detention in Moscow. But while preparing his biography, Savchenko received a letter from Kozin's fellow Lubyanka inmate Alexander Yukhin, who had been chief engineer at the Stalin automobile factory in Moscow. He wrote that he had been detained on the third floor of the secret police's headquarters, in a cell measuring just fifteen square metres, together with three other prisoners: a journalist from the army newspaper *Krasnaya zvezda* ("Red Star"), an engineer from the War Ministry, and Kozin. Even there, the singer was given preferential treatment. He received books and regular care packages from friends, and their cell was hardly ever searched.

Kozin had told Yukhin that he had been arrested because he had been asked by a Polish general in Khabarovsk, in the far east of the Soviet Union, to perform for his newly formed battalion. They were set to be evacuated, and Kozin was accused of planning to flee with them, which would amount to treason. After giving another concert in the same city, this time for local NKVD staff, he was arrested and sent to the Lubyanka.

The interesting part about Yukhin's letter, aside from that Kozin sang Sinti and Roma songs for him during their exercise period in the prison courtyard, was that Kozin basically admitted everything he was accused of during the endless nightly interrogations, to avoid being tortured. Kozin and Yukhin were separated in February 1945.

Musicologist Inna Klause concludes that Kozin's preferential treatment might have had nothing to do with his fame, but was rather the result of his ratting on his fellow prisoners—just as witnesses like Varlam Shalamov claim happened in Magadan.

The most famous victim of Kozin's betrayal in Kolyma was the stage director Leonid Varpakhovsky (1908–76). The NKVD arrested him in Moscow on 22 February 1936, likely because his superior, the renowned director Vsevolod Meyerhold, had reported negatively about his political leanings to the People's Commissariat for War. In early March he was brought before a special tribunal and sentenced to three years' exile in Kazakhstan for "supporting counter-revolutionary Trotskyism".

In Alma-Ata, then the capital of Soviet Kazakhstan, his theatre career took off. Varpakhovsky even received a commendation from the Kazakh government for his achievements, and his family was allowed to join him there.

His life progressed undisturbed for several months, until he was arrested again on 8 November 1937. This time the NKVD dug in deeper, and he was sentenced to ten years in a labour camp. It was the beginning of a nightmare that only worsened when his wife, the pianist Ada Milikovskaya (a pupil of Heinrich Neuhaus) was arrested too, on 9 May 1939. She was charged with spying for Japan and was sentenced to death—executed at the age of thirty. Their three-year-old son Fyodor was raised by Varpakhovsky's sister.

Varpakhovsky was sent to one of the camps along the Baikal–Amur railway and in September 1940 was transferred to Kolyma. There he caught the attention of a staff member from the cultural division, who took him off forced labour and assigned him to the camp's Culture Brigade. It would save his life.

From the summer of 1942, Varpakhovsky was not only the stage director, but also the respected artistic leader of the outfit, which consisted mostly of political prisoners. He staged dozens of productions in Magadan's Gorky Theatre.

During rehearsals he fell in love with another prisoner, the singer Ida Ziskina. She was serving an eight-year sentence as the wife of a "traitor of the people" who had been tried and executed in 1936. Her sentence ended six months after the play's run, but Varpakhovsky would not be freed until 1947. So, after her release, Ida remained in Magadan, where she gave birth to their daughter in 1949. Only after Stalin's death in 1953 could the family finally leave Kolyma.

In October 1947, five months after his release, Varpakhovsky was arrested again. It appeared he had been betrayed by Vadim Kozin. This is the plot of Shalamov's 1965 story "Ivan Fyodorovich", which takes place in a prison camp, where the titular older commandant has recently married the twenty-year-old Komsomol member Rydasova. He has appointed her head of one of the camp's larger divisions, which she rules with an iron fist.

In one scene, during a meeting of the camp directors, it is revealed that "a denunciation has been received from a singer, stating that director Varpakhovsky has cooked up a plan to enact the May Day parade as a procession, with church banners and icons. This naturally constitutes a covert counter-revolutionary activity."

"Madame" Rydasova at first finds nothing objectionable or suspicious about Varpakhovsky's plans. A theatre buff herself, she had taken him under her wing two years earlier by bringing him to Magadan and giving him free rein in staging plays for amateurs. No sooner does he fall in love with a Jewish singer than someone turns on him. Rydasova consults her husband, who takes the denunciation seriously and says, "It's not only about the church banners, but the fact that Varpakhovsky is living with a Jewish woman—one of the actresses—that he gives her roles—she is a singer. What kind of man is this Varpakhovsky?" To which she replies, "He is a fascist, he was sent here from a special camp. He's a director and has worked with Meyerhold; wait, I remember now, I've got it written here somewhere."

And as for the man who betrayed him, she says, "That singer is a reliable person. A homosexual, but not a fascist." As punishment, Ivan Fyodorovich sends Varpakhovsky with a touring company that performs for prisoners in the Kolyma mines. The severe weather conditions and the harsh landscape make the tours physically punishing. Dusya Ziskind, as Varpakhovsky's beloved is called in the story, must remain behind in the camp.

At the end of the story Varpakhovsky writes to Rydasova, begging her for mercy. But it is in vain: even before finishing the letter, she has devised new punishments. Varpakhovsky is forced to work in a mine, and his beloved is sent to a women's agricultural labour camp. Eventually, Ivan Fyodorovich also falls from grace and is kicked upstairs as a government minister.

✻

In reality, Varpakhovsky was not reconvicted of counter-revolutionary activities, but he did spend eight months in solitary confinement. A new court case ensued, in which he was accused of using music from Mozart's *Requiem* for a scene about the execution of a partisan. He successfully defended himself and was acquitted by a higher court.

Varpakhovsky was then moved to Ust-Omchug, a town some 3,000 kilometres from Magadan. As artistic leader of the Central House of Culture, he staged twelve plays and twenty concerts. He remained there until Stalin's death, when he and his family moved to Tbilisi so he could lead the Griboedov Theatre there. In 1957, fully rehabilitated, he could move back to Moscow.

The Moscow theatre world received Varpakhovsky like a long-lost son. He was immediately named chief director at the Yermolova Theatre. Five years later, he moved to the Maly Theatre, the drama equivalent of the Bolshoi, where he would evolve into one of the most innovative directors of the Russian stage. There were days when as many as five of his plays were performed in various theatres across the city.

Vadim Kozin was freed in September 1950. To prove this, he showed his biographer Savchenko a document stating that in 1945 he had been sentenced to eight years in prison but was released in 1950 due to "good work and exemplary behaviour". Kozin then pointed to a passage and said, "The part about 'reason for conviction' is empty, it's left blank! See? Nothing about sex." As always, he was hoping to erase every reference to his homosexuality.

The big question is why he stayed in Magadan after his release. He never once discussed it with anyone. Among the many theories is that he had too many rivals in Moscow, who, fearful of competition and protective of their own careers, are said to have used their political connections to intimidate Kozin into staying away.

Savchenko can imagine that it was easiest just to stay in Kolyma, where everyone knew and admired him. But for Ida Ziskina, Varpakhovsky's wife, the truth lay elsewhere. According to her, Kozin (as in Shalamov's story) did in fact have a hand in her husband's arrest. During an orchestra rehearsal, Varpakhovsky had held a brief memorial for their German concertmaster Sofia Gerbst, who in desperation had committed suicide after a rehearsal. Soon the rumour (attributed to Kozin, who apparently harboured a grudge against Varpakhovsky) spread that the memorial had been organized as a veiled protest against the Soviet prison camps.

Almost immediately after his release, Kozin was named artistic leader of the F. (for Felix) Dzerzhinsky Vocal and Dance Ensemble, which was made up primarily of policemen. Every one of their performances began with the song "The Sacred Lenin Banner". Kozin himself always sang at the end of the evening.

The new job effectively made him a member of the secret police, which in turn made his former fellow inmates suspicious of him. He would continue to lead the ensemble until 1953. A year later, he was given a post at the Gorky Theatre, first as librarian, but from 1955 to 1959 also as a singer in the "highest category", which translated into quite a decent salary. In return, he wrote a musical ode to the city called "Magadan Evenings".

In the two years after Stalin's sudden death on 5 March 1953, some two million prisoners returned to their families. From then on, people only went to Kolyma of their own accord—contract labourers, hunters and members of the Komsomol—all hoping to get rich quick. These new arrivals were often ardent fans of Kozin.

In 1955–6 Kozin undertook a concert tour in the far east and Siberia, organized by the Gorky Theatre, which had fallen on hard times since Stalin's successor Khrushchev dismantled the gulag system. The singer had not performed outside Kolyma for more than ten years and would now give 205 concerts in the space of ten months. After that, Kozin toured central Russia for the first time: 193 concerts in sixty-two cities in nine months, racking up rave reviews. News of his triumphs made its way back to Kolyma—"Local Man Makes Good"—but the tour would not take him any further westward than Voronezh, some 500 kilometres south of Moscow.

The journal he kept during his travels reveals that he would very much have liked to go to the European region of Russia—that is, to Moscow and Leningrad. There, after all, was his biggest audience. He wrote that he was not sure which authorities were preventing this—those in Moscow or in Magadan. It is entirely possible that his early release pertained only to the (fictitious) charges of anti-Soviet agitation, and that the sentence for homosexuality was still in effect. This might explain the roadblock to performing in the capital. Moscow and Leningrad would remain off-limits to him for the rest of his life.

That he was suddenly allowed to return to the stage felt like being rehabilitated for something he hadn't done in the first place. He also railed in his diary against having been silenced for so long, when he could appear in Khabarovsk, for instance, for the first time in fifteen years. Later, he sounds even more bitter and angry when he writes that he hates his work, loathes the concert stage and is anxiously awaiting the day when he can retire. Those responsible for his misfortunes he calls, without naming names, "scoundrels".

He was clearly sombre about the future; he mistrusted everyone and was lonely. He was exhausted from the twenty-five concerts he was required to give every month on tour. When the local Philharmonic in the city of Kuybyshev offered him a job, he turned it down to return to Magadan—in his words—to die.

Kozin was arrested again in October 1959. He was living a quiet life at the time, working as the archivist of a union cultural centre in Magadan. The following February he appeared before the local judge. From that day on, his songs vanished from the airwaves and the printed media. The judge sentenced him to three years in prison for homosexual actions and for corrupting a minor. To this day it is not clear whether these charges were invented or if he indeed had sought contact with underage youths.

Savchenko's preface includes a quote from Kozin's official statement during his second detention, in which he talks openly about his sexual development and preference. He traces his sexuality back to his school days, when he was supposedly abused by a female teacher and was forced into a relationship with her. But here, too, one has to take Kozin's words with a grain of salt: he was under severe pressure and feared for his life.

Life did not change much for him in Magadan after his conviction. It's not known whether he was able to keep his job as an archivist, but he was still able to perform, sometimes as a soloist with Eddie Rosner's jazz orchestra. Only in Magadan, of course, for his concerts were no longer broadcast on the radio.

After being released for good in 1963, Kozin got a job as librarian at the Pushkin Library in Magadan. There would be no comeback at the Gorky Theatre, except for the occasional one-off concert. He did, however, sing for anyone who offered him a lift—this is how he kept his repertoire and reputation alive among the few people in Magadan who still knew him. The authorities had destroyed all his recordings, and there was a ban on so much as mentioning his name in the media. He had been reduced from national hero to a common busker.

But, contrary to what he himself believed, he was not forgotten in the Soviet Union. He even received visits in the sixties and seventies from prominent Soviet figures like the poet Yevgeny Yevtushenko, who had been invited for a reading in Magadan; he requested a meeting with Kozin, which was granted without hesitation. Everyone in Magadan knew they could drop in on Kozin and his cats in his cramped bedsit stuffed with books, newspapers, LPs and a piano. They usually found him tinkering with cassette recorders and the hundreds of cassette tapes of his songs. Anyone who wanted to hear him sing was more than welcome.

His occasional public appearances in Magadan sometimes included new numbers. For instance, he sang at tributes in 1965 for the poet Sergei Yesenin (who had committed suicide in 1925) and the writer Konstantin Simonov, setting their texts to music.

In 1968, his sixty-fifth birthday and fortieth anniversary as a performing artist were celebrated with a concert. Kozin sang both before and after the interval, accompanying himself at the piano. There were ten new numbers, half of them written by himself. These included the cycle *I Love This Country*, dedicated to the city of Magadan and exploding with patriotism. And what would the concert have been without the Roma and Sinti songs?

Unsurprisingly, it was an emotional evening. You could hear a pin drop in the auditorium, and Kozin's passionate performance repeatedly reduced the audience to tears.

Another such concert, equally emotional, was held in 1970. Three years later he would perform in Magadan for the last time.

In 1972 the Russian cellist Dmitri Ferschtman was on tour with an orchestra, and they performed in Magadan. Five decades later he tells me about being introduced to Kozin. "Our impresario at the time was gay. He knew Kozin and introduced us. He fell for me at once. At that meeting were two other men, former prisoners and also gay, a good twenty years younger than he. They acted like his servants. He would often go out, eating and drinking with them."

Ferschtman, now seventy-five, had never heard of Kozin before that meeting in Magadan. "What do you expect? His recordings weren't sold anywhere. He had been erased. It happened to so many homosexual musicians."

But while most prisoners made a beeline for Moscow after serving their time, Kozin stayed put. "He wasn't a fighter," Ferschtman says. "He wasn't the kind of person to make the effort to fit in. He was tainted."

Kozin didn't reappear in the national press until the early 1980s. Outside Magadan no one even realized the singer was still alive. In 1985, after a fierce battle with the authorities, the Melodiya label was given permission to reissue Kozin's LPs, and across the country even teenagers were demanding his records. Kozin was alive and well and revered like a pop star.

In that same year, he sat for an interview with Edvin Polyanovsky, a correspondent from the government newspaper *Izvestia*. The journalist, too, assumed Kozin was no longer alive until a new record of his appeared. He went to visit him at his house at the end of the world—and was shocked by the poverty he encountered.

At first the newspaper refused to publish Polyanovsky's article "due to [the singer's] history". The interview appeared only in 1990 in the minor newspaper *Nedelya* ("This Week") and went more or less unnoticed.

Two years after Polyanovsky's visit, Anna Zelenskaya made a documentary about Kozin entitled *Two Portraits and a Soundtrack*. Now the entire country knew that the entertainment idol was still alive. But the real turnaround in Kozin's fortunes came after the dismantling of the Soviet Union in late 1991. In April 1993, the Russian Ministry of Culture announced that the aged singer would be named People's Artist of the Russian Federation, and Kozin was given a star on Moscow's Star Square (equivalent to Hollywood's Walk of Fame). Both *Izvestia* and *Vechernyaya Moskva* ("Evening Moscow") published gushing articles about him.

But even now, things did not go as Kozin had expected. He never officially became a People's Artist (rescinded, according to the commission, because of his 1960 conviction for soliciting minors), nor an honorary citizen of Magadan. A half-hearted consolation concert was organized in Magadan in 1993 to celebrate his ninetieth birthday. The tribute lasted six full hours, with appearances by countless Russian artists, while Kozin himself sat on a throne onstage. He was given a cash bonus and the flat next to his was refitted (with the financial support of a fishing business) as a music salon, complete with red carpets and a grand piano.

Kozin died a year and a half later. His obituary in the newspaper *Kultura* ("Culture") on 24 December 1994 praised him as a great singer, an artist of the people who had been hard-handedly torn from his audience and thrown into a labour camp. And this was the truth.

✻

Later in the 1990s, Kozin was memorialized in both Magadan and St Petersburg. There were plans to erect a museum to him in his hometown, but nothing came of it. In 1999, however, the music salon in his former residence in Magadan was made into a small museum, although there has never been a real exhibition and no one has bothered to catalogue his massive archive of countless unissued recordings.

Never mind that his name is immortalized on Star Square; Russians still have an ambiguous relationship with Kozin because of his homosexuality. Everyone in Magadan knows about his legal troubles and conviction for pederasty back in 1960, but in 2003 a staff member at the Kozin museum gave only "anti-Soviet agitation" as the reason for his imprisonment. Not a word about his homosexuality.

Kozin's biographer Savchenko does mention it but tries to smooth it over by claiming that the underage boy whom Kozin supposedly had sex with was actually a KGB agent. There is no proof of this. Myths and legend follow Kozin even beyond the grave. But true or not, the fact is that under Stalin he was repeatedly imprisoned, he failed to be rehabilitated under Khrushchev, and under Yeltsin he was, in the end, forgotten entirely.

7

A Nun at the Keyboard

It is March 1953. An attractive, dark-haired woman in a blue taffeta dress is performing Mozart's Piano Concerto No. 23 in a Moscow concert hall. The audience listens in rapt admiration. The music is a welcome distraction from the terror that has engulfed the country. Throughout the Russian capital, people are being arrested, tortured and executed at will. No one knows what the next moment will bring. Not even in the concert hall, where an NKVD agent is stationed in every corner. Hands behind their back, they glower menacingly at the orchestra and the soloist, as if they might be planning a surprise escape.

The concert is broadcast live by Radio Moscow. In the control room, the telephone rings. It's Stalin's secretary. The producer is to call back in exactly seventeen minutes. It's an order. The producer's face tightens in fear; he's so jittery that he can barely write down the number correctly.

Seventeen minutes later, the concert concludes and he dials Stalin's number. "I want a recording of tonight's performance," the dictator says. "I'll send someone to pick it up." In a trembling voice, the producer accedes. But as it happens, the concert was not recorded; it was a live broadcast. Panic all around. The producer charges into the auditorium and tries to keep the audience from leaving, reassuring them that "nobody's going to get killed, I promise you". Some, however, have already left. So the NKVD agents go outside to round up random passers-by: farmers and labourers, none of whom have any idea who Mozart is.

Then the pianist speaks up. She refuses to repeat the performance. Back in the control room, the producer asks, "Do you want to get killed, Maria Veniaminovna?" "Like my father and brother? Like that?" she answers coolly.

The producer turns to the conductor and asks if another pianist is available. Impossible, he says, everyone will hear the difference, even Stalin. "I hope this office isn't bugged," the pianist remarks. The conductor, trembling now too, realizes his comment could cost him his head.

The producer tries again with the pianist, offering her 10,000 roubles. Twenty thousand, she replies. The conductor cannot take the pressure and drops dead of a heart attack. Immediately, a man from Radio Moscow goes to fetch a new conductor, one living in the same block of flats where the NKVD is busy arresting the residents. He is driven, still in his pyjamas and dressing gown, to the concert hall. He is the only conductor left in Moscow who hasn't been arrested or killed.

When the recording is completed and the producer hands a freshly pressed record to the impatient NKVD agent, the pianist slips a note into the record sleeve, claiming, "I wish to convey a special message from my heart."

The record is delivered to Stalin's dacha. He is furious that it has taken so long. He places it on the turntable in his study, where he sometimes shuts himself up for days listening to music and pinning newspaper clippings to the wall. He is momentarily irritated by a recording glitch (the first few beats have been recorded twice).

Then he sees the note the pianist had slipped into the sleeve. It reads: "Joseph Vissarionovich Stalin. You have betrayed our nation and destroyed its people. I pray for your end and ask the Lord to forgive you. Tyrant." The dictator bursts into laughter at such tough language. But then he stiffens, has a stroke and keels over. Not long thereafter he breathes his last breath.

It is a key scene from the 2017 black comedy *The Death of Stalin*, directed by Armando Iannucci. The absurdity of the Kremlin is brilliantly portrayed by a cast of American and British comedians. Steve Buscemi plays the joke-telling Khrushchev and Russell Beale is Lavrenty Beria, the head of Stalin's secret police and Khrushchev's main rival for Stalin's favours. Beria's grotesque puffiness typifies the paranoid, bloodthirsty cruelty that surrounded Stalin's final years. They were all terrified of their boss, who would invite them round for drink-drenched dinners and private screenings of cowboy films, and, as the only sober one present, he would wait to see who would make a slip of the tongue and thus earn himself a place on the execution list.

In *The Death of Stalin*, only Maria Veniaminovna Yudina fears no one. You hear it in her Mozart piano concerto. Fear stands no chance against her majestically erect posture; her taffeta dress is like a suit of armour. Yudina is played in the film by the Ukrainian actress Olga Kurylenko, seen earlier as a Bond girl in *Quantum of Solace*, one of the most violent James Bond films ever made. That might explain the icy cheek in the way her Yudina stands up to Stalin.

But aside from Yudina's intrepidness, not much about the story is true. The pianist Yudina who actually played that Mozart concerto looked nothing like the glamorous young Kurylenko, but was rather a heavy-set woman of forty-eight with unruly dark hair and a grim expression. Instead of a silk dress she wore the floor-length habit of a Russian Orthodox nun and worn-out basketball shoes. Her name was indeed Maria Veniaminovna Yudina, and she is said to have recorded Mozart's Piano Concerto No. 23 on Stalin's orders. And the year of that incident? According to Shostakovich it was 1944; according to my own research, 1948.

Whether Stalin played that record the day he died, as the film suggests, is impossible to verify. That he had a stroke after reading a heretical note from Yudina is, in any case, pure fiction.

More than perhaps with any other Soviet musician, Maria Yudina's life lends itself to mythologizing, like in *The Death of Stalin*. This is primarily thanks to her own self-image as a woman with a moral, religious mission who used music not only to counter evil but also to heal the human soul. She put such effort into her playing that it looked as though she was kneading dough or even laundering clothes. And it sounded that way, too: harsh and loud. As her pupil and friend Maria Drozdova once said, "she was never purely interested in technique or hours of practice, like other pianists. Yudina played at another level of consciousness."

Admirers heard something metaphysical in her playing, an entirely unique vision. Her distinctive, often contradictory interpretations only added to her celebrity, while some of her colleagues (and, more importantly, the authorities) had issues with her musical approach and wrote her off as "abnormal" and "deranged". Read the religious and philosophical comments in the margins of her scores and one might tend to agree. Dmitri Shostakovich claims she regarded Bach's *Goldberg Variations* as a series of illustrations to the Holy Bible.

She wrote in her diary in 1916: "Everything divine or spiritual has revealed itself to me through art, via the branch called music.

This is my calling. I believe in it, and my strength is in it. This is how my life here has meaning. I am a link of the chain of Art."

Shostakovich, a classmate of Yudina's at the Petrograd Conservatory and himself not one to gush, was deeply impressed by her robust playing style. Having heard her play his preludes and fugues, he wrote to her: "This is not at all what I wrote, but please play it like this! Please, play it only like this!"

At the same time, Shostakovich had little patience with the religious aura she created. In his posthumous *Testimony*, he writes (with a rather sexist slant): "Some people claim that Yudina had a unique, profoundly philosophical approach to the works she played. I don't know; I never noticed it myself. On the contrary, I always thought that much of it depended on her mood. As with every woman." And: "Everything Yudina played, she played 'differently than anyone else'. It made her fans go wild. Personally, there were many things in her interpretations I didn't understand. But when I asked her why she did something in a certain manner, the reply was usually something like, 'I feel it that way.' What's philosophical about that?"

"Everything," Yudina would have answered. She spread her religious zeal not only in the concert hall but among her friends, more through her playing than anything else. "She always played as though she were giving a sermon," Shostakovich once remarked, and the poet Joseph Brodsky would later call her a "biblical pianist".

When I ask Vitali, a Moscow acquaintance of mine and himself a concert pianist, about Yudina and her playing, he brings it more down to earth: "When she played Mozart or Beethoven, you would gnash your teeth for the first five minutes. But [then] you would forget her *forte* or *mezzo-forte* and focus on the melody, which was always very special."

"Don't forget, she was typical of the Russian intelligentsia," Vitali continues. Aside from music, religion and philosophy, she was interested in literature, theatre and history. She became enamoured with classical antiquity, and, after finishing conservatory, she studied historical philology at the University of Petrograd and tutored ancient Greek. You see these interests in her essays and memoirs, as well as in her many letters to a variety of intellectual figures like the composers Shostakovich and Stockhausen, the philosophers Theodor Adorno, Mikhail Bakhtin and Pavel Florensky, and the writers Boris Pasternak and Nadezhda Mandelstam. Her literary taste leant towards banned books, writers and poets.

I wonder whether there is any connection between that literary bent and her advocacy of contemporary music forbidden by the Soviet authorities. For if anyone was the symbol of nonconformism in Soviet music, it was Yudina. Her concerts later in life, some say, could be compared to the protests of dissidents, some of whom were her close friends.

But most of all she lived as a nun. She helped others obsessively, doling out her earnings from concerts and teaching to less fortunate artists. And then, short of cash herself, she borrowed money from everyone she knew. Her sister Vera said, "It was always the same—no money, no money, no money. When she died, she was 14,000 roubles in debt. But no one wanted to be repaid; they were happy to do something for a genius like her."

Her chronic shortage of money also played out in the literary soirées she gave at her home. Yudina couldn't afford snacks or drinks to offer her guests, so she went to the Moscow Conservatory distribution office for ration coupons to buy boots, which she then resold to purchase vodka and herring.

During the Stalin terror she sent care packages to prisoners in the gulag. And yet even though the secret police kept a close eye on her, she was never arrested. The authorities could not get a grip on her; her eccentricity seemed to intimidate them. It was as though she was surrounded by a protective aura.

Maria Veniaminovna Yudina was born on 9 September 1899 in Nevel, Belarus. She was the fourth child of Veniamin Gavrilovich Yudin, an assimilated Jew who had worked himself up from poverty in the shtetl to become a well-respected country doctor in the Vitebsk Governorate. The town's makeup was mainly Jewish (three-quarters of its residents), but also Belarusian, Polish and Lithuanian. It enjoyed an exceptional cultural life.

Yudina's first piano instructor was Frieda Levinson, a pupil of the famous Anton Rubinstein. When, around the age of thirteen, Maria's talent became evident, her father sent her to study in St Petersburg, where she enrolled in the class of the renowned piano pedagogue Leonid Nikolaev.

A few years later she met Yevgenia Otten, a well-known religious writer, who introduced Yudina to the religious-philosophical group Resurrection. This was a group of leftist intellectuals who discussed literary, religious and political issues as they pertained to the aesthetics of communism. The philosopher and literary critic Mikhail Bakhtin was also a member. Yudina became so enthralled by the Russian Orthodox rites that she converted in 1919. From then on, faith was her priority; music was solely a means to approach God.

She had already become acquainted with Bakhtin in Nevel, where he had given a lecture on Kant and the neo-Kantian philosophers and had visited her parents' home. They soon hit it off, discussing theological and religious subjects. They even appeared together at Nevel's community centre: Bakhtin with a lecture, Yudina with a concert. This was when she began wearing the long black robes that would become her trademark; the trainers and a house full of cats came later.

Her classmate Shostakovich thought her general behaviour disturbing and her attire bizarre.

> As a musician she was excellent. But we never became very good friends; this was not possible. Yudina was a decent person, a good person. But her goodness was so overblown. She suffered from religious hysteria. It's awkward to talk about it, but it was so. At the drop of a hat, Yudina would fall to her knees or kiss your hands. It could get embarrassing. We both studied with Nikolaev; he would make some remark to her and there she was, back on her knees. Also, I didn't much care for her clothes, all those monk's robes, the habits. She was a pianist, not a nun. So why did she walk around in a habit? Hardly a show of modesty.

Her eccentric behaviour in no way hindered her development as a pianist. When she graduated in 1921, the conservatory director wrote on her diploma, "A great and virtuosic talent. *Forte* at times exaggerated." The evaluation: "Very good."

Sviatoslav Richter later regarded her expressive *forte* as a show of rebellion. He recalled his own teacher, Heinrich Neuhaus, having asked Yudina after one of her concerts during World War II why she emphasized her *fortes* so much. Her answer, delivered just as *forte*, was, "We are at war."

✻

After conservatory Yudina studied philosophy, focusing on Augustine and the Orthodox theological treatises of Vladimir Solovyov, Alexei Losev, Lev Karsavin and Pavel Florensky. She became good friends with the latter three; the intellectual and spiritual legacy of the all-round man of letters Florensky, who would be executed in 1937 during Stalin's Great Terror, became a tenet of her artistic and personal life.

Yudina's spiritual pursuits did not get in the way of her piano career. In the year she graduated, she made her first solo appearances with Beethoven's Piano Concertos Nos. 4 and 5, a concerto by Nikolai Medtner, and works by Ernst Krenek and Paul Hindemith. Two years later, she was appointed to the faculty of the Petrograd Conservatory.

She was already a headstrong woman who spoke her mind freely. In June 1922, she wrote to the authorities, demanding the release of Patriarch Tikhon of Moscow, who was under house arrest in the Donskoy Monastery for refusing to relinquish church relics to the cash-strapped Bolsheviks. The letter was signed "your faithful and devoted madwoman".

Two months later, Patriarch Veniamin of Petrograd and several loyal church brothers were executed, likewise for refusing to turn over religious treasures. She might have eased off, realizing the danger of her outspokenness, yet she stuck to her principles. When, in 1925, she was officially asked to join and support the Russian Communist Party, she replied that although she agreed with many aspects of the Party, her ideological and religious beliefs prevented her from doing so.

Anyone else would have faced severe repercussions, but not Yudina. One explanation for this could be that in those days Stalin, focused on consolidating his power, directed his wrath primarily at his political foes rather than eccentric artists.

This was not the case five years later, when on 9 March 1930 Yudina gave a historic recital at the Leningrad Philharmonic. The programme was Beethoven's *Moonlight Sonata*, the Intermezzi by Brahms, Chopin's Sonata in B minor, Prokofiev's Piano Sonata No. 4, and Mussorgsky's *Pictures at an Exhibition*. The crowd queued up all the way from Nevsky Prospect to the doors of the concert hall in the hope of getting a ticket. After the concert, the euphoric audience showered Yudina not just with flowers but also icons. Those icons would be her undoing.

Two days later she was summoned by the director of the Philharmonic, the young Pavel Serebryakov, known to be an agent of the secret police. He had been deluged with letters denouncing Yudina. (Eager to demonstrate his zeal, he apparently wrote some of them himself.) He knew full well what a gifted pianist she was, but orders were orders.

During their meeting, he asked Yudina if she believed in God. She said yes, which was dangerous because the Bolsheviks had forbidden religion. He then asked if she was spreading religious propaganda among her pupils. She replied that the constitution did not forbid this. These two answers sealed her fate.

An account of that meeting, by an anonymous writer, appeared a few days later in the newspaper *Krasnaya gazeta* ("The Red Gazette"); the headline read: A Nun's Habit at the Conservatory. The article was accompanied by a caricature depicting Yudina as a nun, surrounded by kneeling students. The caption read: "Preachers have come to the conservatory."

Yudina was fired on 6 May. The official reason given was that she was "an exponent of mysticism".

Now she was fair game. Aware of the danger she faced, friends arranged a professorship for her at the conservatory in Tbilisi, the capital of Georgia, safely removed from the centre of power. She would remain there from 1932 to 1934, when she moved back to Moscow and carried on with her career, despite her damaged reputation. For the next two and a half decades she taught piano alongside Heinrich Neuhaus at the Moscow Conservatory and gave lessons in chamber music and art song at the Gnessin Institute.

In 1935 she performed Prokofiev's Piano Concerto No. 2 on tour. The composer was so pleased with her interpretation that he wrote the composition *Things in Themselves*, Op. 45, for her. She reprised the piano concerto in Moscow in 1935 and 1938. The latter concert, conducted by Prokofiev himself, was a triumph for the composer and soloist alike.

Stalin's purges were then reaching their apex. Writers, actors and artists were being arrested left and right, accused of anti-Soviet agitation and either sent to the gulag or executed outright. Yudina ignored it all and forged ahead, performing works by contemporary composers like Prokofiev, Shostakovich, Alban Berg and Stravinsky.

She did suffer one trauma as a result of the Great Terror—a personal rather than professional one. She had fallen in love with a talented student, the engineer Kirill Saltykov, fifteen years her junior. According to friends, they were to be married. But in July 1939, Saltykov, an avid mountain climber, was killed in a hiking accident in the Caucasus. The words of her spiritual mentor Pavel Florensky—that the more one loves another, the more one must suffer—seemed truer than ever. After Saltykov's death, she turned even more zealously to religion as a source of comfort.

Like many of her fellow musicians, Yudina gave countless wartime concerts in factories and on the front. But mostly she was active on the radio. Soldiers worshipped her—from their fan mail one feels their gratitude for her presence via the airwaves.

Among the ensembles she performed with was the Beethoven Quartet, one of Russia's premier chamber ensembles. They were exempted from the evening curfew, so they could perform live (their programmes typically offered music by Shostakovich, Schubert and Tchaikovsky) for the radio's world service: a late-night concert for the Soviet listeners, which was then repeated at one o'clock in the morning in a special broadcast for France, and yet another airing an hour later for England. She would walk to and from the station, even in the winter, in her old gym shoes.

During the war Yudina had become such an avowed Soviet loyalist that, according to her sister Vera, she considered joining the Communist Party if it would help bring her country closer to victory. "She also took a nursing course and wanted to go to the front. But she spent the entire war on the radio. She was a patriot in the truest sense of the word."

In her memoirs, Yudina wrote that all she could have done in the hospitals was to wash the wounded with her tears, and she therefore sought another way to aid the war effort. Her friend Alexandra de Lazari recalls in the documentary *Maria Yudina: Portrait of a Legendary Pianist* (2000, dir. Jakov Nazarov) that in January 1942 Yudina performed in the Moscow Conservatory's recital hall in the freezing cold. The audience was bundled up in fur coats and felt boots. Yudina's bare arms were blue from the cold; occasionally she stopped playing to warm her hands over a small wood-burning stove.

In 1943 she was even flown by military aeroplane into the besieged city of Leningrad to perform for the starving inhabitants. She saw her patriotic duty as part of her sacrifice to God.

After the war, a new wave of terror gripped the nation, with the regime's paranoia now aimed at "foreign" influences. This is where Yudina's famous radio broadcast of Mozart's Piano Concerto No. 23 comes in. To get an idea of what really happened, it is perhaps best to turn to Shostakovich's *Testimony*. For, although much of the book's material is disputed, it is certainly more reliable than the farce depicted in *The Death of Stalin*. Stalin telephoned the producers of the national broadcasting authority in 1944 (says Shostakovich) or 1948 (according to my own research) to enquire whether there was a recording of the piano concerto that Maria Yudina had played on the radio the previous day. Shostakovich writes: "They told Stalin that of course there was a recording. There was not: the concert had been broadcast live from the studio. But they were too scared to say 'no' to Stalin. You never knew what the consequences could be. A human life meant nothing to him. The only option was to be obedient and subservient. Say yes. One must always say 'yes' to a maniac."

Stalin wanted the record to be delivered to his dacha. In a panic, the radio producers summoned Yudina and mustered an orchestra. They recorded the concerto that very night. The orchestra musicians were scared to death, but Yudina remained calm. If the dictator wanted a recording so very badly, then have it he would.

Later, Yudina told Shostakovich that the conductor's nerves got the better of him and she had to send him home. "A second conductor was brought in. But this one, too, was so nervous that he only confused the orchestra even more. The third conductor managed to finish the recording."

By dawn, the recording was completed. One single copy was pressed and delivered to Stalin, who listened to it at his leisure and was entirely satisfied with it. Shortly thereafter Yudina was given an envelope, compliments of the dictator, containing the enormous sum of 20,000 roubles. She then wrote Stalin a thank-you note that is said to have read, "I thank you, Joseph Vissarionovich, for your support. I will pray for you night and day and ask the Lord to forgive your great sins before the people and the country. The Lord is merciful, and he'll forgive you. I shall give the money to my church for renovation work."

From anyone else, such a letter would have meant a one-way ticket to the gulag. But not Yudina. Was Stalin cowed by her reprimand? According to Shostakovich, the dictator was superstitious. Or is the whole story a myth? For no one has ever seen that letter or, for that matter, the record itself.

The late Russian conductor Lev Markiz, with whom I spoke in The Hague in May 2021, thought neither ever existed. "It's a myth," he said, "like so much about Yudina."

Markiz had studied chamber music with Yudina and the two became friends. "She never made any concessions and had no patience with other people's machinations. She was very much herself, and generous, too. Nearly all her earnings went to feed her cats Nelly and Kisan, the two most important creatures in her life. She often sent me out to buy food for them."

He remembers her asking him to go to the manager of a concert hall to cancel her performance that evening. "She didn't have a telephone and was convinced she was having a heart attack," he said.

While Markiz made no bones about Yudina's eccentricities, he did so with love and respect, as when he talked about her teaching methods. "It was very strange. She would sit in a chair and listen to us play, without saying a word. Nor did she look at the clock, which meant we would sometimes go until deep into the night and have to take a taxi home because the metro had stopped running by then." As he told this his dark eyes glistened and laughed.

I'm fairly sure that Markiz was right about that letter to Stalin. How else could you explain that in 1950 Yudina was suddenly allowed to fulfil her wish to travel abroad? Until then, she had been forbidden to leave the country. But when East Germany commemorated the bicentenary of the death of Johann Sebastian Bach, she was allowed to attend the memorial concerts in Leipzig. As soon as she arrived on this sacred soil, she went barefoot to the composer's grave to offer a personal tribute.

A second trip abroad followed in 1954, when Yudina went to Poland for the celebration of Soviet–Polish friendship. In Warsaw, she played works by Lutosławski, Shostakovich and others. These performances were filmed but were never shown in the USSR. Even today, bureaucratic secrecy reigns, and these recordings remain under lock and key.

That would be Yudina's last trip abroad. Every new request to leave the country was met with silence.

Yudina's advocacy of contemporary composers would continue to get her into trouble. In 1960, she was fired from the Gnessin Institute "due to religiousness incompatible with communist morals and due to openly propagating anti-Soviet art, such as works by Stravinsky". To her friends, she said coolly, "This autumn I will be professor emerita. They kicked me out of the Gnessin Institute because of my superiority—forgive me if I put it that way—but also because of my Europeanism, because of the excellent exam results in my class, because of my students' affection for me, because of my open belief in God."

Yudina nevertheless persevered with what she saw as a sacred mission. Alongside traditional concerts with nearly all the top conductors of the day—Gennady Rozhdestvensky, Dimitri Mitropoulos, Kurt Sanderling, Otto Klemperer—she fearlessly promoted contemporary music. During concerts she also read aloud from religious and philosophical treatises and recited poems by two banned poets: the late Nikolai Zabolotsky (once persecuted by Stalin) and Boris Pasternak.

Pasternak was one of her best friends. She would organize literary evenings in her flat on Begovaya Street, where in 1947 he gave a reading of several chapters from his novel *Doctor Zhivago*, nine years before its completion. He also read his poem "A Star of Nativity", which very much impressed Yudina. She wrote to him: "If you had written nothing else but 'A Star of Nativity', it would still be enough to ensure your immortality on earth and in heaven. I beg you to give me a copy of it."

Yudina had met Pasternak in December 1928, when she asked him to translate poems by Rainer Maria Rilke for her—verses the German composer Paul Hindemith had used for his song cycle *Das Marienleben*. It was the beginning of a long and mutually influential friendship. Yudina could (and did) recite Pasternak's poetry from memory, declaiming it onstage as a prelude or encore to a concert.

A letter from 8 December 1953 displays the extent of her fondness for him: "Dear Boris Leonidovich, I miss you terribly, yourself, your poetry, your voice, everything about you."

She was a regular visitor to Pasternak's dacha in Peredelkino, the writers' village near Moscow. There, in 1960, she played at his funeral and read out passages from the Bible. Like Yudina, Pasternak was a believer. As his son Yevgeny put it, "Yudina was a close friend of my father because she was an artist. She possessed an incredibly rare and precious inspiration. Her entire demeanour, her attitude towards the outside world and to art were rooted in her devotion to the Word. And to serve the Word is exactly what Pasternak devoted his life to."

No one could have predicted that the vice of power would be tightened even further. But the next year, in November 1961, Yudina would again experience the cruel caprices of the regime. She was to perform in the recital hall of the Leningrad Philharmonic. The programme, in addition to music by Beethoven, Stravinsky, Krenek and Webern, included a piece composed specially for her, the *Musica Stricta* by Andrei Volkonsky. (She had performed *Musica Stricta* earlier that year, in February, at the Moscow Conservatory. Permission for this concert and even for a recording had been granted reluctantly, but at the last minute the recording was scrapped. Yudina was furious. "Truly scandalous," she fumed. "Shakespeare was right." And at that she recited, by heart, Sonnet 66 in Pasternak's translation, the relevant line being "And art made tongue-tied by authority".)

The audience demanded encores of both the Volkonsky and Webern. Yudina stood in front of the piano and showed the hall her fingers, covered with bandages. "I cut my fingers opening tins of fish for my cats," she explained, revealing the deep wounds on her hands. "So I am finished. My spirit is willing, but my flesh refuses. I cannot play any more." Then she recited poems by Zabolotsky and Pasternak.

Furious at her reciting Pasternak, the Philharmonic's management, under instructions from the KGB, wasted no time in banning Yudina from appearing there for five years. She would never again see the inside of the concert hall, with its stately white columns and excellent acoustics.

Even these harsh measures did not force Yudina to comply with the authorities, nor did she break with contemporary music. She continued to correspond at length with masters like Theodor Adorno, Karlheinz Stockhausen, Pierre Boulez and Igor Stravinsky. In doing so, she became a key player in the group of Soviet musicians who were in close contact with composers from the West. Musicians like Yudina and her colleagues Gennady Rozhdestvensky, Andrei Volkonsky and Alexei Lubimov were the first to perform music by forbidden or unknown Western and Soviet composers including Stockhausen, Boulez, Stravinsky, Olivier Messiaen, Alfred Schnittke, Arvo Pärt, Alexander Lokshin, Alban Berg, Arnold Schoenberg, Anton Webern, and many others. She was the ultimate ambassador for atonality.

She also continued to give money to anyone who needed it more than she did. When she could no longer afford her flat in Moscow, one of her fellow religious zealots invited her to join his commune in the woods on the outskirts of Moscow. Gleb Udintsev, the son of one of the residents, recalls that "it was a meeting place for all kinds of famous intellectuals, musicians and painters. The atmosphere in the community suited Maria Veniaminovna to a T. She was delighted with the invitation and moved to the space above Professor Artemyev. I remember it being quite a job to get her grand piano upstairs, where she rehearsed. Often, especially in the summer, we could hear the thundering of her chords."

Yudina made herself known again in 1965, when the dissident writer Andrei Sinyavsky was arrested. He had been publishing his works in the West since 1959 under the pseudonym Abram Terts. She thought this unacceptable, arguing that he had given in to the Soviet authorities' ban on his work and that his only goal in publishing his books abroad was to satisfy his readers. She felt that one had to do everything openly, regardless of the situation. Sinyavsky's actions brought tears to her eyes. Her friend, the art critic Anatoly Kuznetsov, said: "These were the tears of a martyr who grieved for the suffering of the world, of humanity, and of every individual; one who grieved for the suffering of Russia."

Yudina gave her last solo concert on 12 March 1968 in Moscow's Tchaikovsky Hall. The setting—a bonbon of an auditorium, with white seats and wainscotting—was just the place to bring together her love for classical antiquity and the music of Stravinsky. She played the piano version of his ballet *Orpheus*: one could not imagine a more fitting farewell.

Leonid Rusanovsky and I watch videos of her. He recalls seeing Yudina perform in Leningrad shortly before her farewell concert. "She played Bach. And it was phenomenal. Her rhythm wasn't accurate, but, like Klavdiya Shulzhenko, she had a feel for timing. I remember how much I enjoyed the purity of her playing."

Needing to support herself somehow, at the end of the 1960s Yudina applied to libraries, cemeteries, and post and telegram offices for work. Referring to her application to the Moscow telegraph office, she said, "They all want me here, but me being a retired woman, the personnel department cannot hire me. I shall write to the minister."

She did not get the job. Whether she wrote to the minister is uncertain. If she did, she probably never received a reply—the authorities, after all, had been ignoring her for years.

Yudina died on 19 November 1970 in Moscow. A handwritten notice of her death, with the date and place of the funeral, was tacked to the door of the chamber-music hall at the Moscow Conservatory next to a poster advertising a Beethoven programme featuring the pianist Emil Gilels. A sad sight, but she herself would not have been much bothered by it.

On the eve of the funeral, her friends organized a memorial service in the foyer of the main hall of the Moscow Conservatory (from which she had been fired all those years ago). Mourners had to ask Shostakovich's permission to attend. The pianists Sviatoslav Richter, Maria Grinberg and Vera Gornostaeva played next to the coffin.

A few days after the burial at the Vvedenskoe Cemetery, Yudina's old, out-of-tune Bechstein grand was hoisted out the window of her flat. Years earlier she had sold the instrument to raise money for friends in need, and since then she had rented it from its new owner. The instrument dangling mid-air seemed to echo her motto: "The only path to God is through Art."

No one knows what happened to her cats.

8

The Lost Legacy

Takke-takke-takke-tak. The thick block of lead, sixty centimetres by sixty centimetres, glides over the small metal wheels of the electrically operated bridge to the press. At the other end, it will emerge as a metres-long sheet. A factory worker uses giant pliers to push it back through the press, which rolls the sheet even longer and thinner. *Sssss-boom! Takke-takke-takke-tak*.

"We repeat the process until we achieve the desired thickness," says Alexander Tugarev, director of the Moscow metal factory MZOTsM (Moscow Factory for the Production of Non-Ferrous Metals).

At the end of the production line, two burly labourers slice the sheet, now six metres long, into ten pieces and lay them in a bin. Then a bell rings and a crane hoists the bin onto a cart. *Zoof-boom-takke-takke-tak-boom!* I'm fascinated by the sight of sputtering, super-heated ore being transformed into thick bars, and the associated ear-splitting roar.

"We manufacture about one hundred tons of metals per month," says Tugarev. "Compared to other metal factories, it's not much. But we still produce for all of Russia as well as for foreign customers. Our zinc is even sold in the Netherlands, where it's used for roofing. In the Soviet Union it used to be all about quantity, because demand was so high. Unlike now, quality was not a priority."

In a second division of the factory, long, thin sheets of beryllium copper are pulled through hot-air ovens, stretching them until they are as thin as foil. The products will eventually be used in the electronics industry for conductors and contacts. A floor higher, I arrive at the smelting ovens. Workers with ash-smeared faces lay bronze bricks onto the glowing fire.

The work here might remind one of the heroic posters from the Soviet Union's heyday, the kind that still adorn the front façade of the factory's warehouses. But, for my part, I immediately associate it with Alexander Mosolov's *Iron Foundry*, a hellish racket lasting about three and a half minutes that aimed to depict the steel plates being rolled through the presses. The piece was the final movement of the ballet suite *Steel* (1926–7) written for the revolution's tenth-anniversary celebrations. The work was apparently also performed in Belgium and the USA in 1930.

Initially, this ode to the machine, to industry and to the labourer was widely praised both in the Soviet Union and abroad. But, within a few years, *Steel* lost its popularity. The working class didn't care for Mosolov's music; it was belittled as petit-bourgeois anarchism, while critics called it a formalistic perversion of a contemporary subject. Criticism became so harsh that the work was eventually pulled from the repertoire. When the attacks on Mosolov intensified in 1929, the score itself vanished. Only *Iron Foundry* survives.

Now that I'm actually here at the MZOTsM, it dawns on me how loud the boom and hiss of the industrializing Soviet Union must have sounded: like a giant engine room that never stopped. Production continued day and night. There was a centuries-long backlog to catch up on, and the creation of "the new man", communism's greatest promise, required a vast amount of energy—or, better put, it could only be stamped out of a mould with a massive input of force.

Mosolov was erased from history during Stalin's reign of terror. Until the 1980s no one remembered any of his compositions. The same was true elsewhere—his excommunication at home led to oblivion abroad. With one exception: *Iron Foundry*. Just three and a half minutes was all that was left of him.

Iron Foundry fit neatly in the 1920s worldwide trend of translating technical innovation and industrialization into music. Arthur Honegger's *Pacific 231* (1923), which depicts a steam locomotive, and Ernst Krenek's opera *Jonny spielt auf* (1927), about a jazz violinist in the everything-goes Weimar Republic, also portrayed modern times. But futuristic works like these had no place in the Soviet utopia: new rules concerning socialist realism, issued in 1932, stipulated that music's primary function was to be accessible to a wide audience.

Music was intended first and foremost for factory workers and rural farmers who were essential to building the new socialist society. Labourers had to be able to sing or hum music while at work; compositions were meant to boost productivity. Sing-along numbers with a socialist message, embedded in the collective repertoire, elbowed out the love songs of Vadim Kozin and Klavdiya Shulzhenko, even though these were still a favourite of many in the working class. Serious music by Prokofiev, Zaderatsky, Weinberg and Mosolov was tolerated at most as a treat for the intelligentsia, as a propaganda tool in the capitalist West, or as a means of re-educating criminals.

Before socialist realism became law, many musicians in the USSR actively rode the waves of the international avant-garde and set out to give it a Soviet tint. Alexander Mosolov and his friend Nikolai Roslavets were two of the key figures in this movement. Both, however, would clash with the proletarian culture politics of the 1930s and thereafter fall victim to Stalin's terror. While they evaded execution, they were banned all the same. Their work vanished from every imaginable institution, as though it had never been written; their names were scrapped from books and encyclopaedias; they were retouched out of photographs. They became non-persons.

Alexander Mosolov (1900–73) was the son of a respectable lawyer from Kyiv. His mother, a former singer with the Bolshoi Theatre, gave him his first music lessons. When he was four the family moved to Moscow, where his father died a year later. After a brief affair with the Ukrainian composer Boris Podgoretsky, his mother married the successful painter Mikhail Leblan, with whom she could continue living a cosmopolitan lifestyle. The family regularly travelled abroad: to Berlin, Paris and London. At home they spoke not only Russian but also French and German, the languages of the Russian elite.

During the Great War, Mosolov, like many of the progressives among the Russian elite, came to the conclusion that the tsarist system had become obsolete and only a revolution could save the country. In 1916 he volunteered for the front, but, being underage, he was turned down. After the February Revolution of 1917, he had a brief stint at the People's Commissariat for State Control, for which he thrice personally delivered mail to Lenin. This made a deep impression on him.

At the beginning of the October Revolution, he fought as a volunteer in the First Cavalry Regiment of the Red Army on the

Polish and Ukrainian fronts and was twice decorated with the Order of the Red Banner. When civil war broke out at the end of the Great War, he battled the enemies of the new Russia. A serious injury in 1920 put an end to his soldiering days; suffering from post-traumatic stress disorder, he was discharged from the army in 1921.

A year later he enrolled at the Moscow Conservatory to study composition, first with Reinhold Glière and later with Nikolai Myaskovsky, graduating in 1925. His final project was a cantata, *The Sphinx*, based on an Oscar Wilde poem of the same name.

Mosolov wasted no time in plunging into Soviet music life, which seemed to offer endless possibilities for experimentation. "His music from that time sparkled with enthusiasm for the new day," the seventy-one-year-old Leonid Rasunovsky tells me at his home in Amsterdam. He had become acquainted with Mosolov in the early 1970s, when the composer gave a lecture at the Moscow Conservatory. "What he composed wasn't at all 'cacophony', as the authorities claimed, it was really quite melodious. Like so many other artists in Russia, the revolution was a great inspiration for him, like the sudden eruption of a volcano. He was a utopian—he believed everything was possible."

Mosolov's star rose, and he became a favourite of Russian concertgoers. Sergei Prokofiev praised his work, and he was admitted to the ASM (or ACM, the Association for Contemporary Music); thanks to his advocacy, contemporary Western composers like Alban Berg, Paul Hindemith, Darius Milhaud and Arthur Honegger were performed in the Soviet Union. He was the first Russian to publish a review of Hindemith's work.

While he was primarily active as a concert pianist, between 1924 and 1929 Mosolov also wrote his best works (some of which garnered international attention): a symphony, a string quartet, *Iron Foundry*, a piano concerto, a piano sonata and various art songs including *Four Newspaper Announcements*, Op. 21. One often hears in his music the same ironic humour as in Prokofiev.

Also, like Prokofiev, he was a bit of a dandy. In some photos it even looks like he's wearing eye makeup, which, while for artists was not at all unusual, gave him a jaunty, uppish look and would be used against him later on.

The success of his String Quartet No. 1 at the 1927 ISCM Festival in Frankfurt convinced him to turn to full-time composition. In 1927 and 1928, he was secretary of the Russian division of the ISCM, and a year later the Bolshoi Theatre invited him to contribute to the speculative ballet *The Four Moscows*—his movement was to depict what Moscow might look like in the year 2117. (The other three movements were to be contributed by Leonid Polovinkin, Anatoly Alexandrov and Dmitri Shostakovich. In the end, nothing came of the project.)

Mosolov's rapid ascent annoyed his conservative, "proletarian" opponents within the RAPM. An article in the journal *Muzyka i revolyutsiya* ("Music and Revolution") in 1927 warned against his tendency to approach music solely from the viewpoint of innovation; his compositions were said to be "constructivist".

The Austrian Mosolov expert Christian Heindl points to the irony of this criticism, because Mosolov did in fact write music for the proletariat and hoped to contribute musically to shaping the new Soviet Union. The only difference with his adversaries is that he used other, more intellectual means.

The music politics of the new regime spelt bad news for Mosolov. From 1927 onward, he found little opportunity to get his music performed and could barely eke out a living. After 1930, Soviet publishers stopped printing his music, and opera and concert halls were reluctant to perform it. Only *Iron Foundry* was still put on in 1931.

His friend Vladimir Derzhanovsky, co-publisher of the journal *Sovremennaya muzyka* ("Contemporary Music"), wrote in his diary in 1927: "Poor Mosolov: despite his success in Frankfurt (excellent reviews) and his five-year contract with Universal Edition he is penniless, goes to eat with his mother once a day and smokes the thousands of papirosy he procured in May."

Mosolov's bad luck was to live during Stalin's period of forced industrialization and collectivization of the agricultural sector. These ruthless, deadly nationwide reforms were coupled with a massive cultural attack on the middle-class intelligentsia. The struggle was focused on the "bourgeois specialists", the socially engaged pre-1917 intellectuals who since Lenin's "New Economic Policy" (NEP) had assumed key posts and enjoyed a privileged status. They were accused of "deviating to the right" of Marxism-Leninism and were purged during show trials. Between 1928 and 1931, some 138,000 civil servants were fired and replaced by young, fanatical communists.

The wave of purges in the cultural sector began right away in 1928 with the announcement of the first five-year plan. Cultural institutions like the State Publishing House, theatres and conservatories, which were once led by the intelligentsia and well disposed to these so-called bourgeois specialists, were now forced by the proletarian class warriors to carry out drastic personnel changes. In 1929–30, experts and intellectuals were replaced by ideological party bureaucrats with hardly any expertise. A typical example of these changes was the ousting, in September 1929, of the People's Commissar for Education, Information and Science, Anatoly Lunacharsky, an art-lover and intellectual who had put culture in the service of socialism. He was replaced by Andrei Bubnov, a former military strategist and member of the agitprop department of the Central Committee.

At first, Mosolov seemed to be on solid footing with the new cultural authorities, but that hope was dashed soon enough with his "industry opera" *The Dam*. The work, an initiative of the Leningrad State Opera and Ballet Theatre, was a prestige project intended to set the tone of the evolution of Soviet cultural politics with an opera about industrialization and agricultural collectivization. In 1929 the theatre assembled a commission consisting of three specialists known to be supportive of progressive music. They deliberately chose Mosolov above a proletarian artist, believing that Mosolov, who was not highly placed in the musical hierarchy in the late 1920s and was thus spared during the purges, would be the ideal composer to put "the idea of nation-building into compactly organized sound material". Moreover, he was an "optimist", a catchword of the new times.

Delighted with the commission, Mosolov set to work on an avant-garde composition that wholly satisfied the political norms of the day, including the hard-handed enforcement of collectivization. The opera depicts the construction of a dam in the south of the Soviet Union and the locals' fierce resistance (including sabotage) to it. An intermezzo in the final act shows a film clip of the completed dam with water cascading from it. Two superstitious village women tell of the ringleaders of the resistance, the monk Gavriil and the wealthy *kulak* Pushchin, having been arrested by the secret police. The message was that a *kulak* would never change his ways voluntarily and had to be brought around by brute force.

So, in fact *The Dam* was entirely in line with new ideology. But it all went sour when the cultural revolution reached the Leningrad State Theatres in September 1929. A reorganization committee suggested expanding the artistic management, giving representatives from local unions, the local party committee, the Komsomol, the artists' union, factories and businesses more say in artistic policy. This new, all-powerful body was henceforth called the Artistic Political Council.

The first orchestra rehearsals for *The Dam* in May 1930 met with the council's full approval. The council secretary showered Mosolov with praise, claiming to have heard "the class enemy" in the roles of the *kulak*s, and he left the rehearsal completely satisfied with the vitriol it engendered. This was precisely the goal of the authorities. By now, the composer had secured an "ideological position" with Radio Moscow as leader of "the musical expression of the newspapers" and later as leader of the "sound brigade".

In September of that year, though, a purge in the theatre's management team signalled a shift in government policy. Director Lubinsky was accused of sabotaging the purging committee's work and of partisan use of bourgeois specialists. He was replaced by a Party apparatchik, Veniamin Bukhshtein, who had little knowledge of music and lost no time locking horns with the stage director. Following a public performance of Act I of *The Dam* at the end of the year, the Artistic Political Council reconvened.

This time, most of Leningrad's composers, Shostakovich among them, were summoned to the plenary sitting. They unanimously defended Mosolov's opera. But then it happened. After a speech by Vitali Kilchevsky, one of the most fanatical activists of the RAPM, the Artistic Political Council did an about-face. Representatives from the labourers' caucus suddenly found the work "strange". Then the new director, Bukhshtein, said that *The Dam* brought Soviet opera into disrepute and that the staging must be called off. The council voted unanimously to cancel the rehearsals. On 31 December, RABIS (the Trade Union of Art Workers magazine) reported that the opera *The Dam* was to be pulled from the repertoire "because it did not meet the demands of the day, and the construction of the *kolkhozes* [collective farms] was not accurately depicted".

I am aware of the difficulties of writing a work like *The Dam* while keeping within the parameters of socialist realism. It is well-nigh impossible to overlook the coercion and violence that went into the creation of the socialist utopia. I notice it when, on a work visit, I see a group of people swimming in the Volga outside the industrial city of Rybinsk, more than 300 kilometres to the north of Moscow. The river widens so much as it approaches Rybinsk Reservoir that locals call it "the sea". They also know that in this sea is a submerged city, Mologa. "It's miles upstream," says one of the swimmers, Sasha, pointing to a golden stripe of water on the horizon, "so you can't see it." (Except that in hot summers, when the river's level drops a few metres, bones sometimes stick out above the water.)

In 1935, Stalin announced the construction of a huge dam at the confluence of the Volga and the Mologa to power a new hydroelectric plant at Rybinsk and provide electricity to Moscow. The first plan was for the dam to raise the water level to 98 metres above sea level. The majority of the surrounding land would be submerged, but not the town itself. But in 1937 it was decided to raise the water level by another four metres, to 102 metres above sea level, nearly doubling the size of the reservoir. And this was the death knell for Mologa.

They began clearing the region that same year, and it continued until 1941. In total, 130,000 people were displaced. "They were sent to villages and cities in the surrounding areas," says Snezhana Yevseyeva, the director of the Mologa Museum. "Most of the people went quietly, because Stalin's terror was already in full swing. Others applauded the dam, because they believed it was good for the fatherland." A handful of residents resisted.

When the dam was finished, in April 1941, they started letting the reservoir fill up. NKVD units were sent to Mologa to clear out the remaining residents. But some three hundred of them refused to leave; they holed themselves up in their homes, chaining themselves to stoves and doors. They drowned along with their beloved town, 663 neighbouring villages, 140 churches and three monasteries.

The dam and the hydroelectric plant were both built by forced labourers—most of them political prisoners. "Officially 150,000 of them died during construction," Yevseyeva says, "but we assume the number was much, much higher because the first crews were Uzbeks who weren't accustomed to the harsh climate of northern Russia, and they died in droves during the first couple of months."

The museum, which opened in 1997, consists of four rooms in which old photographs and some archaeological artefacts and antique furniture recall the lost city. "During the political thaw under Khrushchev people started talking openly about a Mologa museum," says Yevseyeva, "but only under Gorbachev did the plans seriously take shape. They finally became reality under Yeltsin."

A few streets further, in a retirement home, lives the eighty-four-year-old Valeria Kapustina. As a child she was among the displaced Mologans. Together with her mother, who passed away six years earlier, she wrote a tribute to her former city in the form of fourteen collections of poems and short stories.

For Valeria, Mologa was a paradise whence she was driven by the diabolical Stalin. Her constant nostalgia for the city of her youth was only amplified by the loss of her father, brother and fiancé during the Second World War. "Our family had to flee the city because my father, a former tsarist officer, was not a member of the Communist Party," she says at her dining table, surrounded by photos of her late loved ones. "Party members were given more time to prepare. But all we could take were our boots, a coat and a fur hat. Later, our house was transported to Rybinsk by boat. After that, my family never uttered a word about Mologa."

Like Snezhana Yevseyeva, Valeria isn't surprised that people left without putting up a fight. "Everyone was scared to death of Stalin," she says. "Luckily we have a good leader now, Vladimir Vladimirovich Putin, who was sent by God and who loves his people."

Then it is time for her poetry about the nature and the fields surrounding Mologa. Valeria stands up and in a tender voice recites a lengthy poem by heart. The starry sky, one's first love and Mother Russia are praised in rhyme. For a few minutes, an idyll comes to life in that overstuffed room, only to vanish back underwater.

Mosolov could have set the atmosphere these poems evoke to music, with no objection from the authorities. But the part about the city purposely drowned by Stalin?

Mosolov's fortunes sank after the rejection of his opera. In spring of 1931, he was fired from Radio Moscow for supposedly being "musically counter-revolutionary" and was replaced by an RAPM loyalist. Nevertheless, the score to *Iron Foundry* was reprinted in 1931—the first printing of this popular work was sold out and there was still a demand for it both at home and abroad. The State Publisher, which by then employed members of the RAPM, tried to block a second edition and even, claimed Mosolov, intended to destroy the plates. But intervention by the Viennese music publisher Universal Edition via the Soviet Foreign Ministry resulted in permission for a reprinting exclusively for the foreign market. Only later that year would the score be made available in the Soviet Union.

The fuss over the score was really about an incident surrounding the work's success abroad. In August 1931, the German communist and cultural activist Rudolf von Liebig had written a letter to the People's Commissar Bubnov to complain about a choreographed version of *Iron Foundry* at the Hollywood Bowl in Los Angeles. He called the work "shallow and misleading" because it portrayed only the noise of the machines and not "the spirit of the factory". Worse yet, said von Liebig, the performance reminded the audience of reports in the "reactionary press" of forced labour in the Soviet Union, something that could harm the image of the communist utopia.

The letter was passed on to Glaviskusstvo (the department for literary and artistic affairs), where inspector Moisei Grinberg of the music department lambasted the work. He called Mosolov a "class-hostile" representative of the "extreme right wing" of Soviet composers who imitated modern-day Western, bourgeois-decadent, urban models and aimed to depict Soviet realism in a "negative and biased" light. Grinberg opposed allowing the score to be made available and called in the censors.

That the *Iron Foundry* score was re-issued anyway despite such harsh criticism shows that the State's and the Party's support for proletarian art organizations was waning. *Iron Foundry* was still not blacklisted by the censors. "Bourgeois" and Western-inspired music could apparently be performed, so long as it served the advancement of socialism.

Notwithstanding these positive signals, Mosolov was dissatisfied with his situation. He had done his best to submit to the new rules, and again it wasn't good enough. So, he decided to try his luck elsewhere and went on a folksong-collecting expedition in Turkmenistan, Kyrgyzstan, Tajikistan and Armenia. It was a safe move: the trip was paid for by a state cultural fund, and he would be the first Russian composer to write a symphonic suite based on a Turkmen folksong.

But here, too, he afforded himself some risky artistic licence: his compositions were thickly orchestrated and he employed polytonality—contrary to the strictures of socialist realism—and this raised the hackles of his adversaries.

Vexed by the constant criticism, in March 1932 he appealed directly to Stalin, complaining that none of his works had been printed since 1929 and nothing of his had been performed since 1930. (Remarkably, he also pointed to countless performances in the provinces, until 1931, of *Iron Foundry* and the reprinting of its score.) "Since 1926 I have been the target of permanent harassment. It has become intolerable. I must compose, and my works must be performed! I must test my works against the masses: if I fail, then I know what I must do."

He also asked Stalin to "influence the proletarian musicians and their minions, who have been badgering me for the whole of the past year" and to either allow him to work in the USSR or "authorize my departure abroad, where I, with my music, could be more useful to the USSR than here".

He must have been so desperate by then that he lost sight of how dangerous those words were. A few years later they would certainly have cost him his life. But for now, nothing happened— nor did any reply come from the great music-lover in the Kremlin.

And yet he must have been surprised when, on 21 April 1932, his Piano Concerto No. 2 on Kyrgyz themes was allowed to be premiered at the Moscow Conservatory. The reason for the authorities' sudden forbearance became apparent three days later, when the Central Committee issued a resolution stating that socialist realism would henceforth be the new norm in all art forms. This meant partial rehabilitation for Mosolov, insofar as he stuck to folkloric elements, which were allowed under the new rules.

But Mosolov was unhappy with his new situation, for the simple reason that he was still not free to compose as he wished. At times this frustration led to open rebellion. As it did on 31 January 1936, three days after *Pravda* published its infamous attack on Shostakovich's *Lady Macbeth of Mtsensk*. At the restaurant of the Press House, the meeting place of the Moscow intelligentsia, Mosolov denounced the critique in a drunken tirade, as though it were an attack on his own work. Four days later, he was expelled from the composers' union. (In the end, it was just a temporary suspension; he was readmitted several months later.)

Commissions for orchestral works over the next few years took him once again to the southern regions of the USSR for research: in addition to Soviet Kyrgyzstan, he travelled to Dagestan, Georgia, Armenia, Turkmenistan and Ukraine. He also went to the White

Sea Canal (also called the Belomorkanal), the construction of which some years earlier had claimed the lives of at least 25,000 forced labourers. During this trip he made no bones about his irritation at his life as a forced "folkloric composer".

By now Stalin's terror was operating at full throttle. At every level of society, betrayal was normal among careerists seeking advancement and survival. Surprisingly, Mosolov was not one of its victims—yet.

On 18 September 1937, *Izvestia* published a scathing article about him written by the "Brothers Tur", a playwright duo (not brothers at all) named Leonid Tubelsky and Pyotr Ryzhey, who produced popular propaganda pieces for Stalin's secret police. The gist of their message was the need to be vigilant for espionage. In this particular article, they accused Mosolov of spending his time in Central Asia and leading a rowdy and "debauched existence" in taverns rather than writing the opera he had been commissioned to do. The bottom line was that he was guilty of "counter-revolutionary activities"—in other words, he was an enemy of the people.

It is still unclear why the Turs smeared Mosolov in the first place. Their assignment most likely came from vengeful musicians within the RAPM, who simply disliked Mosolov and used the repressive climate to lash out at him (even though plenty of the leaders of their own organization also fell prey to the terror). Or it could be that the Kremlin wanted to expand its campaign against formalism in Soviet music with the same savagery as with the writers' union and actors' union.

Interestingly, the composers' union came to Mosolov's defence. In a letter to *Izvestia* it rebutted the Turs' accusations and demanded a written rectification. The paper's editors did not print the letter and ignored the demand.

Mosolov's fate was thus sealed. He was arrested on 4 November 1937; seven weeks later, a military tribunal, invoking the infamous Article 58, Paragraph 10, convicted him of counter-revolutionary propaganda. The sentence: eight years in a "corrective labour camp"—that is, hard labour in the gulag. The camp, on the Sheksna River, was just on the opposite (north) side of the enormous Rybinsk Reservoir and in the same region where the late opposition activist Alexei Navalny was imprisoned in March 2021.

His case was reviewed some six months later, on 15 July 1938, probably the result of an appeal by his former teachers Glière and Myaskovsky to Soviet president, Mikhail Kalinin. His sentence was reduced to a five-year prohibition on residing in Moscow, Leningrad or Kyiv, and he was released on 25 August.

Surprisingly, his work—as after his outburst in 1932—could still be performed, although the ban prevented him from attending those concerts. In November 1938, his Concerto for Harp was premiered to great success in Moscow during the opening concert of "A Decade of Soviet Music". The first movement was reprised during the festival's final concert, along with works by leading Soviet composers of the day: Shostakovich, Khachaturian, Dunaevsky, Muradeli and Koval.

A few weeks later, *Izvestia*—the very newspaper that had defamed him two years earlier—honoured Mosolov by printing, on the occasion of Stalin's sixtieth birthday, his setting of a drinking song to a text by the Komsomol poet Alexander Zharov.

Now that he was back in the regime's good graces—some of his works, in particular his patriotic songs, were republished—Mosolov submitted a request to the Council of People's Commissars to have his exile lifted. In 1941 his request was approved, and he moved back to Moscow the following year.

After the Second World War, Mosolov led a solitary, withdrawn life. He was plagued by his past as a former avant-gardist and his work was rarely performed. At the end of his life he enjoyed renewed inspiration, thanks in part to Nina Meshko, a well-known choral conductor seventeen years his junior who specialized in folkloric music. He had met her in the 1960s in Murmansk, where she led the Northern Russian Folk Chorus. They married and lived together in Moscow until his death in 1973.

"Meshko inspired Mosolov to write new music," says the violist Leonid Rusanovsky. "The regime had crushed him: those months in the camp had turned a talented artist into a misanthrope. His music written after his release was inconsequential, but that changed once he met Meshko. He had gone from avant-garde to folkloric, but still he retained some of the old Mosolov. It's like with Malevich, who first painted portraits, then abstract work, and at the end of his life returned to portraiture with avant-garde elements. Meshko rekindled his creativity, and her status as a famous choral conductor and singing teacher offered him a kind of protection."

But, like his early compositions, much of his later work has been lost. Mosolov himself inflated the myth of his missing early work, spreading the story that sometime in the 1920s, a burglar had stolen a large yellow suitcase containing his manuscripts. While he was drawing up an inventory of his oeuvre in 1968, he referred to the suitcase, which he said contained songs to texts by Alexander Blok, Anna Akhmatova and Vladimir Mayakovsky, as well as a complete opera called *The Hero*.

His widow Nina Meshko says he invented the burglary story. The more likely version, she says, is that Mosolov had given the suitcase to the Polish-Russian tenor Sergei Radamsky at a music soirée in 1927. Radamsky lived in the United States and was on tour in the Soviet Union at the time and, at Mosolov's request, took it back to the US for safekeeping.

The musicologist Inna Barsova was one of the first to study Soviet musicians, and, during her visits to the United States in the seventies and eighties with Gennady Rozhdestvensky, she looked for Radamsky and the manuscripts. But the singer had died in 1973, and the suitcase was nowhere to be found.*

Barsova did discover the score to *The Hero* in 1979 on the shelves of Universal Edition in Vienna. She brought a copy back to Moscow for Rozhdestvensky, where it lay for another ten years before it was performed. Since the early 2000s, the work has been staged with some regularity, including in Berlin, Cambridge, Arkhangelsk and St Petersburg.

Why Mosolov kept such a low profile after the war, no one can say. Maybe it was the trauma of his eight months in the gulag. Maybe the dictates of folkloric composition deadened his creativity. Maybe. It's a word that applies to so many events of the dark history of the Soviet Union. But whatever the reason, it does not diminish the tragedy of his life. Only the discovery of the suitcase gone missing in the United States could—maybe—posthumously lighten the burden.

Leonid Rasunovsky and I raise a glass to Mosolov. He suddenly recalls something Mosolov said during that lecture he gave in Moscow in the early seventies: "Freedom comes naked, casting flowers on the heart." It is a quote from a poem by Velimir Khlebnikov. You don't get more Russian than that.

---

* There is a film planned (but as of this writing not yet realized) called *Mosolov's Suitcase*. The trailer can be seen at: https://www.mosolovfilm.com/

9

Stalin's Last Lackey

That the Dutch daily paper *De Volkskrant* referred to Tikhon Khrennikov as "Stalin's last lackey" in his obituary on 14 August 2007 came as no surprise. I was familiar with Khrennikov as the villainous general secretary of the composers' union who from 1948 through 1991 had sabotaged the career of many a Soviet composer by banning their music or publicly condemning it for not meeting the regime's standards of socialist realism and folk qualities. Shostakovich, Prokofiev, Zaderatsky and Weinberg all had the scars to show for it.

Khrennikov's bad reputation was largely thanks to *Testimony*, Dmitri Shostakovich's memoirs, which the composer dictated in the late sixties and early seventies to the musicologist Solomon Volkov. Published after his death and the subject of much debate as to its credibility, *Testimony* is a harsh indictment of Stalin's rule and of all those who helped undermine Shostakovich during those years. The gist of the memoirs was that this ostensibly obedient, conformist composer—Shostakovich—who at party congresses spoke admiringly of the authorities' policies, was in fact a rebel who via his music waged a protest against the communist regime.

Shostakovich portrayed the composers' union as an organization rife with grudges, ambition and conflicts over official recognition and monetary rewards. Khrennikov was made out to be little more than Stalin's flunky, dead set on destroying brilliant modern composers like himself and Prokofiev. He called him one of Stalin's wolfhounds.

Testimony, in the 1970s one of the few sources of information regarding everyday Soviet musical life, makes one thing very clear: Shostakovich lived in mortal fear of Stalin. He writes:

> Fear, that was a collective feeling. I could not escape it. [...] They'll say: what was there to be afraid of? Didn't they leave musicians be? Then I shall answer: that is not so. That world was also in their crosshairs. And how! The fiction that musicians were left alone is now being spread by Khrennikov and his henchmen. And because artists tend to have a short memory, they believe it.

Such harsh accusations blinded me to the notion that Khrennikov—like so many other high-ranking Soviet officials—must also have lived in constant fear of the dictator's whims. Shostakovich does mention in his memoirs that Khrennikov wet himself when Stalin gave him a dressing-down for unintentionally disobeying an order, but that struck me as a one-off incident.

Looking at the photos of a smiling Shostakovich standing jovially alongside a similarly laughing Khrennikov, my first reaction is that these were two men who got along just fine. This doesn't say much, of course, in the context of the Stalin era, when it was commonly accepted that your best friend could stab you in the back to save himself. But perhaps the old Latin proverb *homo homini lupus*—"man is a wolf to man"—applies here: one does whatever it takes to survive in a totalitarian state. Khrennikov himself said that he had to castigate his best friends in public to keep them out of the clutches of the secret police.

Volkov's book is, to this day, the subject of much debate. One side contests its authenticity, the other stands by its accuracy. The American musicologist and Shostakovich biographer Laurel E. Fay determined that each chapter in *Testimony* begins in more or less the same way as previously published texts by Shostakovich. And you have Shostakovich's son, Maxim, who confirmed his father's words after himself fleeing to the West in 1981. He did say in an interview with the *Sunday Times* that *Testimony* was a book "about his father, not by his father". Five years later, he added in a BBC television interview that the book was accurate in its depiction of the hardships under totalitarian rule.

But while Maxim continued to stick up for Solomon Volkov, his stepmother Irina (Shostakovich's third wife) in turn stoked the doubts: "Volkov met Dmitri maybe three or four times," she said. "He was never an intimate friend. He never came to eat with us. So I can't imagine how he managed to collect so much material for such a fat book."

In Moscow, I go to my favourite bookshop Moskva in search of a biography of Khrennikov. The music section hasn't much to offer; today's publishers tend to favour Soviet-era rock and folk singers. But in the section with the legendary series "Lives of Remarkable People" I find a volume about Khrennikov by the musicologist Andrei Kokarev, Khrennikov's grandson. I immediately wonder how objective his take on his grandfather is. And much of what I later read confirms my suspicion that his main aim was to restore Khrennikov's reputation. In January 2021, in an interview with the newspaper *Moskovsky komsomolets* ("The Moscow Komsomolets") about his new book on persecuted composers in the twenties, thirties and forties, he even said that being Khrennikov's grandson did not mean he glossed over the facts. Luckily for him, research confirms that during his grandfather's tenure hardly any musicians were murdered outright by the State. True, but it says nothing of those who were hounded, incarcerated, forced into exile or sent to labour camps.

In the BBC's online archive, a treasure trove for any lover of classical music, I come across the documentary *Gabriel Prokofiev: My Family and Russia*, in which the composer's grandson (himself a composer, London-born and based) visits Russia. In Moscow, he drops in on Kokarev to ask whether Khrennikov liked Prokofiev's music. He answers that his grandfather had three musical heroes: Bach, Tchaikovsky and Prokofiev. But he quickly adds that from 1948, when the regime began its attacks on "formalism" in music, Khrennikov was forced to change his tune. These were just "the rules of the game". That is: say what the authorities want to hear.

They then turn to Prokofiev's ex-wife Lina, who in 1948 was sentenced to eight years in the gulag. Kokarev says that after her release in 1956—three years after Stalin's death—she came to eat at the Khrennikovs' two or three times a week. But when Gabriel presses him on whether Khrennikov had taken concrete actions to get her released, the answer is that his grandfather always helped those whom he could, and that he had more success at it as his career progressed, but in 1948 there was nothing he could do.

The fact remains that even long after Stalin's death, Khrennikov managed to make life difficult for composers. Gabriel Prokofiev also pays a visit to the Russian couple Yelena Firsova and Dmitri Smirnov, both also composers. In the 1970s—they were in their twenties at the time—Khrennikov blacklisted them, Smirnov says. They were not even allowed to give small-scale private concerts. "In the Soviet Union, everything was controlled by the composers' union. We were kept in a cage, in a prison."

Talking about Khrennikov personally, Firsova says, "Sometimes he would help you, but usually only if there was something in it for him. Basically, he bought people."

Kokarev's biography includes a series of photos of Khrennikov over the years. A smiling man with typical Russian peasant looks: broad head, thick dark-blond hair combed straight back, a nose like a duck's bill, small eyes. Your typecast Soviet civil servant. Stalin is said to have chosen him just from his photograph: one look at that face said enough.

The musicologist Olga de Kort-Kulikova is surprisingly mild when I bring up Khrennikov. "You have to see him as the symbol of Soviet music," she says. "He lived through every period in the history of the Soviet Union and had a tragic life. A carefree provincial lad who moved to Moscow to study and enjoy the pleasures of the city, who loved music and was happiest writing songs and pieces for mandolin, transformed against his will into a civil servant. He was just thirty-four when, out of the blue, Stalin named him general secretary of the composers' union, with all that responsibility. From that moment on, he had to set composing aside and abandon his musical personality."

I am reminded that Jascha Nemtsov, the Weinberg expert, told me that Khrennikov always tried to protect union members. "Of course, he had to play his official role and carry out the party's wishes. If he hadn't done so, he would never have been made general secretary. But there are plenty of testimonials to his behind-the-scenes efforts to help people. Remember, he was appointed by Stalin, and to refuse could have cost him his head. I met Khrennikov a few times at the end of his life. He told me he hadn't wanted the job at all but was forced to take it."

He might have taken the job reluctantly, but he often seemed to execute it with fervour. The more I learn about Khrennikov, the more ambiguous a figure he appears.

Tikhon Khrennikov was born in 1913 in Yelets, some 400 kilometres south of Moscow. It's a typical Turgenev, Tolstoy or Chekhov setting: wooden tradesmen's houses and brick factories wind their way through the old city around a tall, green-and-white cathedral that looks out over the Bystraya Sosna River.

Khrennikov's father came from a family of merchants fallen on hard times and was a warehouse employee himself. Tikhon was the youngest of ten children. Like so many others, he would benefit from the social changes brought about by the Revolution of 1917, which allowed talented children from poor families to study. Playing in a mandolin orchestra as a child must have sparked his love of folk music that one hears in his later compositions. When he started piano lessons at the age of nine, his interest turned to composition, and he produced his first waltzes and marches at thirteen.

Three years later he was admitted to the prestigious Gnessin Institute in Moscow to study piano and composition, where he soon became a star pupil of Sviatoslav Richter's teacher, Heinrich Neuhaus. He transferred to the Moscow Conservatory, where his graduation piece was the Symphony No. 1. The jury, chaired by Prokofiev, did not award the piece the highest score—a "5"—but rather a "4", because they considered it too traditional. The ambitious debutant was highly insulted, an omen of the jealousy and rancour that would later mark his tenure as general secretary of the composers' union.

And yet, this "defeat" would be avenged somewhat a few months after the symphony's premiere. The piece was reprised, and its performance was broadcast in the United States, where it was hailed by such acclaimed conductors as Eugene Ormandy, Arturo Toscanini, Charles Munch and Franz Waxman.

By now, 1936, Stalin's terror was in full swing. Khrennikov, on behalf of the Young Composers, seconded Stalin's denunciation of Shostakovich's opera *Lady Macbeth of Mtsensk*. He also denounced Prokofiev's statement calling Shostakovich the Soviet Union's most modern composer and for disparaging Soviet music as "provincial".

Three years later, in 1939, Shostakovich, still nettled, took subtle revenge by writing to Khrennikov about his new opera *Into the Storm*: "You are talented, but you must still listen carefully to Mozart, Bach, Beethoven, Mussorgsky, Brahms, Liszt, Chopin and Tchaikovsky, to be able to distinguish good music from bad."

This tit-for-tat played out with Stalin giving the opera his blessing and the critics and theatre directors following suit. *Into the Storm* was deemed a success, and over the next few months it was put on in eighteen of the twenty opera theatres across the country. It must have given Khrennikov only mixed satisfaction. His opera was a triumph, but only thanks to his denunciation of Shostakovich. And this was nothing to be proud of.

Khrennikov slyly steered clear of ideological battles. He opted for the safest possible tactics and declined to ally himself with any one particular artistic movement. It would save him a good deal of trouble.

This became clear when *Pravda* printed an article on 6 April 1937 entitled "Something Is Amiss in the Soviet Composers'

Union". The article criticized Nikolai Chelyapov, the head of the union's Moscow chapter and editor-in-chief of the journal *Sovetskaya muzyka*, as out of touch with music and art and not in control of the union's affairs. The real reason for the attack, however, was that at a meeting the previous December, his preference for symphonies and oratorios came under fire. By the fall of 1937, Chelyapov's name made it onto the list of "enemies of the people". Shortly thereafter he disappeared without a trace.

The malicious article was the beginning of a wave of repression in the Soviet music world. Countless performers and composers were arrested and murdered. Khrennikov's biographer, Kokarev, defending Khrennikov's role in the affair, concedes that while Chelyapov was indeed unfit for his function, no one could have foreseen that he would be fired, arrested and executed. It was an incident that would mark Khrennikov for the rest of his life—he realized that this could be anyone's fate, even his own. This fear was only augmented later that year when his two older brothers, Boris and Nikolai, were accused of anti-Soviet propaganda, while both had been avowed revolutionaries in 1917 and until the day of their arrest firmly believed in the cause of Lenin and Stalin.

Now that it had touched his own family, Khrennikov sprang into action. He wrote to Lavrenty Beria, the head of the NKVD, and collected funds to pay for a good lawyer. For Nikolai, a mathematics and physics teacher, this turned out to be a good move. He had apparently been falsely incriminated by colleagues, who testified in court that they had been pressured by the NKVD to bring the false accusation. Nikolai was acquitted.

Boris Khrennikov, the boss of a railway station, fared less well. He was accused of membership in a non-existent counter-revolutionary, fascist organization planning to violently overthrow the Soviet regime, and was sentenced to five years in the gulag. He was released in 1943 and died shortly thereafter.

Interestingly, Shostakovich was quite supportive of Khrennikov during those trying times. They met in Leningrad often, happily sitting at the piano playing *à quatre mains*. In photos they look like student and mentor. But, as always, the reality was a different story.

Shostakovich's music exuded pessimism. He wanted to express the suffering of his time. Khrennikov's music, on the other hand, displayed the optimism befitting Soviet propaganda. That optimism meant writing simple melodies, which Shostakovich would have no truck with. So, it's hardly surprising that in these circumstances the two increasingly had artistic conflicts and that their professional relationship became more distant as the years went on.

Meanwhile, Khrennikov's opera *Into the Storm* also came under fire: not only from Shostakovich, but from within the composers' union itself. Some members even compared it to Prokofiev's much-derided *Semyon Kotko*, and the music critic Semyon Shlifstein called the work "banal and vulgar".

Khrennikov was not easily intimidated. During the next meeting of the composers' union, he played excerpts of his music and was applauded for it. Three days later, Prokofiev, in a show of support, told him that in his younger years he had also quarrelled with his critics but, not possessing Khrennikov's self-control, had aggressively countered the critique.

That same year, Khrennikov married the journalist Klara Vaks, who worked at the composers' union press office. They moved into a third-floor flat in a newly renovated residence reserved for composers on what is now called the Chayanov Street, not far from the Belorussky Railway Station. As was usual in housing for the Soviet elite, the block had its own restaurant, club, cinema and library. The young couple also bought a dacha outside Moscow.

Over the next few years Khrennikov's musical output was chiefly for the theatre and the cinema, such as Ivan Pyryev's classic film *They Met in Moscow* (aka *The Swineherd and the Shepherd*, 1941). Khrennikov also composed an opera based on Turgenev's novel *The Torrents of Spring*, but it was left unfinished due to the outbreak of the Great Patriotic War. *They Met in Moscow* became one of the Soviet Union's first hit musical comedies on film, thanks in part to its role as a welcome diversion in wartime.

Like so many other prominent musicians, Khrennikov was called upon to entertain the troops, while his wife and daughter joined the artists and intellectuals who were evacuated to the Sverdlovsk region. In July 1941, he and his colleagues were put to work at the All-Soviet Radio Committee, the national broadcaster. His first assignment was to compose an opera about *Peter the Great*, but a German breakthrough appeared imminent, and he was evacuated by train to the city of Kuybyshev (modern-day Samara) in the Urals. Among his fellow evacuees were artists, dancers and musicians (including Shostakovich). They would return home only after the German retreat in early 1943.

In spring 2018, I walk up the hill from Samara's train station to the city. There is a bronze statue of Shostakovich on Kuybyshev Square, and for the first time I see him depicted in a relaxed pose, in loose-fitting trousers and a flapping overcoat. A self-assured young man. Perhaps this is really how he walked around here. Everyone I talk to here, young and old, is an admirer.

Across from the constructivist building that housed officers during the war is a low-rise block of flats where Shostakovich lived. However, there is no trace of Khrennikov anywhere. When I mention his name to older passers-by, they shrug their shoulders. But fond memories are reserved for the composer who depicted the Siege of Leningrad in his Symphony No. 7, completed here in December 1941 and premiered here in March 1942.

While Khrennikov was ensconced in Kuybyshev, his family did not fare as well. His brother Nikolai died of tuberculosis and his mother died during her evacuation from Yelets after the Germans took control. But none of this personal hardship comes through in his music from that time: his Symphony No. 2, the ballet *Francesca* and his songs mainly exude the optimism meant to buoy his countrymen.

His relatively safe existence was disrupted in early 1945, when he was sent to the Belarusian front, where for two months he and the composer Matvei Blanter gave concerts for the soldiers. There he also composed the film score to Pyryev's *Six P.M.* (a.k.a. *At Six P.M. after the War*, 1944), which would become a success and earn him the Stalin Prize.

Shortly thereafter, Khrennikov was in Berlin to perform at Marshal Vasily Chuikov's headquarters when the city fell to the Russians. The mood was a combination of triumph and relief.

Back in Moscow after the war, his career seemed to take off, but there was always the danger of running afoul of the authorities. At the plenary meeting of the composers' union in 1946, he defended his friend Blanter from accusations of having used blues elements in his music. But this was the last time he would stick out his neck for a colleague.

On 10 January 1948, Khrennikov and a few other composers were summoned to appear before the Central Committee. Party

Secretary for Culture Andrei Zhdanov received them and immediately sat down at the piano to play music as it was "supposed to" sound. Prokofiev and Shostakovich listened in agreement, unaware of what, in just a matter of days, was in store for them.

On 13 January, Zhdanov opened a frontal attack on "formalism" during a closed meeting of the Central Committee. Shostakovich, Prokofiev, Khachaturian, Popov, Kabalevsky, Shebalin and Shaporin were its first victims. Khrennikov was at the meeting as well and is said to have tried to smooth things over, but to no avail. A week later, Alexander Goldenweiser, the former director of the Moscow Conservatory, exacerbated the situation by distancing himself from the work of Prokofiev, Weinberg and Kabalevsky. And when on 10 February an article appeared in *Pravda* summing up those composers' shortcomings, the damage was complete.

At the end of January, Khrennikov was summoned to the Central Committee at eleven o'clock in the evening. (This was normal practice: Stalin worked until late, so everyone else in the Kremlin did, too.) He went straight to the office of Dmitri Shepilov, deputy to chief ideologue Mikhail Suslov. In the corridor he met his colleagues Golovanov, Sveshnikov and Khachaturian. None of them had any idea why they were there.

Khachaturian was the first to be called in. He had a leading role in the composers' union at the time but had recently been accused of modernism and bourgeois decadence in his music. When he came back out, he went up to Khrennikov and congratulated him. "What for?" he asked. "You'll find out soon enough," Khachaturian replied.

Golovanov, the conductor, was next. He was told he was to lead the Bolshoi Theatre, replacing Samuil Samosud. Sveshnikov was promoted to dean of the Moscow Conservatory.

And then it was Khrennikov's turn. The thirty-four-year-old was told he would henceforth be the general secretary of the Union of Soviet Composers. His first task would be to organize the first general assembly of the nation's composers. He had three months. Additionally, he was made chairman of the music category of the Stalin Prize. When he demurred and tried to refuse, Shepilov's answer was simply: "These are Stalin's orders."

In a way, the choice of Khrennikov was a logical one. After the recent unrest in the composers' union, things needed calming down, and Khrennikov fit the bill: he was young, talented, outgoing, had served at the front and wrote accessible, popular music. For Khrennikov himself, though, his appointment felt like a personal tragedy. "When I came home with the news, my wife and I cried about it all night," he said later in an interview. "She said I had to find a way to get out of it. Especially because I was in no way cut out for organizational work. But I had no choice. You just didn't defy an order from Stalin."

So the next day, he reported to the offices of the *orgkomitet*, which ran the union's day-to-day business, in the same building where he lived. This would be his workplace from now on.

Right on that first morning, his deposed predecessor Khachaturian came by to tell him there was nothing to hand over to him, because there were no pressing matters. Khrennikov tried to reassure his shaken colleague that his unexpected promotion would not affect their friendship. "I regard you as a monumental composer," he said, "and I promise that I will only help you in the future."

But in public, his message was quite different. He claimed that Khachaturian had been entirely unfit to lead the composers' union because he never met with the Central Committee or other agencies or individuals useful to composers. Moreover, at the first meeting of the new composers' union he read a statement in support of the regime's attack on formalism.

When Andrei Zhdanov, the instigator of the Central Committee's resolution against formalism, died suddenly in August 1948, Khrennikov at once became the most powerful man in the Soviet music world. He confirmed his standing in a speech to the composers' union in early 1949 entitled "On the Inexcusable Lag in Music Criticism and Musicology". In its intimidating tone, it was Zhdanov all over again. After declaring that music critics had failed to steer Soviet composers onto the path of socialist realism and warning that there were still supporters of formalism among critics, he delivered a few accusations by name.

His attack focused on three groups of composers who would now be blacklisted. The first group comprised the worst culprits: their activities, he said, were "damaging, unpatriotic and intended to undermine the ideological basis for Soviet music". The second group had committed "cosmopolitan errors"—caving in to Western influences and showing disdain for Russian music. The third category distanced itself from the work of union members and thereby withheld assistance to them.

The majority of the denounced musicians were employed at conservatories and music institutions in Moscow and Leningrad. Of the thirty-five in total, half were Jews. This was not necessarily unusual, as Jews were disproportionally represented in Soviet musical life. But the fact that Stalin's antisemitic campaign was then also in full swing throws another light on the attacks.

✼

In his new leadership role, Khrennikov showed his worst side. Not only did he throw his weight around, but he perfected the typical Soviet bureaucratic game of saying one thing in private and another in public to save one's own skin. It was eat or be eaten.

In this respect, it is difficult to judge Khrennikov fairly. While he was vain and clearly enjoyed his power and prestige, he would later claim that under his leadership no single member of the composers' union became a victim of state repression. (You can still read this on Khrennikov's official website to this day.) Kokarev gives his grandfather credit for single-handedly getting Mieczysław Weinberg released from the gulag, for seeing to it that Prokofiev and Shostakovich both were awarded the Stalin Prize in 1949, and for getting the Central Committee to scrap its statement denouncing formalism in 1958.

Gaining access to records concerning the composers persecuted under Stalin and the archives of the composers' union is still difficult, writes the German musicologist Inna Klause in *Der Klang des Gulag*. But, based on the data that have been made public, we can conclude that under Khrennikov the number of composers arrested did not show any discernible decline. In 1950, there was even an increase due to the many arrests in the Baltic republics, where in 1945 a campaign of terror was unleashed against the "elite". Memorial, the excellent organization that researches Stalinist repression, concludes that sixty-eight composers were arrested and sent to the gulag. During Khrennikov's tenure, at least eleven—three Estonians, three Latvians, two Jews, a Pole, a Russian and a German—were given lengthy sentences in prison or labour camps. Their sentences came to an end not thanks to any intervention by the composers' union, but as a result of Stalin's death in 1953. And even then, some had to wait several more years before being released and rehabilitated.

Compared to the three thousand writers arrested under Stalin—some 1,500 of these were executed—the composers got off lightly. In 1948 the union, with 908 members, was the smallest arts organization in the country.

Khrennikov's grandson Kokarev insists that the awful things his grandfather said and wrote must be seen in the context of that fearful time; having to denounce his best friends and his mentor was part and parcel of his position. Khrennikov himself said he wrestled with his actions and did his best behind the scenes to help those he was publicly lambasting. If he was on holiday when a colleague was fired, says Olga de Kort-Kulikova, he would return at once to try to intervene. "He made sure they had food, a roof over their head and medical care, but he had to toe the party line."

The inevitable cronyism often took on convoluted forms. Take the case of Herman Zhukovsky, who was made endlessly to amend his folk opera *From the Bottom of My Heart* in order to receive the Stalin Prize (third class). But once the opera—by now cut to ribbons by the censors—was premiered in April 1951, with Stalin in attendance, the criticism in *Pravda* was so harsh (the opera, it said, gave an inaccurate impression of life on a *kolkhoz*) that the composer himself wrote to Stalin, offering to return the prize. This was a great embarrassment for the jury; two members were fired and Khrennikov only just managed to retain his chairmanship.

The political situation worsened quickly and drastically. On 8 December a letter arrived at the Kremlin from one Anna Begicheva, who wrote: "Comrade Stalin! There are enemies at work in our arts." No one had any clue who this woman was: clearly, she had been invented by Stalin's henchmen to justify unleashing a new wave of repression. Thousands of Soviet citizens were arrested, most of them Jews. They were active in the arts, as scientists or as doctors—but none were composers. Khrennikov was chastised for laxness and ordered to get on with "the struggle against the influential Jews and cosmopolitans", but for now he was able to protect his own union members.

No example of this is clearer than the case of Semyon Shlifstein, the music critic who had panned Khrennikov's opera *Into the Storm* in the late 1930s and had now fallen afoul of the authorities. He turned to Khrennikov for help and was given a job in far-off Yakutia, in the Russian Far East. Not a moment too soon: just three days later the NKVD came knocking at Shlifstein's door to arrest him.

In the early 1950s, Khrennikov invited Betty Glan, the former head of the Central Park of Culture and Leisure, to work on the day-to-day management of the composers' union. Glan was married to a Yugoslav communist, who, due to the 1948 schism between Tito and Stalin, was prevented from living in Moscow. Khrennikov tried (ultimately in vain) to secure him a residence permit and was reprimanded in the process by the head of the arts section of the Central Committee for having submitted the application in the first place. But this incident had no further consequences: as a protégé of Stalin's, Khrennikov was in the clear.

One area in which Khrennikov found himself in the firing line was Stalin's antisemitic campaign, namely because his wife, Klara Vaks, was Jewish. Khrennikov received anonymous messages in his mailbox on a daily basis: threats and cartoons depicting him hanging from a gallows or in an electric chair. This kind of mail was also sent to the Central Committee. Khrennikov was accused of being a Jew under the protection of the composers' union or under the influence of Jews and Zionists. Many of the perpetrators of this were friends and colleagues whom he had invited to his home and were now bent on "cancelling" him.

He suffered from sleeplessness and apathy, and, when these health issues became chronic, he was admitted to a Kremlin sanatorium under the watchful eye of the NKVD. Klara was allowed to visit him only once a week. When he began to have hallucinations due to lack of sleep, it was Klara who got him out of the sanatorium and brought him home.

Khrennikov started composing again, as a distraction from the arrests and show trials. The year 1950 saw the premiere of his comic opera *Frol Skobeyev*. The balalaikas sounded sumptuous in this work about the amorous doings of a seventeenth-century nobleman. Reviews were mild, although some critics were bothered by the lyricism and the bourgeois theme. And then all further performances of the work were banned on the basis of the Central Committee's 1946 decree "On the Repertoire of Dramatic Theatre and the Measures Necessary to Improve It".

Even Khrennikov's own composers' union and the music conservatories were critical of the opera. *Frol Skobeyev* was, they said, a product of "the decay of the bourgeoisie" and played to the "banal tastes" of the public at large. Much more of this kind of criticism and the general secretary could take his place among the maligned formalists and cosmopolitans.

But instead Khrennikov wrote to Stalin, explaining that he had been expressing Russia's national colours, including in the strong character of his hero *Frol Skobeyev*. In short, Skobeyev stood for the new Soviet man.

That last argument won Stalin over. He summoned the chairman of the Committee for Artistic Affairs, Polikarp Lebedev, and asked if he would prefer that the boyars in Khrennikov's opera were communists and sang modern-day songs. After this meeting, the ban on *Frol Skobeyev* was lifted.

While Khrennikov was one of the few who managed to dodge the regime's ideological decrees, he must have realized he was extremely lucky, for after *Frol Skobeyev* he lay low and concentrated on his work for the composers' union. At most, he composed film music.

In mid-May 1951, on two consecutive evenings, Shostakovich performed his *24 Preludes and Fugues* for piano in the union's concert hall. With the attack on formalism now in full swing, a tense atmosphere filled the hall. What kind of criticism awaited Shostakovich's performance? In the audience was the writer Lyubov Rudneva, who would later become a friend of Shostakovich. Thanks to her, we have a complete eyewitness account of the concert.

She describes in detail how exhausted and fragile Shostakovich looked after his performance. The hall was filled with young, admiring composers who regarded each new premiere of his music as an event of note. The pianists Maria Yudina and Tatiana Nikolaeva (the preludes and fugues are dedicated to Nikolaeva) were also in attendance. But in the front rows sat Shostakovich's colleagues, who had the power to persecute. In her report, Rudneva calls them untalented and jealous bureaucrats.

Shostakovich calmly explained to the audience what he aimed to achieve with this new work. He had been inspired by Bach: the bicentenary of his death had been commemorated the previous year in Leipzig, and Shostakovich had heard much exquisite music there. Before travelling to Leipzig, he had studied Rimsky-Korsakov's sixty fugues, written as a sort of training in polyphony.

Tchaikovsky, too, had written a series of preludes and fugues with the same goal. And because for Shostakovich composition was so laborious, he decided to do the same.

His words elicited some discomfort among those in the front rows. They began to whisper among themselves and fumble with their papers. After Shostakovich explained that the preludes and fugues were not a cycle per se but could be played in groups of three of four, his critics opened fire, accusing him of violating "reality" and failing to reflect the music of his contemporaries. And, of course, along came the accusations of formalism.

In 1954 a similar debate would take place concerning Shostakovich's Symphony No. 10, which Khrennikov criticized as an unconvincing musical reflection of life in the Soviet Union. Later that year, when it came time to award the Stalin Prizes, Khrennikov vetoed the symphony's nomination. He did, however, show his true colours as a nationalist hawk by supporting Shostakovich's patriotic cantata *The Sun Shines over Our Motherland*.

It is still unclear how Shostakovich dealt with this seesaw of praise and put-downs. Perhaps he felt trapped in an eternal tragicomedy, with no choice but to go with the flow. When he joined the Communist Party in 1960 and was named first secretary of the composers' union of the Russian Socialist Soviet Republic, he performed his role with aplomb. There was no more exemplary and obedient Party member: he participated in nearly every meeting of the Supreme Soviet and never missed a plenary meeting or political demonstration. Later he would write that he was so uninterested in the politics of music that participation was "torture by boredom" and the best thing to do was to go along with it.

He had become a puppet of the Party, literally applauding when the others did. Lyubov Rudneva recalls seeing Shostakovich clap enthusiastically at a speech in which Khrennikov made disparaging remarks about him. When asked why, Shostakovich replied that he didn't even realize he was being insulted. Another instance of this forced compliance was when he, Khrennikov, Kabalevsky, Khachaturian and Sviridov signed an open letter to *Pravda* in the early 1970s slandering the nuclear physicist and human rights activist Andrei Sakharov. In fact, he sympathized with the dissident scientist, just as he did with the writer Alexander Solzhenitsyn, whom he admired and yet against whom he signed a collective condemnation.

Khrennikov tried to get an obituary of Prokofiev printed in the newspapers after his death on 5 March 1953, but to no avail: since Joseph Stalin had died the same day, the papers devoted entire editions to eulogizing "the father of nations". Five days later, the leaders of the composers' union met to discuss Prokofiev's legacy—a composer whose work for years they had sabotaged at every opportunity. They decided to install a commemorative plaque at the front of his residence, publish a thirty-volume set of his entire oeuvre, provide his widow with a pension, place busts of him in the Moscow and Leningrad conservatories and organize memorial concerts.

Stalin was dead. Finally, everyone could breathe more or less freely and need not fear for their lives. This climate afforded Khrennikov the opportunity to compose a large-scale work: an opera based on Maxim Gorky's novel *Mother*. It was premiered in October 1957.

At one of the performances, Khrennikov was summoned to the box of the Party chairman, Nikita Khrushchev, who was delighted with the opera and praised its lyrical, heroic-sounding music. This was their first meeting, and afterwards Khrennikov dared ask Khrushchev if the Central Committee would consider rescinding the 1948 edict regarding formalism. Khrushchev replied that the Central Committee never did such things, but that in 1958 a new resolution would be introduced minus some of the more egregious aspects of the 1948 one. Composers previously accused of formalism would thus be rehabilitated, and it looked as though Soviet music was heading for a renaissance of sorts.

But reality, as so often throughout Russian history, turned out differently. Having been a loyal vassal to Andrei Zhdanov back in 1948, Khrennikov knew nothing was certain and felt it prudent to tread cautiously—that is, to appease the authorities—as regards Khrushchev's cultural thaw.

Khrushchev's secret speech to the 20th Party Congress in February 1956, which for the first time censured the crimes and hero-worship of Stalin, provoked an ideological struggle about the future of music, fought out on the pages of the *Sovetskaya muzyka* between the "conservatives" and "liberals". For even though a progressive wind appeared to be gathering in the arts, composers and music critics alike were unsure which way it would blow in the political arena.

Their answer came during the Second All-Union Congress in 1957. While Khrennikov's opening speech might have sounded mild compared to his militant tirade in 1948, he still vented arch-conservative opinions. His task, he felt, was to salvage socialist realism from the wreckage of Stalinism. Further liberalization of artistic aesthetics was out of the question. In fact, music had to revert to the doctrines of the 1930s, when socialist realism was "ripening", without the personality cult of Stalin.

Khrennikov's speech dashed the hopes of many composers. The repressive era of Zhdanov had not passed at all; his ideas were only less rigidly applied.

One could interpret Khrennikov's refusal to allow innovation as a sign that his beliefs about Soviet music were sincere, even if his excessive loyalty to the Communist Party was disastrous for cultural life. This approach was confirmed when, less than a week later, the Party ideologist and Central Committee member Dmitri Shepilov addressed the congress, reassuring the conservatives while at the same time giving hope to the progressives. Shepilov, an opportunist who had stood by Zhdanov's condemnation of Prokofiev and Shostakovich, but who in 1956 then contributed to Khrushchev's speech on the excesses of Stalin, seconded Khrennikov that socialist realism must be preserved. It was, he said, the most progressive musical model. Mindful of Lenin's relaxed approach to artists and the arts, he added that "cultural workers" fulfilling their patriotic duty must not be hindered by governmental orders and small-minded interference.

Notwithstanding his more liberal tone, Shepilov's speech made it abundantly clear that artistic policy was still the responsibility of the Communist Party and the government. He reiterated the criticism of Shostakovich and other composers accused of formalism back in 1948. Music, he said, must be "simple and accessible, it must reach out to the people, rich in ideas and emotions; it must be inspirational and reflect these new times, beautiful in melody and artistic perfection."

It was as though Zhdanov were speaking from the grave. The only concession was that decisions made by the Party could always be amended and that despite the ideological flaws in the work of leading Soviet composers, their contribution to the development of Soviet musical culture would not be denied.

The liberals, Shostakovich among them, were likely buoyed by Shepilov's words. When he took the microphone, Shostakovich did not ask for special concessions, but argued that composers be permitted to have creative discussions among themselves. This earned him a round of applause. He then added that "the secretariat of the composers' union [i.e. Khrennikov] has done more to freeze discussion than to develop it".

Open debate was suddenly possible, as an article in *Sovetskaya muzyka* shows. The sharpest edges of Shepilov's keynote address were blunted; the conservatives' hold on power appeared to be losing traction. That notion of artistic freedom was strengthened when Shepilov was removed from the Central Committee in June 1957 for having taken part in an attempt to depose the reform-minded Khrushchev.

Attacks on Western culture ceased and in 1958 the Soviet Union resumed cultural exchanges with the West. Moreover, work by writers and composers banned during the twenties and thirties could once again be published or performed.

Khrushchev understood better than anyone in Soviet politics that he needed the support of the intelligentsia to stand his ground against his hard-right adversaries. So, he did everything he could to get them on his side. In February 1958, he hosted a reception in the Kremlin Palace. It rained VIP speeches: Khrushchev himself addressed the scientists and writers, Bulganin toasted the filmmakers, Mikoyan engaged with the actors and directors. Pyotr Pospelov, a minor party official, praised the musicians for their many new compositions that reflected the heroic ideals of the proletarian revolution.

On behalf of his colleagues, Shostakovich lauded the excellent opportunities for talent development in the Soviet Union. He then gave a toast to the Communist Party, its Leninist Central Committee, the Soviet government and the Soviet people.

Shostakovich knew precisely how to appease the authorities. Especially when one considers that a year earlier, on the fortieth anniversary of the October Revolution, he completed his Symphony No. 11 ("The Year 1905"), a textbook example of socialist realism.

And yet this speech was probably not his own initiative, but rather was foisted on him by the authorities. As the most prominent victim of the government policies of 1936 and 1948, his orchestrated appearance at the Kremlin was surely meant to symbolize the reconciliation between the formerly demonized composers and the Party.

On 28 May 1958, the Central Committee adopted a resolution entitled "On Rectifying Errors in the Evaluation of the Operas *The Great Friendship*, *Bogdan Khmelnitsky* and *From the Bottom of My Heart*" (by Muradeli, Dankevich and Zhukovsky, respectively), repealing their censure. The resolution went on to retract the condemnation of composers including Shostakovich, Khachaturian, Shebalin, Myaskovsky and Prokofiev, who had been accused of formalism—regardless of their occasional "wrong tendencies"—in effect, rehabilitating them.

Oddly enough, neither Stalin nor Zhdanov, the architects of the 1948 decree against formalism, is mentioned in the new resolution. Instead, Molotov, Malenkov and Beria took the fall. They were blamed for exerting misguided influence on Stalin, encouraging him to assume a "subjective approach" to certain artworks. Rather than rescinding the previous resolution, the Central Committee appeared to reiterate its so-called benefits to the development of Soviet music.

Khrennikov's role in all this is unclear. Yet the fact that the resolution not only bolstered his own position but also exclusively addressed music and none of the other art forms that had long suffered under Stalin's heavy-handed rules could be taken as a sign that he might well have had a hand in it.

Khrushchev's cultural thaw made it possible for many Soviet artists to travel abroad, and musicians proved to be ideal cultural ambassadors. Khrennikov took his first foreign trip in September 1958, to the Brussels World's Fair. A year later, he and a group of prominent Soviet composers and performers, including Shostakovich, Kabalevsky, Dankevich, Rostropovich and his wife Galina Vishnevskaya went to the United States. The trip was a personal success as well: Khrennikov's Symphony No. 1 was performed in Philadelphia, Boston and New York.

The tricky diplomacy of being a Soviet composer became evident during a press conference at which Shostakovich was asked how he could sit at the same table with Khrennikov, who had castigated him a decade earlier. Without so much as batting an eye (and with the camouflaging help of his thick glasses), Shostakovich calmly answered that Khrennikov had indeed criticized him in 1948, but that he had returned the criticism, which within the composers' union was perfectly normal. Shostakovich also praised the Communist Party as humankind's most progressive force. He was clearly not planning to turn himself into a dissident.

In 1961 Khrennikov returned to the United States, this time to the west coast. Meeting Stravinsky there, he invited the famous émigré to celebrate his eightieth birthday, on 17 June, in the Soviet Union. Stravinsky, an avowed anti-communist, had already been invited to the White House by President Kennedy that day and turned down the invitation. But he did promise to visit his homeland that autumn.

From the moment Stravinsky stepped out of the aeroplane in Moscow, he was given a hero's welcome. His concerts in Moscow and Leningrad were sold out, all thanks to Khrennikov.

During this period, Khrennikov worked tirelessly to aid needy union members and their families. In the late 1950s, for instance, he sorted Prokofiev's first wife Lina with a flat and a pension after she returned, rehabilitated, from the gulag. In 1974 he convinced KGB chief Yuri Andropov to allow her to emigrate to the UK to join her son Oleg.

Shostakovich, too, got a helping hand. In June 1961, Khrennikov appealed to the Central Committee to rescind the long-standing ban on his opera *Lady Macbeth of Mtsensk*. The committee agreed to listen to the revised version; as Shostakovich was unable to play the demanding piano score himself, he asked his friend Mieczysław Weinberg to do so. He played the complete score, got up and left without waiting for their discussion. Two hours later, Shostakovich went outside with the good news that the ban had been lifted.

The 1979 publication of Solomon Volkov's *Testimony* disrupted Khrennikov's comfortable existence. But, no matter how harsh the criticism, he did not respond publicly. His friends neither refuted nor substantiated the accusations. Only in 2012 did the pianist Evgeny Kissin—once a protégé of Khrennikov's—shed more light on Volkov's book. And the book did not fare well.

Kissin's main criticism is that Shostakovich never witnessed first-hand most of the things of which he accuses Khrennikov. For example, Khrennikov is said to have signed a list of composers to be arrested, while such a list never actually existed.

But Kissin is treading on thin ice when he casts doubt on Shostakovich's assertion that Khrennikov and his cronies actively pushed him to the edge. Because, despite Shostakovich's two Stalin Prizes (in 1950 and 1951), there is no disputing that no single composer had been systematically hounded the way Shostakovich had been, his whole life long. The State propaganda machine pulled out all the stops to destroy him, and the one responsible for that propaganda was Khrennikov. About his fear of the Soviet authorities, Shostakovich is said to have told his friend Lev Lebedinsky: "I am scared to death of them. You don't know the whole truth. From childhood I have been doing things that I wanted not to do. I'm a wretched alcoholic. I've been a whore, I am and always will be a whore."

While in the early 1950s Khrennikov had styled himself as a Maecenas of Soviet musical life, the tide turned in the mid-eighties during the perestroika and glasnost of the new Party leader, Mikhail Gorbachev. Khrennikov's absolute power was a thing of the past.

The composer Vladimir Dashkevich fired the first salvo in February 1987 in the government newspaper *Izvestia*. His article laid the blame for all that had gone wrong with Soviet music for the past four decades squarely at Khrennikov's feet. It also held Khrennikov responsible for the Central Committee resolution against formalism.

A year later, in May 1988, a similar article appeared in the magazine *Sovetskaya kultura* by the pianist Vera Gornostaeva, who had the reputation of being a schemer. Her article was titled "Who Owns Art?".

Khrennikov, still under the illusion of omnipotence, hastened to defend himself. Firstly, not he but Stalin and Zhdanov should take the blame for the persecution of Soviet musicians. Secondly, he had protected members of the composers' union from Stalin's repression, and it was thanks to him that the infamous resolution had been rescinded. And lastly, under the dictatorship his own father and two of his brothers had been arrested and imprisoned, so to accuse him, of all people, of Stalinism was insane.

Pyotr Merkulov, the grandson of the stage director Vsevolod Meyerhold (executed by Stalin in 1940) and an employee of the composers' union, defended Khrennikov and in turn accused Gornostaeva of libel.

My friend, the violist Mikhail Zemtsov, is similarly well disposed towards Khrennikov. "I was in his composition class at the Moscow Conservatory," he tells me. "The consensus was that if anyone else had been in charge of the composers' union, there would have been many more victims."

Even Dmitri Ferschtman won't hear an ill word about him. "He helped me find a place to live," he says. "And besides being a very kind man, he was also a good composer. His music for *They Met in Moscow* is brilliant."

So, judging Khrennikov is not as simple as one might think. Certainly not after his function as general secretary of the composers' union became redundant after the disintegration of the Soviet Union in 1991. In the new Russia, he was a nobody. Forgotten, as if he and his music politics had never existed.

That wall of silence lasted for three years, until his eightieth birthday. It seemed as if his old age softened people's opinion of him, and a gala was planned in his honour. Popular singers like Joseph Kobzon and the conductor Valery Gergiev took part. Gergiev in particular had much to thank Khrennikov for: the elder musician had advised him to programme his concerts in Russia in a way that showed off his patriotism.

In the West, opinions were less charitable. Khrennikov was still seen as a symbol of the Soviet dictatorship and many were unwilling to forgive his past, disregarding the positive work he did for the composers' union. For instance, several months after his ballet *Napoleon Bonaparte* had its premiere in the Kremlin Palace on 3 October 1995, the *New York Times* published an article about him with the headline "Stalin's Music Man is a Kremlin Star Again". There wasn't a good word about him in it. Nor did it even touch on his music, which makes one wonder if its author had even seen the ballet. No matter that the ballet was a success in Russia and also in Europe, Asia and South America, Khrennikov would never again rise above his sullied reputation.

Khrennikov died of a heart attack in 2007, six years after his wife Klara. He was ninety-four years old and had led the composers' union for more than four decades. On his deathbed, he said to his daughter, "Natasha, this is the end. Bury me in Yelets." He wanted to return to his birthplace, to his family, to the world from which he had grown into not only a talented musician, but also the most influential and longest-serving Soviet official in the field of music.

Khrennikov will always remain an ambiguous, controversial figure in musical history. He loyally carried out Stalin's orders until the dictator's last breath. Whether he did so out of vanity, ambition and greed, from the conviction that he was serving the interests of new Soviet music, or simply out of fear—we will never know, if only because we never stood in his shoes.

10

Solidarity with Dissidents

The Rostropovich Festival is in full swing at the end of March 2012. For a full month, an international line-up of musicians will pay tribute to the world-famous cellist, who died five years previously. Nearly every Moscow concert hall takes part in the festivities.

The festival opens with the unveiling of a bronze-and-stone statue of Mstislav Rostropovich on a small square, right across from the imposing block of flats where he, his wife, and their two daughters lived. It is a work by the sculptor Alexander Rukavishnikov and the architect Igor Voskresensky, commissioned by the Moscow City Council.

The larger-than-life cellist is hunched over his instrument. His posthumous face is more creased than I remember, his jaw more forceful. But even if it's not a particularly accurate likeness, it suits him well. Rostropovich had more resolve than any other Soviet musician: when push came to shove, he was prepared to stand up to anyone who dared to defy him and his principles.

On one face of the rough granite pedestal is inscribed a page from music that Sergei Prokofiev wrote for him. I wish there was a crank I could turn to hear the bronze cellist play.

Since the monument's unveiling, older Russians have come to lay flowers on the flat yellow stone jutting out from the base, on which his name is etched. The flowers—roses or carnations—lie in pairs, for in Russia an even number is a tribute to the deceased. Some cross themselves, others say a few words to the bronze giant. A few times I pick up the word *spasibo*—"thank you".

The opening evening, in the Moscow Conservatory, features a concert performance of Shostakovich's *Lady Macbeth of Mtsensk*. Olga, one of Rostropovich's daughters, is the host. A cellist herself, she says she doesn't dare play here in front of a metres-tall photo of her father and her mother, the soprano Galina Vishnevskaya, in the hall. No one can compete with two megastars like these.

My first encounter with Rostropovich was when I discovered classical music as a child. In the early 1970s, my mother bought a Philips stereo system and suddenly the LPs we had been playing on a simple phonograph for years sounded like a live concert. One of these albums was of the Brahms Double Concerto, played by Rostropovich and David Oistrakh; the Cleveland Orchestra was led by George Szell. The recording, made in 1970, had won an Edison Award. As I fidgeted with the volume knob on the new system, I could not get enough of the musical passion, the sublime tenderness and the driving strength of both players. It was Brahms at his best.

The photo on the purple-edged record jacket (which I still cherish) features the three musicians standing in front of the hall where the concerto was recorded. Oistrakh and Szell beam with satisfied smiles, but Rostropovich is laughing out loud. Alongside making music, his greatest strength was his humour. I would witness it time and again whenever I saw him perform.

The same year as the Brahms recording, Rostropovich and his wife had supported the dissident author Alexander Solzhenitsyn, and the authorities retaliated by forbidding the couple to perform abroad or in Moscow or Leningrad for three years. In 1974, sick and tired of the authorities' harassment, Rostropovich left the Soviet Union; his wife and daughters followed him shortly thereafter. A year later they were stripped of their passports. This was the regime's way of striking back at so-called "traitors".

The forty-seven-year-old Rostropovich was at the height of his musical fame and, having taken leave of his adoring home audience, concertized all over the world. And if anyone had rejuvenated the cello repertoire, it was Rostropovich.

Mstislav Rostropovich, nicknamed "Slava", was born on 17 March 1927 in Baku, the capital of Soviet Azerbaijan. His father, Leopold, was himself a brilliant cellist who had studied in Paris with Pablo Casals. His mother, the pianist Sofia Fedotova, was born into a family of Jewish musicians from Orenburg. The couple first lived in Saratov, in the Volga region, where their daughter Veronika was born in 1925. When Leopold landed a job at the newly opened conservatory in Baku, the family moved to the Caucasus.

Life in the Soviet Union in those days was harsh. Constant scarcity—food, furniture, clothing—was part of everyday reality. So much so that Sofia was dead set against having another child. When she became pregnant anyway, she even tried to induce a miscarriage by exercising fanatically. It failed, and the family soon had another mouth to feed. (The poverty of those early years would colour Rostropovich's attitude toward money for the rest of his life. The cellist Dmitri Ferschtman told me he "had never met anyone as money-crazed as Rostropovich. He always wanted to be rich. And his talent made that possible.")

Leopold and Sofia moved to Moscow in 1931, hoping to provide their children with a decent musical education there. After revolution and civil war, there was mass migration from the countryside to the cities. Farmers even brought their livestock with them, installing it on their urban balconies. In less than ten years, Moscow would be transformed from an ancient city with hundreds of churches and monasteries into a dynamic centre of industry and the face of the new Soviet Union. Factories shot up like weeds. Labourers, however, were even worse off than under the tsars, and their only solace was the promise of a better life once socialism took hold.

The Rostropoviches, too, were as poor as ever. Leopold did find work at the Moscow Radio Committee, which made programmes for the state broadcaster, but the huge influx of migrants made housing scarce. After living for a while in a single room in a *kommunalka* they moved to a one-room flat on Kozitsky Lane. Little Slava slept on a camp bed under his parents' Becker grand piano. A while later they moved again, to a small flat at 3 Nemirovich-Danchenko Street, where they would remain until the mid-1950s.

Slava took cello lessons from his father, who by now was teaching at the Gnessin Institute. He remembers being a lazy student, putting away his instrument as soon as his parents left the house and unpacking it again just before they came home, as if he'd been practising the whole time.

At the Moscow Conservatory he studied with his uncle Semyon Kozolupov, who ran the cello department and taught Slava his fiery bowing technique. Kozolupov was a peculiar man, for even though his brother-in-law was a far superior cellist, he refused to give him a teaching post. Despite this small-mindedness, he was an excellent teacher to Leopold's son.

✻

Rostropovich made his debut in 1940 with Saint-Saëns's Cello Concerto No. 1 at an open-air concert in Slovyansk, eastern Ukraine. It was a success, kicking off what promised to be a stellar career. But the German invasion of June 1941 turned everything upside down. Talented Soviet artists were evacuated by train from Leningrad and Moscow to cities beyond the Ural.

The Rostropoviches ended up in Orenburg, where Leopold taught at the local music school. The Maly Theatre of Leningrad, along with its conductors Boris Chaykin and Kirill Kondrashin, had also been sent there. Having such a fine orchestra at hand created a rich cultural climate, and the fifteen-year-old Rostropovich benefitted from it not only as a cellist but also as a pianist and composer. In April 1942, he gave a concert of Soviet composers, and early the next year he appeared as soloist with the orchestra, playing Tchaikovsky's *Variations on a Rococo Theme*, which would later become a staple of his repertoire. That winter, the young cellist earned extra ration coupons by joining a travelling orchestra brigade that entertained villagers in the region. Right around this time, his father died unexpectedly.

The German defeat at Stalingrad in early 1943 meant that Rostropovich could return to Moscow. "He arrived at the train station empty-handed," Dmitri Ferschtman tells me. "There he met a beautiful Armenian woman, and they moved in together the very same day. That's typical of his impetuous character. They were together for two years. There were other girlfriends after that, but then he met Galina Vishnevskaya and forgot the rest."

As his father would have wanted, he resumed his lessons with Kozolupov. He also enrolled in the composition class of Dmitri Shostakovich, with whom he would become friends for life.

After the war, his career skyrocketed. He entered the All-Union Competition and won first prize in the cello category. He played so well that Shostakovich, the jury chairman, did not even want to award a second prize because the difference was so great. The already well-known Sviatoslav Richter, unsurprisingly, won first prize for piano.

Shostakovich's assessment of Rostropovich's musicianship would be confirmed over and over in the years to come. In 1964, he said of the cellist, "Whether he plays Bach or Prokofiev, Haydn or Hindemith, we hear in his playing the taut rhythm of contemporary life, the artist's clear and bold representation of the times we live in."

But Rostropovich was more than just a musician. As his biographer and student Elizabeth Wilson has chronicled, he always spoke up against injustice. While the regime succeeded in intimidating most of his fellow musicians, Rostropovich dared to stick up for friends who were being harassed by the authorities. The 1948 Central Committee resolution against formalism resulted in the firing of his conservatory teachers Shebalin and Shostakovich for "professional incompetence". As one of the few who had the courage to protest (some of his fellow students even supported the action), Rostropovich refused to attend composition lessons any longer. He had no stomach for the witch hunt against his two professors and other composers like Prokofiev, Myaskovsky and Khachaturian. Politics and music, he insisted, were separate affairs.

In 1960, he likewise broke with the violinist Leonid Kogan, with whom he and pianist Emil Gilels had a long-standing piano trio. Kogan, who was married to Gilels's sister, turned out to be a KGB informant—since 1945, no less. The secret police had blackmailed Kogan into passing on information from two American acquaintances who regularly visited him in Moscow. He had no choice: either snitch for the KGB or be packed off to Siberia and say goodbye to his career. Tragic as this might sound for Kogan, it turned out that he had kept a dossier on his trio partners as well. When he found out, Rostropovich put an end to their friendship and their brilliant and celebrated seven-year musical collaboration.

The incident also put Gilels in a bind. He no longer felt he could trust his sister Yelizaveta (Kogan's wife) and henceforth always watched his words when around his family. The siblings' relationship soured to the point that, at the end of his life, Gilels trusted his brother-in-law more than his sister.

The plot thickens: both Kogan and Gilels died under peculiar circumstances in the 1980s. Kogan at age 58 of a heart attack on the train from Moscow to Yaroslavl, and Gilels three years later, at 68, during a check-up at his cardiologist's. Sviatoslav Richter, Gilels's arch-rival, claimed that he had been given an injection of the wrong medicine. Indeed, shortly before the tragedy, a panicked Gilels had said to a friend, the Israeli conductor Uri Segal, "They're murdering me. Just look at my trembling hands. How do they expect me to play a concert?" Segal pinned it all on Gilels's tormentors at the KGB.

In April 1955, at a reception in Moscow's Metropol Hotel, Rostropovich met the Bolshoi Theatre's newest star, the twenty-nine-year-old Galina Vishnevskaya. He and a few other young musicians found themselves sharing a table with the beautiful soprano with the jet-black hair. As usual, Rostropovich regaled his tablemates with a steady stream of anecdotes. At first, Vishnevskaya paid him no notice, partly because she found his given name so hard to pronounce. But, as she stood up to leave, he asked if he could walk her home.

It was a balmy spring evening; Moscow at its finest. As in a romantic movie, they ambled down the boulevards lined with fragrant trees. Animated as always, Rostropovich darted around her like an excited foal. When they arrived at her flat, he produced a box of chocolates before saying goodnight.

Shortly thereafter, they bumped into each other again in Prague, where Vishnevskaya was to appear in Tchaikovsky's *Eugene Onegin* at the Spring Festival. This time they were staying at the same hotel, and at the breakfast table Rostropovich once again launched into jokes and anecdotes. He still had never heard her sing and therefore saw her, as did most others, not as a prima donna but as a beautiful young woman. She soon fell for his spontaneity, sincerity and humour.

Later that day, they happened upon an old woman selling lilies of the valley. Rostropovich bought the entire basket and gave them to Galina. Back at the hotel, he sat down at the piano to play for her and apologized for not being able to attend her performance that evening, as he had a concert of his own. He then sank to his knees and said, "Forgive me, but when we first met in Moscow I couldn't help noticing your beautiful legs. I wanted to kiss your feet. But I'll get up now because you have to get to the theatre. Until tomorrow."

That evening, too, he had flowers delivered to the theatre. And the evening after that, flowers and dill pickles. After four days together in Prague they decided to marry once they were both back in Moscow.

In her 1987 autobiography *Galina*, Vishnevskaya describes Rostropovich's marriage proposal: he came to pick her up in a taxi filled to the brim with red roses. Asked later if he ever regretted such a snap decision, he replied, "Yes—I wasted three whole days of my life."

The couple soon belonged to the upper echelons of Soviet music life and were showered with privileges and distinctions. But a pair of concerts in November 1967 in the provincial city of Ryazan marked the opening of a tumultuous new chapter. The writer Alexander Solzhenitsyn, whom Rostropovich greatly admired, happened to be in the audience. The next day Rostropovich looked him up. It would be the beginning of a long friendship, but one with severe consequences for Rostropovich.

Alexander Solzhenitsyn (1918–2008) was the most famous writer in the Soviet Union at that time. In 1962 the literary magazine *Novy mir* ("New World") published his novella *One Day in the Life of Ivan Denisovich*, an exposé of the extreme hardships millions of Soviet citizens suffered in the labour camps. As part of his anti-Stalinist campaign, party leader Khrushchev had approved publication of the book, apparently underestimating the effect it would have on the Soviet public. That issue of *Novy mir* sold out within a few days. Party zealots, shocked by what they read, turned on the writer and did their best to hinder any further projects. They managed to keep his play *The Tenderfoot and the Tart* from being staged and denied him the Lenin Prize.

After Khrushchev was ousted by these same hardliners following his mishandling of the Cuban missile crisis, pressure on Solzhenitsyn increased. The KGB began surveilling him and confiscated his archives. They also put pressure on *Novy mir* in an effort to prevent publication of his novel *Cancer Ward*. The magazine's chief editor, Alexander Tvardovsky, was already in hot water because it was he who had secured permission from Khrushchev to publish *Ivan Denisovich*.

Undaunted, Solzhenitsyn launched a counter-attack in the form of an open letter to the Fourth Congress of the authors' union. He criticized the censorship of his work, condemned the KGB's harassment and lambasted the union for being too weak-willed to stand up for him. The union did not respond. But when *Cancer Ward* and *In the First Circle* were published abroad in Russian over the next few years, they expelled him.

In summer 1968, the Soviet army invaded Czechoslovakia to quash the Prague Spring. At the same time, Rostropovich appeared at a Proms concert at the Royal Albert Hall in London with the USSR State Symphony Orchestra. Shouts of "Soviet fascists go home!" were directed at the orchestra, but when Rostropovich came on stage the audience calmed down. In solidarity with the Czech people, he played Dvořák's Cello Concerto with such feeling that the audience cheered him afterwards. His loyalty to his country had evaporated. "Without our suspecting it," Vishnevskaya wrote in her memoirs, "the events in Czechoslovakia had slammed the book shut on what had been our good life."

After that, the incidents began to pile up. In October 1969, Rostropovich got a phone call from the writer Lydia Chukovskaya to say that Solzhenitsyn was probably dying; his cancer had returned. He was living in an unheated dacha at the time, at kilometre marker 83 along the Mozhaysk highway. Rostropovich drove out at once and found the writer in bed with acute sciatica; he insisted that Solzhenitsyn move into his—that is, Rostropovich's own—comfortable dacha. The author accepted.

When the Minister of Culture, Yekaterina Furtseva, got wind of this, she ordered Rostropovich to evict Solzhenitsyn. His reply:

"Only if you provide him with a warm roof over his head and he leaves of his own accord."

Many years later, Rostropovich said of the "Solzhenitsyn affair": "When we took him into our house it became clear how every personal conflict was elevated to a political one: if you protect someone who is against us, you are against us, too. I was thrust into a political position not of my own choosing—unlike most of us who had reached the top of the pyramid. We left politics to the politicians. But the way Solzhenitsyn had been treated opened my eyes once and for all."

A new and dramatic chapter began when in 1970 Solzhenitsyn was awarded the Nobel Prize in Literature "for the ethical force with which he has pursued the indispensable traditions of Russian literature". The Soviet authorities were furious, and they forbade the writer from travelling to Sweden to accept the award. But even this did not deter him, and he made sure every new work was published abroad, even if it was banned at home. In doing so, he sealed his own fate.

In September 1973, Solzhenitsyn heard that the KGB had managed to get its hands on the manuscript of *The Gulag Archipelago*. Worried that an unauthorized (i.e. censored) version would hit the foreign markets, he gave his permission for publication, and in early 1974 excerpts from the book appeared in the Sunday editions of Western newspapers. The revelations about the fate of the many thousands of innocent prisoners in the gulag was bombshell news. The West was being shown the true face of the Soviet Union.

The Soviet authorities had no choice but to respond. In February 1974, they expelled Solzhenitsyn to Frankfurt, West Germany; his wife and children were allowed to follow him later.

The Gulag Archipelago was still banned in the Soviet Union, but it did circulate in *samizdat* (the underground press), whereby typed and retyped manuscripts were passed around. This is how all of my Russian friends and acquaintances read it.

Meanwhile, Rostropovich continued to advocate for his friend. His first step was to alert the British embassy via his pupil Elizabeth Wilson, the daughter of the ambassador and later his biographer. From that moment on, the Soviet authorities regarded him as complicit, and there were immediate repercussions.

A few days before Rostropovich was to leave for London to record Witold Lutosławski's Cello Concerto and be presented with a gold medal from the Royal Philharmonic Society, he was informed that the trip was cancelled—a typical way of exerting pressure in those days. Not one to take such things lying down, he turned to the composer Benjamin Britten, who in turn contacted the Soviet authorities. Fearing a scandal, they rescinded the travel ban.

Rostropovich was to appear in London with the Bournemouth Festival Orchestra. On his way to rehearsal, a British journalist asked him whether it was true that he had given Solzhenitsyn sanctuary and what he thought of him being awarded the Nobel Prize. Rostropovich wisely declined to comment on the matter. But at the same time he realized there was no turning back and resolved to compose an open letter after returning to the USSR.

Back at home, Vishnevskaya tried her best to talk her husband out of it, fearing reprisals, but the argument proved fruitless. So, on 31 October, as he was leaving for a tour of Austria and Germany, Rostropovich posted four copies of the letter, each addressed to a major Soviet newspaper: *Pravda, Izvestia, Literaturnaya gazeta* and *Sovetskaya kultura*.

At first there was no response. But when he was confronted with journalists and television crews upon arriving at the concert hall in Bregenz, Austria, he knew his aim had been accomplished. Just before the concert, the organizers handed him the English and German translations of his letter. Apparently realizing there was no stopping him, the Soviet authorities leaked his letter to the Western media and decided to leave him be for the moment.

Back in his hotel, Rostropovich was met by officials from the Soviet embassy who politely asked him for an explanation. Fearful of a cultural crown jewel like Rostropovich seeking asylum in the West, they treated him with kid gloves for the rest of the tour.

Only upon his return to Moscow did he realize the full ramifications of his actions. During his absence the campaign against the political dissident movement had intensified. Some of the measures were so extreme that it almost felt like a return to the dark years of the Stalinist terror. The Soviet press referred to Solzhenitsyn as an "internal emigrant" who was hostile to all aspects of Soviet life, while the "imperialist West" hailed him as a great Russian writer.

Although Rostropovich expected to be reprimanded in some way, he also counted on his international reputation offering some protection. That was an idle hope: when he was to perform Beethoven's Triple Concerto with Sviatoslav Richter and David Oistrakh on the occasion of the composer's two hundredth birthday, the Ministry of Culture informed him that he would not be allowed to play.

Richter and Oistrakh were told to find a new cellist, but they refused. So the first concert was cancelled. But the second concert went ahead, with Rostropovich. When the soloists walked on stage, they were given a seven-minute standing ovation.

✿

Shostakovich, an admirer of Solzhenitsyn but not a friend, privately condemned Rostropovich's actions to a civil servant at the Ministry of Culture. According to the civil servant, Shostakovich pressed him to do everything they could to save "Slava": "He is our pride, our country made him great and brought him international fame."

The authorities then put Shostakovich to work to repair as best he could the damage to both parties. He even considered flying to West Germany, where Rostropovich was on tour, to convince him to stop publicly defending Solzhenitsyn. The writer himself never forgave Shostakovich for this.

In her memoirs, Vishnevskaya recalls Shostakovich often admonishing her husband: "Don't waste your energy. Work, play. You're living here, in this country, and you must see everything as it really is. Don't have any illusions. There is no other life. Just be thankful you're still allowed to breathe!"

Just how significant Solzhenitsyn was to many of his countrymen became clear to me at his funeral in Moscow on 6 August 2008. An hours-long service was held in the sixteenth-century Donskoy Monastery, replete with all the pomp and liturgy of the Russian Orthodox Church. Many hundreds of admirers had come to pay their last respects. They varied in age and religious tint, but they had one thing in common: admiration for him and his books about the gulag. "He was the first one to tell the world what was going on in the Soviet Union," says the writer and former dissident Yelena Dyakova. "We stole—and devoured—copies of *Ivan Denisovich* from the library. And then came *The Gulag Archipelago*, which we rewrote by hand in order to distribute it via *samizdat*. Alexander Isaevich Solzhenitsyn was a saint, and a great writer."

Then-President Medvedev also attended the service. He crossed himself more than anyone else there—but the wrong way around, like a clumsy convert. Solzhenitsyn's widow, sons and grandchildren observed it with resignation. Next to me, an admirer of the author shrugged his shoulders and sighed, "It's all politics. The president's not here for Alexander Isaevich, that's for sure."

The hymns were followed by a three-volley salute, and then the military band played a march—Solzhenitsyn, after all, had been a captain in the Red Army before he was sent to the gulag for critical comments he made about Stalin in letters to a friend. As the military band marched off, I noticed that attached to the banner one of the soldiers carried was a black ribbon, the army's symbol of mourning.

After Medvedev (surrounded by a bevy of female secretaries) left, civilians were allowed to approach, and they thronged to get a glimpse of the coffin. In the crowd was a Russian emigrant, Natalie Lobastov, who had travelled specially from Australia for the funeral. "My whole family was wiped out under communism," she told me, "and Alexander Isaevich was the first to write about it. To this day, no one has been called to account for those crimes." She pushed further, clutching two roses.

Behind her in the queue was the thirty-five-year-old poet Sergei Brel, a good friend of mine. "Aside from being a great writer, Solzhenitsyn was also this country's historian of the twentieth century," he said as he placed a collection of his poetry on the grave and crossed himself.

Was Rostropovich ever afraid during those days of resistance? As one of the Soviet Union's most celebrated musicians, he had a lot to lose. For an answer to this question, I pay another visit to the violist Leonid Rusanovsky. He had met Rostropovich in 1969, when the latter conducted the student orchestra of the Kyiv Conservatory. When I ask what it was like to play under him, he says, "He was one of us. There was no distance whatsoever between him and the students. But, at the same time, he was off limits, because we knew how important he was. Musicians like him were the elites. And, of course, he enjoyed the protection of the party bigwigs. That's why he dared to stick up for Solzhenitsyn."

The same went for Shostakovich at that time, says Rusanovsky. "You could always fall out of favour, but only under Stalin did you have to fear for your life. That's why Shostakovich adapted and Rostropovich rebelled—after the dictator's death, he could openly side with a dissident."

In April 1971, the London Symphony Orchestra, led by Benjamin Britten, played in Leningrad during the "British Music Days". The programme included Britten's Cello Concerto (with Rostropovich as soloist) and his Piano Concerto (featuring Sviatoslav Richter). The venue, built to hold an audience of 2,000, was packed to double capacity. After all, foreign stars like Benjamin Britten were a rarity in those days.

Despite the success of the concert, the authorities had not forgiven Rostropovich his efforts on Solzhenitsyn's behalf. As punishment, the state impresario sent him on a tour of the Central Asian Soviet republics and Kamchatka, where, after spending many hours in aeroplanes, he was made to perform in draughty auditoriums for indifferent audiences. Moreover, the Bolshoi Theatre's management forced him to step down as conductor, and he was henceforth forbidden to play concerts abroad. But perhaps the nastiest move of all was that his students were thereafter regularly questioned by the KGB.

After that, Rostropovich was allowed to perform only sporadically in Moscow: in 1972, he played a concert with concertos by Lutosławski, Haydn and Dvořák; and in 1973, he conducted a student orchestra performance of Shostakovich's Symphony No. 14.

Not only in Moscow, but elsewhere in the Soviet Union, too, his performances were scaled back. He was banned from performing in Kyiv, Leningrad and Riga, and even concerts in small provincial venues were suddenly cancelled. And if he was allowed to perform, his name never appeared on concert posters, in programme books or in the local press, meaning that he often played for empty auditoriums. "He told me that in those days he had become wallpaper," Dmitri Ferschtman told me. "And this while he had breathed new life into the repertoire by popularizing the cello as a solo instrument. Until he fell out of favour, he played upward of thirty-five cello concertos a year."

Nor was he mentioned in reviews. Like so many fallen celebrities during the Stalinist terror, he had become a non-person: entries excised from the *Great Soviet Encyclopaedia*, with new persons or topics pasted over them. The only good thing that happened to Rostropovich in those years was that he was allowed to tour the Caucasus together with the composer Aram Khachaturian, performing in Yerevan and in his hometown, Baku.

The authorities' promise of reinstating permission to perform outside the USSR, however, were hollow. One day he was summoned by a high-ranking official of the Central Committee, who said (freely quoting Lenin), "Whoever is not for us, is against us." To which Rostropovich shot back, "When I play Dvořák's Cello

Concerto, which I do very well, can you tell whether I'm for or against you?"

The pressure continued to mount. In April 1972, Rostropovich was allowed to play a few concerts in Austria and Hungary, but when in January 1974 Yehudi Menuhin invited him to Paris to perform for UNESCO, the organizers received a phone call from Moscow that Rostropovich was indisposed and could not attend. Menuhin didn't believe a word of it and rang Rostropovich directly. Galina Vishnevskaya answered and told him her husband was not at all sick; in fact, he was the picture of health.

Menuhin put pressure on both the Russian Minister of Culture and the state impresario Gosconcert. With success: Rostropovich went to Paris and performed Beethoven's *Archduke Trio* with Menuhin and the pianist Wilhelm Kempff.

In his Paris hotel, he bumped into his friend David Oistrakh, who invited him for a stroll. He said to Rostropovich, "I admire your purity, your courage, everything you do. But tomorrow you will read a letter to *Pravda*, signed by me, in which I denounce you. I beg you to find the strength to forgive me." He then told Rostropovich a story of an incident during the Great Terror that had destroyed him as a person. At that time, around 1936, Oistrakh and his wife Tamara lived in a block of flats where one day the secret police came and rounded up practically the entire building. Just the Oistrakhs and one man, in the flat across the hall from his, were left. Tamara had packed a valise for him with clothes and biscuits should they come to get him too. This usually happened at around four in the morning. One morning they heard knocking on the building's outside door. They leapt out of bed, terrified. Minutes lasted an eternity. They heard the footsteps on the stairs and waited for the knock. It came: at the door to the other flat.

What Oistrakh then said had been true for an entire generation: "This is what Soviet power did to people. They were forced to adopt a second nature, to think and act differently." These words applied to himself, but also to Shostakovich. They had to live with the reality that the regime could destroy their career at any given moment.

I can only vaguely imagine Oistrakh's fear. But one incident in my own life gave me a taste of how people must have felt every day during Stalin's terror.

In August 2009, I was doing some reporting in Kabardino-Balkaria, a Russian republic in the North Caucasus. I had gone to its capital, Nalchik, to interview the human-rights activist Magomed Abubakarov about the local authorities' ongoing intimidation of the Muslim inhabitants. They were steadily accused of Islamic terrorism, when all they did was protest the misappropriation of state funds. Rather than going to schools and hospitals, public money disappeared into the pockets of corrupt politicians.

Abubakarov and I were barely finished with the interview when I was accosted by a small battalion of heavily armed policemen, who at gunpoint demanded to see my correspondent's accreditation, my passport and my Moscow registration. In that last document they discovered a misspelling and hauled me off to the police station. I was fingerprinted while a semi-literate agent wrote down the official charges. "Why don't you write about the Mt Elbrus instead of human rights?" he asked as he struggled to copy my name onto the form.

I was then taken by convoy to the courthouse, where several hours later a hastily summoned judge appeared: a fat, sympathetic man who could have stepped straight out of Gogol's *Dead Souls* and was at most a bit irritated at having been roused from his afternoon nap. Leaning against the wall of the small courtroom, a very young FSB agent kept guard, a pistol tucked into the waistband of his jeans. He had a supercilious smirk on his lips, as though he alone were in charge that day. And that turned out to be the case, because, after the judge had asked a few random questions about the Netherlands ("a land of cheese and tulips near Latvia, correct?"), the FSB boy whispered something to him that spoiled his good humour. He adjourned the sitting with the announcement that he would return the next morning at ten o'clock with the verdict.

By now it was evening. Abubakarov advised against driving back to Pyatigorsk, in the nearby region of Stavropol where I had been staying the past few days, saying they might stage a car accident to make sure I did not make it to court the next day. Who "they" were was by now quite clear.

So, he took me to the local hotel, a tall building whose marble-and-bling lobby was populated by the local elite: men in suits, all of them, like the FSB lad, with a pistol tucked into their waistband. This threatening tableau was underscored by the Kalashnikov-wielding security men in bulletproof vests at the entrance. Not exactly a carefree holiday resort, that Nalchik.

"If anyone knocks on your door tonight, don't open up. Call me," Abubakarov said as he took me to my room on the top floor. "Recently another foreign correspondent was dragged out of his room and beaten up out on the street, probably by the FSB. Slide some furniture against the door just to be on the safe side, and lie low until I come get you in the morning."

I tried to phone my wife in Moscow and my colleagues at the newspaper in the Netherlands, but my mobile's battery was nearly empty, and I was without a charger. Shut off from the world, I spent a sleepless night, certain that I would meet the same fate as my unfortunate colleague. For the first time ever, I truly feared for my life.

The next morning, the court ruled that because of the misspelling in my registration I would be expelled from the country. The judge carefully avoided making any eye contact with me as he read out the sentence. "One less busybody," the FSB agent, who had undoubtedly dictated the terms, must have thought.

Once back in Moscow, I appealed the decision. When the case was brought to court a month later, I was acquitted immediately after a telephone call between Kabardino-Balkaria and Moscow. For years thereafter, I could not tell anyone about that night in Nalchik without bursting into tears.

Once Solzhenitsyn had left the country, Rostropovich hoped his own situation would improve. He was allowed to conduct *Die Fledermaus* at the Moscow Operetta Theatre, but a planned recording of *Tosca* with the Bolshoi and Vishnevskaya in the lead role nearly didn't go through, because the theatre director had replaced her with Tamara Milashkina. Vishnevskaya was furious and threatened to quit the Bolshoi, so Furtseva, the Minister of Culture, backed off and reinstated the diva.

The Bolshoi musicians were upbeat about their first day of recordings in the Melodiya studio. But their euphoria was short-lived, for a few days later Rostropovich was told the recording would be halted after all. Indignant, he went to the director of Melodiya, who dodged the issue but then admitted that the project had been scrapped. Rostropovich was livid. He said, "You've given me a clear choice: either I leave the country or I kill myself." He slammed the door on his way out.

Six months later he would find out what was behind the cancellation. Five lead singers from the Bolshoi Theatre had been granted an audience with Pyotr Demichev, member of the Central Committee in charge of cultural affairs. They went to him as communists, not as musicians, to denounce Rostropovich. They were afraid the cellist would contaminate their theatre with wayward ideology.

For Rostropovich and Vishnevskaya, this was the last straw. They wrote to General Secretary Brezhnev, requesting permission to live abroad for two years (the accepted euphemism for "permanently"). Just a few hours after delivering the letter to Demichev, they were given Brezhnev's personal blessing to go.

Rostropovich had hoped the authorities would beg him to stay in the Soviet Union, but they did not, and there was no way back now. "He didn't expect the Soviet authorities to let him go," Dmitri Ferschtman tells me. "For all those years, he had enjoyed a certain degree of KGB protection, which made it possible for him to stick up for Solzhenitsyn. Now they just wanted to be rid of him."

Furtseva told Rostropovich he had to leave the country by 4 June, because that was when the Tchaikovsky Competition would begin. From its inception, Rostropovich had chaired the international jury for the cello division, and the authorities were afraid that, if he were still in Moscow but not on the jury, the rest of the jury members would boycott it out of solidarity.

That spring, he performed in Lithuania and Czechoslovakia. Then came rehearsals for another production of *Die Fledermaus* at the Helikon Theatre. But there, too, he was no longer welcome, and, after hearing this, he walked to the theatre's courtyard and wept as though jilted by a lover.

In those days, he became religious (he had been raised an atheist), as though to forge a tie with the Russia he was about to leave behind and to find the strength to endure the humiliation. Shortly before his departure, he organized a service in a small church on Nezhdanova Street for a small group of friends.

Elizabeth Wilson's biography gives the address of the church, but I'm unable to find it on my map of Moscow. This is not so strange, because after the fall of the Soviet Union in 1991 many Moscow streets reverted to their pre-revolution names. Gorky Street, for instance, went back to being Tverskaya Street, and Herzen Street is now Bolshaya Nikitskaya. I dig out a Falk map of Moscow, 11th edition, which I bought back in 1988. Nezhdanova Street (named after the opera singer Antonina Nezhdanova) was renamed Bryusov Lane, after Jacob and Robert Bruce, two seventeenth-century counts of Scottish descent (Jacob had been a general under Peter the Great; Robert was the high commandant of St Petersburg). The church is a terracotta-coloured chapel diagonally across from the Rostropoviches' flat.

I revisit it during a return visit to Moscow in February 2020. I ask the young clerk in the icon shop if Rostropovich and Vishnevskaya really did come here. "I can't help you," she warily replies. "Rostropovich has been dead for so long, and I've only just started working here."

I decide to take that as a yes and walk further into the intimate chapel. I want to imagine Rostropovich standing here, deep in thought, perhaps prayer, as he said farewell to everything Russian that was sacred and precious to him. At the iconostasis, several young women in head scarves stand silently in prayer. They light candles that shed such a mysterious glow over their faces that it might sow doubt in even the most convinced atheist. If it was here that he could reach a higher plane, then it's not at all a bad choice.

On the way to the exit, I notice an old woman sitting at a table selling votive candles. They vary in size, priced from 50 to 100 roubles. Cautious and courteous, I ask her the same question. This time I get the answer I was angling for: "In the Soviet days, this was the only church in Moscow that stayed open," she says. "Many famous artists from the Bolshoi came here. So it's very likely that Rostropovich visited, too. After all, he lived right across the street."

On 10 May 1974, Rostropovich gave a farewell concert in the Great Hall of the Moscow Conservatory. He had permission to put together a student orchestra; the all-Tchaikovsky programme included the *Nutcracker Suite*, the *Rococo Variations* and the Symphony No. 6 (*"Pathétique"*).

All music-loving Moscow turned out for the concert. Even in the aisles, there was standing room only. Before a note had been played, the audience had given the cellist a lengthy standing ovation. Many had tears in their eyes.

After the last sombre notes of the *Pathétique* had died out, the crowd erupted in wails of "Don't go, don't go, don't go!"

Shortly thereafter, Rostropovich gave his last lessons at the conservatory. For his students, it was as though life had ground to a halt. Then he visited his mother's grave, and that of Prokofiev. He also went to see Shostakovich, who broke into tears when his friend told him he was leaving the country for good.

Two weeks later, on 26 May, Rostropovich flew to London. His luggage consisted of one large suitcase, two cellos and his Newfoundland dog Kuzha. Vishnevskaya, Shostakovich's wife and several students were there to see him off.

He was in for one final humiliation before boarding. Customs agents would not allow him to bring the gold medals he had been awarded by the State. They even accused him of trying to smuggle gold out of the country.

Four hours later, he landed at Heathrow. Vishnevskaya and their daughters would join him in July, after the end of the Russian school year.

Undeterred, Rostropovich and Vishnevskaya pursued their careers in exile. Between 1977 and 1994, Rostropovich earned a small fortune as the conductor of the National Symphony Orchestra in Washington, DC, which he then invested in Russian art that he displayed in his seven houses worldwide. After his death, soaring conservation costs forced Vishnevskaya to put the collection up for auction at Sotheby's in London. But even before the first rap of the hammer, the oligarch Alisher Usmanov bought the entire collection for nearly $45 million. He then donated it to the Russian state; it is now housed at the Konstantinovsky Palace in St Petersburg.

I visited the palace in 2008. The collection is extraordinary: it includes rare glass objects, porcelain and dinner service; Fabergé eggs; and twenty-three works by Ilya Repin.

Sixteen years after their departure, during Mikhail Gorbachev's more reform-minded presidency, Rostropovich and Vishnevskaya's Soviet citizenship was restored, and they made their first visit back to their homeland. (Meanwhile, *The Gulag Archipelago* was also freely available in the USSR.) After this visit they returned to Paris, where they had settled after their years in America.

When in summer 1991 communist hardliners led a coup attempt on Gorbachev known as "the August Coup" and tanks rolled through the streets of Moscow, Rostropovich took the first flight to his fatherland to join the newly elected Russian president, Boris Yeltsin, in defending the White House, the government headquarters, which was under attack from mutinous army units. He hoped his celebrity would contribute to the reformers' goals—anything but a return to the old, repressive regime that had ruined the lives of so many of his friends.

A photo from those days shows him sitting in one of the long corridors of the White House, a pistol in his left hand on the armrest. His free arm is draped around the shoulders of a sleeping man, probably the owner of the gun.

His symbolic heroism earned him Yeltsin's friendship. When a standoff between the president and Russia's parliament two years later dissolved into an armed struggle, Rostropovich once again hurried to Moscow to stand by Yeltsin. With the parties still fighting, he led the National Symphony Orchestra in a concert on Red Square, a dramatic act that must have made him feel like a protector of democracy. And, once again, he earned Yeltsin's gratitude; no wonder that Yeltsin's widow Naina was present at the opening of the 2012 Rostropovich Festival.

After the fall of the USSR, the couple divided their time between their homes in Paris, Moscow, St Petersburg, London, Lausanne and New York. He continued to perform, mostly as a conductor, but occasionally as a cellist. In 1995, he recorded the Bach cello suites in the basilica in Vézeley, France.

Rostropovich was diagnosed with cancer in early 2006. Doctors managed to suppress it, but, when it returned a year later, he decided to return to Moscow, where he was admitted to the Blokhin Cancer Institute. He died on 27 April, a month after his eightieth birthday. "We always thought he was immortal," says

Dmitri Ferschtman. "He had such energy and strength. I remember that after the funeral of Kirill Kondrashin in Amsterdam in March 1981, we put away forty of those little bottles of jenever from his hotel minibar. The next morning, we had a rehearsal in the Concertgebouw, and he was as fresh as a daisy. He gave concerts that afternoon and evening as though it were nothing."

The day after his passing, he was laid in state in an open casket in the main hall of the Moscow Conservatory, where he had studied and taught. Then his body was taken to the Cathedral of Christ the Saviour near the Kremlin (which Stalin had blown up in 1931 and Yeltsin had rebuilt with even more bling than the original). Thousands of Russians, including President Putin, came to pay tribute to him.

Rostropovich was buried in the cemetery of the Novodevichy Convent. A year later, a simple Russian Orthodox cross headstone bearing his name was placed at his grave. Vishnevskaya was buried alongside him in 2012. Across the broad central walkway is Boris Yeltsin's tomb, under an enormous, unruly memorial sculpture of the Russian tricolour flag.

On the second evening of the Rostropovich Festival in 2012, I attend a wonderful orchestra concert in the 1,500-seat Tchaikovsky Concert Hall, itself a unique experience, because the audience seems to have stepped straight out of the 1970s Soviet Union. People are conservatively dressed—no nouveau-riche or hipster looks—and are serious music aficionados.

The Rostropovich Academy Symphony Orchestra opens with the overture from Wagner's *Die Meistersinger von Nürnberg*. Then comes Elgar's Cello Concerto, with the sixteen-year-old Russian Vsevolod Guzov, a past Rostropovich stipend recipient, as soloist.

Guzov plays with the same kind of passion, elegance and strength as Rostropovich, but without the same sound. He blushes at the audience's cheers, like a girl at a debutante ball. I have to laugh at the many "intermezzi" of anecdotes and memories of Rostropovich the orchestra members share during the concert.

The encore is *Slava! A Political Overture* by Leonard Bernstein, written for Rostropovich's inaugural concerts with the National Symphony Orchestra. I catch audience members dabbing their eyes.

EPILOGUE

In the early morning of 24 February 2022, Russia invaded Ukraine. What Vladimir Putin had intended as a brief campaign to bring its neighbour under Kremlin rule instead widened into a war lasting almost three years and costing many thousands of Ukrainian lives.

Kindred peoples who had long lived in harmony were now sworn enemies. Ukrainians broke with family members in Russia who, influenced or not by Russian state propaganda, had taken Putin's side.

For cultural life, too, the war had disastrous consequences. In Ukraine they yanked Russian literary classics, including Dostoevsky, Turgenev and Brodsky, from library shelves and school curriculums. Russian composers whose music might exude Russian nationalism, such as Tchaikovsky, could no longer be performed. Likewise, Russian authorities banned the performance of works by Ukrainian composers like Valentyn Sylvestrov. Early on in the war, Moscow police even broke off a concert of his music midway.

Now, while Ukraine fights for survival, Russia seems to have reverted to the Stalin years. Suddenly, betrayal and mistrust are commonplace. Even family members report one another to the police if one of them dares to criticize Putin's war—accusations that could result in lengthy prison sentences.

Nearly a million well-educated Russians, including countless leading figures in the cultural sector, left the country during the first months of the war. Conversely, those who remained in Russia have gone to great lengths to prove their loyalty to the regime. For instance, some symphony orchestras wore T-shirts emblazoned with a "Z", the symbol of the invasion that also adorned many Russian tanks. World-class performing artists, even those living abroad, have openly expressed their admiration for Putin, echoing his message that Ukraine belongs to Russia and that the invasion was justified.

Gone, it seems, are the days when on an ordinary summer afternoon in Moscow you could hear singing on the Arbat. Back in 2019 I followed that sound to the statue of the chansonnier Bulat Okudzhava. Never mind that he's been interred at the Novodevichy Cemetery since 1997: millions of Russians, young and old, still know his melancholy songs by heart.

That time, it was a group of schoolchildren from the provinces singing in front of his bronze likeness. As an homage, but also because they just liked his music. With their red windbreakers and rucksacks, these youngsters could have stepped straight out of a Komsomol youth camp. One of them played the guitar, as did Okudzhava. And suddenly the wistful "Prayer" echoes down the street. Passing Muscovites looked on and smiled, as though reminded of the days when so many things were prohibited there, and they listened to Okudzhava in secret.

It begins:

> As long as the earth still turns,
> As long as the light is bright,
> Lord, grant each one
> What he lacks in life.

Each stanza ends with the line: "And don't forget about me."

This is Russia, but also Ukraine, in all its suffering, joy, tragedy, zeal and greatness, but most of all in its compassion for the harsh fate of the common man.

The terror that artists in the Soviet Union endured came to an end more than thirty years ago with the sudden collapse of the communist regime. Under Boris Yeltsin, the first president of a democratic Russia, the arts appeared to enjoy the independence they had been denied during seventy years of Soviet stranglehold. Even through Vladimir Putin's first two terms as president, the cultural sector appeared relatively secure—partly the outcome of Putin's social contract with the Russian people: do what you want, but keep your nose out of politics.

Yet now that the country is at war, and the West the bogeyman, it is as though the authorities have revived their attack on "formalism", and artists whose patriotism is deemed inadequate can expect the same kind of persecution as Prokofiev, Shostakovich, Mosolov and Zaderatsky. It is not an optimistic scenario. In that case, all one can do is hold on to the old Russian saying *nadezhda umirayet posledney*—"hope dies last".

ACKNOWLEDGEMENTS

I am not a musicologist, but a historian specialized in Russian history. This book therefore does not offer analyses of musical compositions. I have concentrated on the lives of the composers and musicians I am familiar with and whom I admire, and I wondered how they fared and conducted themselves during the Stalin years.

During my research, I soon realized that even today little is known about the repression of musicians in the Soviet Union. The state archives that were opened in the 1990s have been largely reclosed these days, as though the Russian state wants to shield the blemishes of the past from the general public. But fortunately I could turn to the excellent literature concerning this dark subject. First and foremost is the book *Der Klang des Gulag* by Inna Klause, an unparalleled standard work.

Due to the outbreak of the Covid-19 pandemic in March 2020, I was unable to travel to Russia in person to find answers to my remaining questions. But I was fortunate to have many inspiring conversations with Russian musicians and musicologists living in the Netherlands, Germany and, just before the lockdown, Russia itself. I extend my sincerest thanks to Marina Brokanova, Dmitri Ferschtman, Olga de Kort-Kulikova, Lev Markiz, Jascha Nemtsov, Yekaterina Vlasova, Vsevolod V. Zaderatsky and Mikhail

Zemtsov—Russian musicians and experts who were a source of information never before written down. My friend Hans Driessen, from whom I learnt Russian, was always prepared to read along and, like a critical but good-natured mentor, saved me from some grave errors. My publisher Mizzi van der Pluijm encouraged me, in times of doubt, to complete the book. Evi Hoste, with her love for Russia and its music, was the ideal editor. Without her sage advice, this book would have turned out very differently indeed. And then there is my mother, Lot Krielaars, who passed away in 2019 at the age of ninety-five. She was the one who sent me to music lessons as a child and instilled in me a love of classical music. When I think of her, I often hear Schubert's *Moments musicaux* played by Sviatoslav Richter, a pianist she admired.

The biggest thank-you goes to my wife, Henriette Schenk, with whom I have shared my life for thirty-five years, and who, as a singer, followed me to Russia, sharing my love of that country and its people. There is almost nothing finer than listening to music with her. I dedicate this book to her.

AMSTERDAM, AUGUST 2021

BIBLIOGRAPHY

Chapter 1. Richter's Secret

Bezemer, J.W. and Jansen, Marc, *Een geschiedenis van Rusland. Van Rurik tot Poetin*, Amsterdam: G.A. van Oorschot, 2008

Dorliac, Dimitri, *Sviatoslav Richter. Visions Fugitives. Mémoires de Dimitri Dorliac*, Paris: Magellan & Cie, 2005

Frolova-Walker, Marina, *Stalin's Music Prize: Soviet Culture and Politics*, New Haven, CT: Yale University Press, 2016

Grossman, Vasily, *Everything Flows*, tr. Robert Chandler, New York: NYRB Classics, 2009

Jansen, Marc, *De toekomst die nooit kwam. Hoe Rusland worstelt met zijn verleden*, Amsterdam: Uitgeverij Van Oorschot, 2019

Kotkin, Stephen, *Stalin. Volume I: Paradoxes of Power, 1878–1928*, New York: Allen Lane, 2014

———, *Stalin. Volume II: Waiting for Hitler, 1928–1941*, New York: Allen Lane, 2017

Monsaingeon, Bruno, *Sviatoslav Richter: Notebooks and Conversations*, London: Faber & Faber, 2005

Moskalewa-Richter, Anna, von Reincke, Dagmar, and Moskalew, Walter, *Svetik: A Family Memoir of Sviatoslav Richter*, London: Toccata Press, 2015

Schlögel, Karl, *Das Sowjetische Jahrhundert. Archäologie einer untergegangenen Welt*, Munich and Frankfurt: C.H. Beck, 2017

Sebag Montefiore, Simon, *Stalin: The Court of the Red Tsar*, London: Weidenfeld & Nicolson, 2003

———, *Young Stalin*, London: Weidenfeld & Nicolson, 2007

Chapter 2. Yellow Shoes and Fancy Cars

Dekker, Angela, *Verloren verleden. Een eeuw Russische emigrés in Parijs*, Breda: De Geus, 2007

Fairclough, Pauline, *Classics for the Masses: Shaping Soviet Musical Identity under Lenin and Stalin*, New Haven, CT: Yale University Press, 2016

Fitzpatrick, Sheila, *The Cultural Front: Power and Culture in Revolutionary Russia*, Ithaca, NY: Cornell University Press, 1992

Frolova-Walker, Marina, *Stalin's Music Prize: Soviet Culture and Politics*, New Haven, CT: Yale University Press, 2016

Ginzburg, Yevgenia, *Krutoi marshrut. Khronika vremen kul'ta lichnosti*, Moscow: AST, 2007

Jaffé, Daniel, *Sergey Prokofiev*, London: Phaidon Press, 1998

Kotkin, Stephen, *Stalin. Volume I: Paradoxes of Power, 1878–1928*, New York: Allen Lane, 2014

———, *Stalin. Volume II: Waiting for Hitler, 1928–1941*, New York: Allen Lane, 2017

Maes, Francis, *Geschiedenis van de Russische Muziek. Van Glinka tot Sjostakovitsj*, Nijmegen: SUN, 1996

Morrison, Simon, *The Love and Wars of Lina Prokofiev*, London: Harvill Secker, 2013

———, *The People's Artist: Prokofiev's Soviet Years*, Oxford: Oxford University Press, 2009

Moynahan, Brian, *Leningrad: Siege and Symphony*, London: Quercus, 2013

Nestjew, I., *Prokofjew. Der Künstler und sein Werk*, Berlin: Henschelverlag, 1962

Nest'eva, Marina, *Sergei Prokof'ev. Solnechnii genii*, Moscow: AST, 2019

Nestyev, Israel V., *Sergei Prokofiev: His Musical Life*, tr. Rose Prokofieva, New York: Alfred A. Knopf, 1946

Olof, Arthur, *De kunst om te overleven. Russische muziek in de eeuw van Dmitri Sjostakovitsj*, Amsterdam: Stichting Autres Directions, 2019

Prokof'ev, Sergei, *Dnevnik, 1907–1933*, Paris: sprkfv, 2002

———, *Pis'ma, vospominaniia, stat'i. K 110-letiiu so dnia rozhdeniia*, Moscow: Muzei-kino, 2007

Prokofiev, Sergey, *Diaries 1924–1933: Prodigal Son*, ed. and tr. Anthony Phillips, Ithaca, NY: Cornell University Press, 2012

Shostakovich, Dmitri, *Story of a Friendship: The Letters of Dmitri Shostakovich to Isaak Glikman, 1941–1975*, tr. Anthony Phillips, Ithaca, NY: Cornell University Press, 2001

Vishnevskaya, Galina, *Galina: A Russian Story*, tr. Guy Daniels, New York: Harcourt Brace Jovanovich, 1984

Vlasova, E.S., *1948 god v sovetskoi muzyke. Ne iskusstvo dlia iskusstva, a iskusstvo dlia mass*, Moscow: Klassika-XXI, 2010

Volkov, Solomon, *The Magical Chorus: A History of Russian Culture from Tolstoy to Solzhenitsyn*, New York: Alfred A. Knopf, 2008

———, *Shostakovich and Stalin: The Extraordinary Relationship Between the Great Composer and the Brutal Dictator*, New York: Alfred A. Knopf, 2004

Wilson, Elizabeth, *Shostakovich: A Life Remembered*, London: Faber & Faber, 2006

Chapter 3. The Lost Notes

Applebaum, Anne, *Gulag: A History of the Soviet Camps*, London: Allen Lane, 2003

Grossman, Vasily, *Everything Flows*, tr. Robert Chandler, New York: NYRB Classics, 2009

Klause, Inna, *Der Klang des Gulag. Musik und Musiker in den sowjetischen Zwangsarbeitslagern der 1920er- bis 1950er- Jahre*, Bonn: V&R unipress, 2014

Maes, Francis, *Geschiedenis van de Russische Muziek. Van Glinka tot Sjostakovitsj*, Nijmegen: SUN, 1996

Nemtsov, Yasha, '"Ich bin schon längst tot." Komponisten im Gulag: Vsevolod Zaderackij und Aleksandr Veprik', *Osteuropa* 6, 2007, pp. 315–40

Zaderatsky, Vsevolod V., *Per aspera…*, St Petersburg: Kompozitor, 2015

———, 'Vsevolod Petrovich Zaderatsky (1891–1953): A Lost Soviet Composer', tr. Anthony Phillips, JMI International Centre for Suppressed Music, 2006

Chapter 4. The Russian Vera Lynn

Fairclough, Pauline, *Classics for the Masses: Shaping Soviet Musical Identity under Lenin and Stalin*, New Haven, CT: Yale University Press, 2016

MacFadyen, David, *Estrada?! Grand Narratives and the Philosophy of the Russian Popular Song since Perestroika*, Montreal: McGill-Queen's University Press, 2002

———, *Red Stars: Personality and the Soviet Popular Song, 1955–1991*, Montreal: McGill-Queen's University Press, 2001

———, *Songs for Fat People. Affect, Emotion and Celebrity in the Russian Popular Song, 1900–1955*, Montreal: McGill-Queen's University Press, 2002

Shul'zhenko, Klavdiia, *Kogda vy sprosite menia…*, Moscow: Molodaia Gvardiia, 1981.

Chapter 5. Celebrated, Persecuted, Rehabilitated

Elphick, Daniel, *Music behind the Iron Curtain: Weinberg and his Polish Contemporaries*, Cambridge: Cambridge University Press, 2020

Fanning, David, *Mieczysław Weinberg: In Search of Freedom*, Hofheim: Wolke Verlag, 2019

Frolova-Walker, Marina, *Stalin's Music Prize: Soviet Culture and Politics*, New Haven, CT: Yale University Press, 2016

Geiger, Friedrich (ed.), *Komponisten unter Stalin. Aleksandr Veprik (1899–1958) und die Neue jüdische Schule*, Dresden: Hannah-Arendt-Institut, 2000

Gvizdalianka [Gwizdalanka], Danuta, *Mechislav Vainberg. Kompozitor trekh mirov*, St Petersburg: Kompozitor, 2022

Klause, Inna, *Der Klang des Gulag. Musik und Musiker in den sowjetischen Zwangsarbeitslagern der 1920er- bis 1950er-Jahre*, Bonn: V&R unipress, 2014

Chapter 6. The Vanished Singer

Almond, Marc, 'In Search of Vadim Kozin', [podcast], BBC World Service, 2015

Applebaum, Anne, *Gulag: A History of the Soviet Camps*, London: Allen Lane, 2003

Fairclough, Pauline, *Classics for the Masses: Shaping Soviet Musical Identity under Lenin and Stalin*, New Haven, CT: Yale University Press, 2016

Gold: Lost in Siberia, [documentary film], dir. Theo Uittenbogaard, 1994

Klause, Inna, *Der Klang des Gulag. Musik und Musiker in den sowjetischen Zwangsarbeitslagern der 1920er- bis 1950er- Jahre*, Bonn: V&R unipress, 2014

MacFadyen, David, *Songs for Fat People. Affect, Emotion and Celebrity in the Russian Popular Song, 1900–1955*, Montreal: McGill-Queen's University Press, 2002

Roberts, Sophy, *The Lost Pianos of Siberia*, London: Doubleday, 2020

Savchenko, Boris, *Vadim Kozin*, Smolensk: Rusich, 2001

Shalamov, Varlam, *Kolyma Stories*, tr. Donald Rayfield, New York: NYRB Classics, 2018–2019

Solzhenitsyn, Alexander, *The Gulag Archipelago*, tr. Thomas P. Whitney, London: Penguin Press, 1974

Chapter 7. A Nun at the Keyboard

Hanslik, Aleksander, 'A Pianist *"d'execution transcendante"*: Remembrance of Maria Yudina on the 50th Anniversary of Her Death', in Norman Lebrecht, *The Whole Truth about Maria Yudina*, [online], Slipped Disc, 2020, https://slippedisc.com/2020/12/the-whole-truth-about-maria-yudina/ (accessed 30 June 2024)

Kotkin, Stephen, *Stalin. Volume I: Paradoxes of Power, 1878–1928*, New York: Allen Lane, 2014

———, *Stalin. Volume II: Waiting for Hitler, 1928–1941*, New York: Allen Lane, 2017

Mandelstam, Nadezhda, *Hope against Hope: A Memoir*, intro. Maria Stepanova, tr. Max Hayward, London: Everyman, 2023

Shostakovich, Dmitri, *Testimony: The Memoirs of Dmitri Shostakovich*, ed. Solomon Volkov, tr. Antonina Bouis, New York: Limelight Editions, 2004

Wilson, Elizabeth, *Playing with Fire: The Story of Maria Yudina, Pianist in Stalin's Russia*, New Haven, CT, and London: Yale University Press, 2022

Chapter 8. The Lost Legacy

Geiger, Friedrich (ed.), *Komponisten unter Stalin. Aleksandr Veprik (1899–1958) und die Neue jüdische Schule*, Dresden: Hannah-Arendt-Institut, 2000

——— and Eckhard, John (eds.), *Musik zwischen Emigration und Stalinismus. Russische Componisten in den 1930er und 1940er Jahren*, Heidelberg: J.B. Metzler, 2004

Klause, Inna, *Der Klang des Gulag. Musik und Musiker in den sowjetischen Zwangsarbeitslagern der 1920er- bis 1950er- Jahre*, Bonn: V&R unipress, 2014

Schwarz, Boris, *Music and Musical Life in Soviet Russia, 1917–1970*, London: Barrie & Jenkins, 1972

Sitsky, Larry, *Music of the Repressed Russian Avant-Garde, 1900–1929*, Westpoint, CT: Greenwood Press, 1994

Taruskin, Richard, *Defining Russia Musically: Historical and Hermeneutical Essays*, Princeton, NJ: Princeton University Press, 2001

Vorob'ev, Igor', *Russkiy avangard i tvorchestvo Aleksandra Mosolova 1920–1930-kh godov*, St Petersburg: Kompozitor, 2006

Chapter 9. Stalin's Last Lackey

Alexievich, Svetlana, *Secondhand Time: The Last of the Soviets*, tr. Bela Shayevich, New York: Random House, 2016

Fay, Laurel E., *Shostakovich: A Life*, Oxford: Oxford University Press, 2005

——— (ed.), *Shostakovich and His World*, Princeton, NJ: Princeton University Press, 2004

Frolova-Walker, Marina, *Stalin's Music Prize: Soviet Culture and Politics*, New Haven, CT: Yale University Press, 2016

Khrennikov, Tikhon, *Kak eto bylo. Tikhon Khrennikov o vremeni i o sebe*, Moscow: Muzyka, 1994

Kokarev, Andrei, *Tikhon Khrennikov*, Moscow: Zhizn' zamechatel'nykh liudei, 2015

Maes, Francis, *Geschiedenis van de Russische Muziek. Van Glinka tot Sjostakovitsj*, Nijmegen: SUN, 1996

Schwarz, Boris, *Music and Musical Life in Soviet Russia, 1917–1981*, Bloomington, IN: Indiana University Press, 1983

Shostakovich, Dmitri, *Testimony: The Memoirs of Dmitri Shostakovich*, ed. Solomon Volkov, tr. Antonina Bouis, New York: Limelight Editions, 2004

Tomoff, Kiril, *Creative Union: The Professional Organization of Soviet Composers, 1939–1954*, Ithaca, NY: Cornell University Press, 2006

Vlasova, E.S., *1948 god v sovetskoi muzyke. Ne iskusstvo dlia iskusstva, a iskusstvo dlia mass*, Moscow: Klassika-XXI, 2010

Wilson, Elizabeth, *Shostakovich: A Life Remembered*, London: Faber & Faber, 2006

Chapter 10. Solidarity with Dissidents

Cliff, Nigel, *Moscow Nights*, New York: HarperCollins Publishers, 2017

David Oistrakh. Artiste du Peuple?, [documentary film], dir. Bruno Monsaingeon, France/Germany, 1994

Rostropovich, Mstislav, and Vishnevskaya, Galina, *Russia, Music, and Liberty: Conversations with Claude Samuel*, Portland, OR: Amadeus Press, 1995

Vishnevskaya, Galina, *Galina. A Russian Story*, London: Sceptre, 1984

Volkov, Solomon, *The Magical Chorus: A History of Russian Culture from Tolstoy to Solzhenitsyn*, New York: Alfred A. Knopf, 2008

Wilson, Elizabeth, *Mstislav Rostropovich: Cellist, Teacher, Legend*, London: Faber & Faber, 2007

AVAILABLE AND COMING SOON FROM PUSHKIN PRESS

Pushkin Press was founded in 1997, and publishes novels, essays, memoirs, children's books—everything from timeless classics to the urgent and contemporary.

Our books represent exciting, high-quality writing from around the world: we publish some of the twentieth century's most widely acclaimed, brilliant authors such as Stefan Zweig, Yasushi Inoue, Teffi, Antal Szerb, Gerard Reve and Elsa Morante, as well as compelling and award-winning contemporary writers, including Dorthe Nors, Edith Pearlman, Perumal Murugan, Ayelet Gundar-Goshen and Chigozie Obioma.

Pushkin Press publishes the world's best stories, to be read and read again. To discover more, visit www.pushkinpress.com.

I LIVE A LIFE LIKE YOURS
JAN GRUE

A LINE IN THE WORLD
DORTHE NORS

STALKING THE ATOMIC CITY
MARKIYAN KAMYSH

CLOUDS OVER PARIS
FELIX HARTLAUB

THE WOLF AGE
TORE SKEIE

A WOMAN IN THE POLAR NIGHT
CHRISTIANE RITTER

A LIFE IN THE MAKING
FRANZ MICHAEL FELDER

MAZEL TOV
J.S. MARGOT

DAYS IN THE CAUCASUS
BANINE

ON LOVE AND TYRANNY
ANN HEBERLEIN

THOSE WHO FORGET
GÉRALDINE SCHWARZ

YOUNG REMBRANDT
ONNO BLOM

THE WORLD OF YESTERDAY
STEFAN ZWEIG

NO PLACE TO LAY ONE'S HEAD
FRANÇOISE FRENKEL

DREAMERS
VOLKER WEIDERMANN

THE LIMITS OF MY LANGUAGE
EVA MEIJER

A CHILL IN THE AIR
IRIS ORIGO

RED LOVE
MAXIM LEO

A WORLD GONE MAD
ASTRID LINDGREN

ON THE END OF THE WORLD
JOSEPH ROTH

SORROW OF THE EARTH
ERIC VUILLARD

A SORROW BEYOND DREAMS
PETER HANDKE

MEMORIES: FROM MOSCOW TO THE BLACK SEA
TEFFI